Indonesians
Portraits from an Archipelago

To

MARGARET + RUSSELL

FRom
THE JAKARTA MAYNARDS

CHRISTMAS
1984

Indonesians
Portraits from an Archipelago

Photographs by
IAN CHARLES STEWART

Text by
IAN CHARLES STEWART & JUDITH SHAW

INDONESIA
PARAMOUNT CIPTA
CONCEPT MEDIA
SINGAPORE

Photo editors: Ian Charles Stewart & Hasan-Uddin Khan
Art director: Hasan-Uddin Khan
Designers: Design Objectives Pte Ltd

Production coordinator: Patricia Theseira
Typesetting by Computype Pte Ltd
Colour separations by Colourscan Co Pte Ltd
Printed and bound in Singapore by Tien Wah Press (Pte) Ltd

Photographs by Ian Charles Stewart
except those on pages 184 & 185 by Gene Christy
and on page 184 by Nora Suryanti
and on pages 216, 217 & 218 by Virginia White
and on page 218 by Edith Somerset
Text by Ian Charles Stewart and Judith Shaw
Preface by H. Mahendra

Published by Concept Media Pte Ltd,
19 Tanglin Road, #06-52, Singapore 1024 and
Paramount Cipta Ltd, P.O. Box 280,
KBY Jakarta Selatan, Indonesia.
First printing — October 1983
Second printing — April 1984
Photographs: © Yayasan Bhakti Putra.
Book: © Paramount Cipta & Concept Media.

ISBN: 9971-83-772-2

CONTENTS

Preface

Indonesia has long been looked upon as a country of great scenic beauty and a wealth of natural resources. Both are true, but greater resources and a much warmer beauty can be found in the people of this vast land. The motivating force behind the decision to create *Indonesians: Portraits from an Archipelago* is the wish to share, particularly with non-Indonesian readers, this as yet unrecognised but abundantly visible wealth.

This book is about people, the many different peoples who live on the islands of the Indonesian archipelago. It offers a composite portrait of the many different environments and cultural backgrounds that co-exist here, as well as the underlying traditions that bind these differing cultures together. These common traditions are based on simplicity, belief in the Good, tolerance, and respect for others. Most important is an all-pervading spiritual sensitivity, and a strong belief in God. Many different religions exist side by side in Indonesia, and most people participate in at least one.

This book is not about the high culture of Indonesia, or the great ceremonies of the royal courts. It portrays ordinary people living their daily lives, much of which is engraved on their faces. The slant is rural rather than urban; low-key rather than dramatic and unusual. It aims at giving the reader an understanding of the country and people as they are today, with their long traditions in tenuous balance with the demands and intrusions of the modern world. Although their ethnological characteristics will not change in the foreseeable future, attitudes, behaviour and way of life are likely to be greatly influenced by the tide of Western-style modernisation sweeping the country. No-one can predict what effect this modernisation will have on peoples with a traditional culture strongly rooted in rural, agricultural society, but certain changes in living patterns are already visible. Thirty years from now this book may portray only the Indonesia of the "good old days".

The concepts and traditions that form the basis of Indonesian culture are different from those underlying Western societies. These differences influence the day-to-day behaviour of the people and are reflected in the photographs in this book.

One of the dominant concepts at all levels of Indonesian society is *gotong royong*, or mutual help, which stresses social unity and the inter-connectedness of people. The Indonesian does not look at himself as an individual in the sense that the term is used in the West. Rather he is part of a group—family, clan, village—and develops his identity in relation to that group. Such deeply entrenched traditions as *gotong royong*, however, today face the challenge of change. Many Indonesians in the big cities have begun to appreciate privacy; some have adopted an individual life style. But the acceptance of *gotong royong* as a principle in national life puts heavy restrictions on the development of too extreme an individualistic outlook among the population in general.

Another strong tradition in Indonesian society is the decision-making process known as *musyawarah untuk mufakat*, "deliberation leading to consensus". In Indonesia, the majority seldom rules; neither are decisions simply handed down from above. Rather the people who must implement the decision reach agreement on the correct path before a decision is taken. This technique is slow but effective, because everyone involved is behind the action decided upon. *Musyawarah untuk mufakat* is the method applied in the People's Consultative Assembly, the House of People's Representatives, the Cabinet, and the Supreme Advisory Council. Voting is only used in Indonesian democracy when no consensus can be reached.

One of the themes of this book is the development, in even the remotest parts of the archipelago, of an emerging Indonesian culture that transcends the differences of the various regions. The national motto is *Bhinneka Tunggal Ika*, "Unity in Diversity". Despite vast cultural diversity, the national identity is becoming stronger all the time. The thrust toward Indonesian cultural unity is not new. In 1331 Gajah Mada, one of the most famous ministers of the Majapahit Kingdom made what has come to be known as the *"Palapa Vow"*, swearing never to rest until the whole archipelago was united under Majapahit rule. Indonesia's telecommunications satellites, which interconnect the entire nation in all its far-flung diversity and also bring Indonesia closer to the rest of world, are named *Palapa* to commemorate his resolve. It is hoped that, in some small measure, this book can do the same.

- H. Mahendra -

Introduction

Indonesia is the world's largest archipelago, with more than 13,000 islands stretching over 4,800 kilometres across the seas between Asia and Australia. The six major islands are Sumatra, Java, Bali, Kalimantan, Sulawesi and Irian Jaya. Maluku and Nusa Tenggara, which make up Indonesia's two remaining divisions, are groups of islands running from Sulawesi to Irian in the North and from Bali to Timor in the south. The country is divided into twenty-seven provinces. The two newest are Irian Jaya and East Timor, which joined the Republic in 1969 and 1976 respectively. More than sixty percent of Indonesia's 160 million people live on Java. With the exception of the tiny island of Bali, also densely inhabited, population is relatively sparse throughout the rest of the country, much of which is forest and jungle. Less than half the land is arable.

Indonesia straddles the equator, and the climate is mostly tropical. Rainfall varies, from the semi-arid islands of Nusa Tenggara to the lush rain forests of Sumatra, Kalimantan and Irian Jaya. Irrigated rice fields, called *sawah,* have been used in Java and Bali for thousands of years, and whole societies have grown up around the apportionment and control of water. Wet-rice cultivation occurs on some of the outer islands, where water and suitable land are available. On other islands corn, sago, and cassava are dietary staples. In most areas fish is an important source of protein.

Indonesia is the home of a large variety of plant and animal life, much of it found nowhere else in the world. Among the more unusual species are the orangutans of Kalimantan and North Sumatra, West Java's one-horned rhinoceros, and the dwarf buffalo of Sulawesi. The world's largest flower, the *Rafflesia Arnoldi,* is found here, as are thousands of species of orchid. The "Wallace Line" falls between Bali and the island of Lombok in West Nusa Tenggara. Animals and plants on islands to the west of that line are most clearly related to the flora and fauna of Asia; plant and animal life on islands to the east are similar to those of New Guinea and Australia.

There is a greater wealth of ethnic diversity in Indonesia than perhaps anywhere in the world. More than 300 ethnic groups and about 365 languages co-exist here, although *Bahasa Indonesia,* the national language, is now spoken everywhere. The reason for this incredible variety of peoples lies in Indonesia's position *vis à vis* Asia and Australia. Until relatively recently, geologically speaking, Indonesia was connected to Asia and Australia by three land bridges. Sumatra, Java, Bali and Kalimantan were one land mass extending north into peninsular Malaysia and Indo-China; Sulawesi was connected to the Philippines and north to Taiwan and Japan; New Guinea and Australia were also joined. Primitive humans, along with many species of animal, were able to walk into what is now Indonesia from Asia. Fossil remains of Java Man, an upright-striding hominid, date back at least one million years. Time brought more sophisticated cultures to Indonesia, as well as stone-age technology. When the ice age ended in Europe, Indonesia was no longer connected to the mainland. Waves of migrants came by boat from China, Thailand and Vietnam. Reflections of these cultures can be seen in bronze drums and gongs, polished ceremonial tools, and designs still vibrant in Indonesian decorative arts today.

Although enjoying sporadic periods of unifying cultural influence—under the Sriwijaya Kingdom in the 12th and 13th Centuries, and the 14th-Century Majapahit Kingdom, for instance—the different areas of the archipelago were often politically fragmented. Islam, which entered the islands in the 13th Century, was a strong unifying factor; today the vast majority of Indonesians are Muslim. The era of European influence began in the 16th Century when the Portuguese arrived in Maluku. They were followed by the Dutch in the 17th Century and the English, who ruled Indonesia for a few years from 1811-1816. The Dutch were the major colonial power in the archipelago, exercising control first through the Dutch East India Company, established in 1602 and later through the Dutch government.

In 1945 Sukarno and Mohammad Hatta proclaimed Indonesia's independence. After nearly five years of guerilla war against the Dutch, Indonesia was recognised as an independent, sovereign nation in the final days of 1949. Sukarno was Indonesia's first President from 1950 to 1965. The "New Order", under President Suharto, began in 1968. He was elected for a third term in 1983.

Indonesia's national philosophy, *Pancasila*, is embodied in the preamble to the 1945 Constitution. Its five points are "Belief in the One Supreme God; Just and Civilised Humanity; Unity of Indonesia; The People's Sovereignty guided by the wisdom of unanimity in deliberation among representatives; and Social Justice for all the people of Indonesia".

Young men in ceremonial dress, Nusa Tenggara.

Indonesia

The maps at the beginning of every chapter indicate the places shown in the photographs. Major islands, cities and towns are also given, but much has been omitted in the interest of clarity.

Andaman Sea

South China Sea

BRUNEI

Banda Aceh

MALAYSIA

Medan •

Strait of Malacca

MALAYSIA

Mt Menyapa ▲ 2000

SIMEULUE

Lake Toba

SINGAPORE

R. Mahakam

NIAS

Pekanbaru

Pontianak

KALIMANTAN

R. Kapuas

SUMATRA

Balikpapan •

• Padang

MENTAWAI ISLANDS

R. Barito

▲ *Gunung Kerinci* 3800

BANGKA

Palembang

• Banjarmasin

Indian Ocean

Java Sea

Makassar

Sunda Strait

• Jakarta

MADURA

• Bandung

•Surakarta• Surabaya

• Yogyakarta ▲ *Mt Bromo* 2392

BALI

JAVA

LOMBOK

SUMBAWA

Indian Ocean

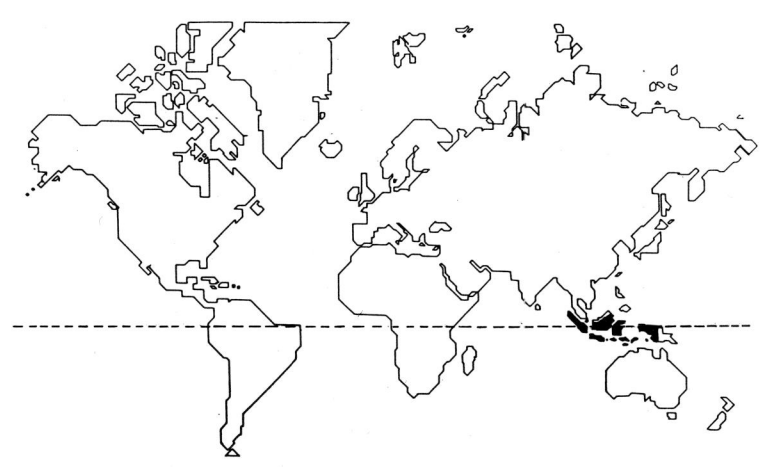

PHILIPPINES

Philippines Sea

Sulawesi Sea

HALMAHERA

•Manado

Maluku Sea

Halmahera Sea

Equator

BACAN

•Sorong

•Biak

Palu

OBI

R. Memberamo

•Jayapura

MALUKU

ULAWESI

Gulf of Tolo

BURU

SERAM

IRIAN JAYA

BALIEM VALLEY

Seram Sea

•Timika

•Kendari

AMBON

TOYANDU

R. Digul

•Ujung Pandang

KAI ISLES

ARU ISLES

Banda Sea

PAPUA NEW GUINEA

Flores Sea

TANIMBAR ISLES

•Mapi

JSA TENGGARA

FLORES

Arafuru Sea

SUMBA

Savu Sea

TIMOR

Timor Sea

•Kupang

0   100   200Km

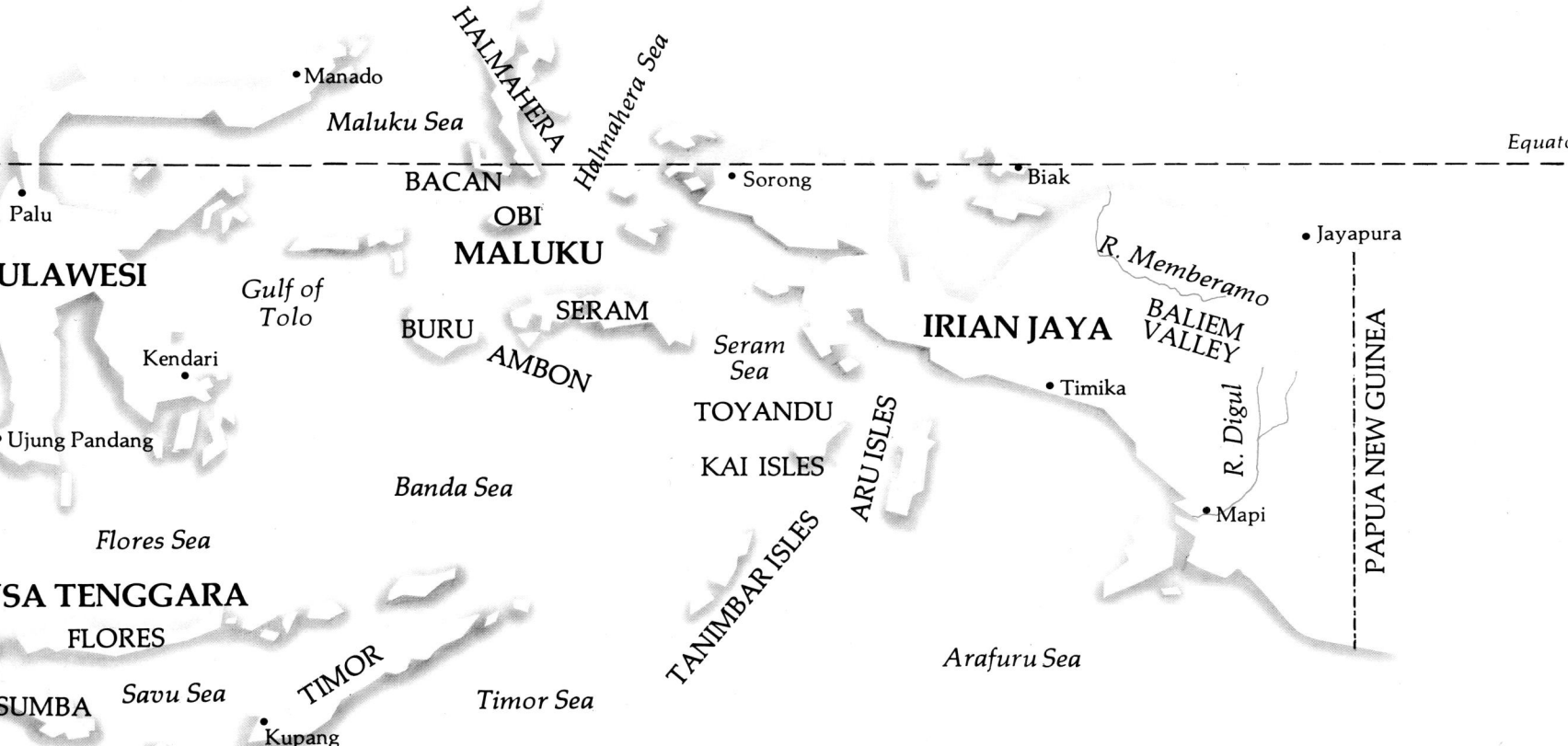

Sumatra

Sumatra. An island where tigers, elephants and rhinos still roam the forests; where head-hunters have only just left off their bloodthirsty purusits. Sumatra's northern tip faces India, its northeast coast borders Malaysia and the Strait of Malacca, and across the Sunda Strait Java is less than twenty-five kilometres away. The fifth largest island in the world, Sumatra is a land of coastal swamps, inland mountain chains, crater lakes, and thousands of square kilometres of nearly impenetrable jungle. Natural resources are plentiful: Sumatra exports oil, natural gas and tropical hardwoods, as well as the rubber, coffee, sugar, palm oil and tobacco that have been grown here for centuries.

Ideally located as a port of call for Asian travellers, Sumatra has a long history of foreign contact. The first visitors walked in more than a million years ago when Sumatra, Java and Bali were connected to the mainland. Groups of primitive humans, *Homo Erectus* and early *Homo Sapiens* drifted south from China and Southeast Asia. Some of these migrants settled in Sumatra; others moved on to Java or across to western Borneo. Millennia passed. Neolithic peoples from China and what is now Vietnam came by boat, bringing agriculture, pottery, and metal-working technology with them. They settled in Sumatra, mixing with the local people or driving them inland. More migrants came and the cycle was repeated again and again, continuing well into the modern era.

Today, Sumatra is the home of many different peoples. The tall, dark-skinned dignified Acehnese in the north; the Batak people of Lake Toba, the creative, shrewd Minangkabau and the Kubu of the south, whose lives are scarcely different from their nomadic stone-age forebears. Together with the island's other ethnic groups they present a richly varied tapestry of race and culture.

Aceh, Sumatra's northernmost province, first appeared in historical records as the 6th-Century Buddhist State of Poli. By the time Marco Polo reached the area, it was already strongly Muslim. A people whose lifeblood is trade, it is no surprise that they enthusiastically embraced this religion, brought by traders. But Islam in Aceh, though always visible, is understated and has been, to a certain extent, adapted to fit local needs. This flexibility of religious interpretation is characteristic of Indonesia as a whole and can be seen throughout the archipelago in varying degrees.

Nias is an island about 120 kilometres off the west coast of North Sumatra. The Niah were valued as slaves on Sumatra, especially by the Acehnese, and slave raids were common on the island. In addition, the Niah were enthusiastic fighters and head-hunters, and villages were often at war with one another. Niasan architecture reflects a very real need for defense. Houses are strongly fortified, with barred windows and trap-door entrances through the

A devout young girl in Muslim dress praying.

15

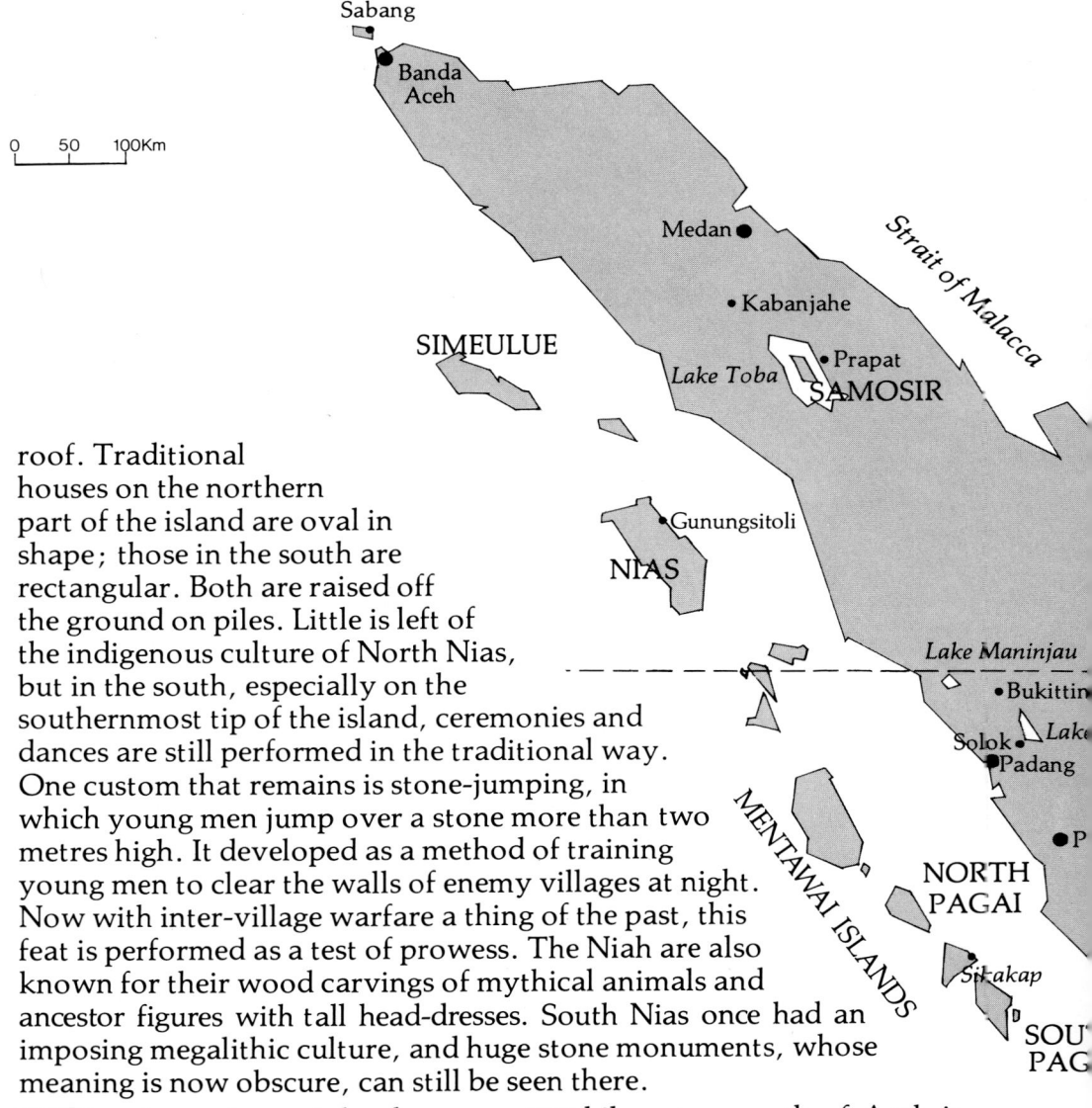

roof. Traditional
houses on the northern
part of the island are oval in
shape; those in the south are
rectangular. Both are raised off
the ground on piles. Little is left of
the indigenous culture of North Nias,
but in the south, especially on the
southernmost tip of the island, ceremonies and
dances are still performed in the traditional way.
One custom that remains is stone-jumping, in
which young men jump over a stone more than two
metres high. It developed as a method of training
young men to clear the walls of enemy villages at night.
Now with inter-village warfare a thing of the past, this
feat is performed as a test of prowess. The Niah are also
known for their wood carvings of mythical animals and
ancestor figures with tall head-dresses. South Nias once had an
imposing megalithic culture, and huge stone monuments, whose
meaning is now obscure, can still be seen there.

Back on the mainland, a mere 350 kilometres south of Aceh is
the land of the Tapanuli, whose heartland is the area around
Lake Toba in North Sumatra. Called Batak by outsiders, they
have maintained their cultural identity although surrounded on all
sides by people with very different traditions. There are six Batak
subgroups, with the Toba, Karo and Mandailing being the largest. All
Batak groups share a basic language and similar culture, although
minor differences are evident. They have in common, however, a
reputation for plain speaking that is notorious throughout Indonesia.
Unlike the refined Javanese who hides his feelings behind a mask of
good manners, the Batak always says what he means.

South of Batakland in the area around Bukittinggi live the
people known as Minangkabau. Intensely Muslim, the Minangkabau
have a social system in which name and control of property pass
down through the female line. It used to be the case that when a
woman married, the groom either moved in with her family or, if he
preferred, only visited at first, gradually moving in his belongings as
the relationship became established. If there were marital difficulties,
he would gradually move them out again. Today marriage customs
among the Minangkabau are not very different from marriage
customs elsewhere in Sumatra, although they are still usually
matrilocal. Management of the family fields is the responsibility of the
women; a Minangkabau man is more likely to be found working the
land of his mother or sister than that of his wife's family. It may seem
strange that a patriarchal religion like Islam should exist comfortably

baru

Equator

k

•Jambi

ng Kerinci

BANGKA

● Palembang

•Bengkulu

ENGGANO

•Telukbetung

Sunda Strait

in such a strongly woman-oriented society, but in fact much of pre-Islamic Sumatra shows evidence of the same social organisation. In Aceh marriages are often matrilocal, with the bride staying in her own village after marriage rather than moving to the home of her husband's family. In the area around Mt. Kerinci in South Sumatra the system is strictly matrilineal and matrilocal. A father there is not influential in the affairs of his children, but rather is an important figure to his sister's children. The Minangkabau people are excellent craftsmen and business people. They are also active in national politics and a high proportion of government officials and civil servants come from this part of Sumatra.

The Mentawai islands lie south of Nias and include the islands of North and South Pagai. More primitive than their neighbours to the north, the Pagai islanders have a history in which weaving, metal-working and domesticated animals played no part. This lack of development can be explained in terms of *punen*, holy periods, which could last anywhere from a few days or weeks to several years. During *punen* most purposeful activity was taboo, including all work in the fields. Food had to be gathered wild or stolen from other villages.Obviously, agricultural pursuits requiring sustained effort, such as growing rice or caring for animals, were not possible. Taro was the staple food, supplemented with yams, banana, sugarcane, durian and fish. Today, *punen* has virtually disappeared, and is observed only on Sundays. During the past few decades, rice cultivation has been developed with the encouragement of missionaries and government officials. Contact with the outside world has increased with the development of a timber industry, and the ancient ways are quickly being lost. The grass skirts so prevalent even ten years ago have now given way to batik sarongs and Western clothing.

In the eastern coastal region live the Kubu, the most primitive of Sumatra's many ethnic groups. Similar in lifestyle to some of the island's earliest inhabitants, they wander in small family groups through the forests between Jambi and Palembang, trading simple woven products for food. Their houses, used for only a few weeks or months and then abandoned, are made of bamboo and palm fronds raised from the ground on bamboo piles. As logging and oil exploration have become more intense in the region, the government has addressed itself to the problems of a country rapidly modernising around these people. Small resettlement villages have been set up at the forests' edge in the hope that some Kubu will give up their nomadic ways and learn to live a more settled way of life.

Sumatra serves as a fitting introduction to Indonesia as a whole because it exhibits many of the contrasting—and sometimes conflicting—features that characterise this rapidly changing nation. Modern bustling cities cheek by jowl with deep jungle, a rich variety of ethnic groups, advanced technology and primitive life-styles, and a wide range of religious beliefs. Sumatra, with one foot firmly planted in traditional culture, is moving quickly into the modern age.

A Minangkabau wedding procession displays a charming mixture of old and new. The bride wears traditional West Sumatran wedding garb with its distinctive golden head-dress, while her attendants cover their heads in the Muslim style.
Minangkabau society, although intensely Muslim, is both matrilineal and matrilocal: descent, name, and property are passed down from mother to daughter. When a woman marries, the groom is invited to live·with the bride's parents, and, if the family can afford it, a new room is added on to house the young couple.

OVERLEAF: *A village landscape near Bukittinggi, West Sumatra. The Minangkabau house in the left foreground shows new extensions.*

Two men from Aceh sitting in their cool open mosque. Islam was brought to Indonesia in the 13th Century by traders from the Middle East. The first converts were made in Aceh, North Sumatra, and the Acehnese are still considered some of the strictest adherants of Islam in the country.

In Indonesia, unlike many Muslim countries, women are permitted to pray inside the mosque, although they sit apart from the men. These young women wear the obligatory white kerundung *which covers everything except the worshiper's face—even hands and feet must be covered. The main mosque at Banda Aceh shows a wealth of intricate detail and a mixture of styles from Arabia, India and Malaysia. As in all mosques, no human or animal forms are portrayed.*

Aceh was once famous for its fine unglazed pottery. The craft is still practised, but to a much lesser degree. Here a potter puts the finishing touches on a group of earthenware bowls. They will dry in the sun before being fired in a home-made kiln. The finished bowls are packed in baskets and taken to market by local transport—in this case, by bicycle.

Living on a small island about 120 kilometres off the west coast of North Sumatra, the people of Nias, like this man (top right), can dream idly of the outside world without having it thrust upon them. They have been able to make a more relaxed adjustment to change than their neighbours on the mainland. A Niah girl (above) takes a break from tending her garden; and a family relaxes in the shade of the entrance porch of their house. This young woman (right) wears a modern version of traditional Niasan ceremonial dress.

28

Mother and child peer out at the world through barred windows. Although not found on modern houses, these horizontal slats are seen on the windows of all older buildings on North and South Nias. This house (above) shows the high sloping roof and skylight windows typical of indigenous Niasan architecture. A modern extension has been added to the right. Seen from the inside, the house is spartan but hospitable. It has three small bedrooms, a kitchen and a large family room. Today more and more people are foregoing the raised houses of their ancestors in favour of conventional houses on the ground.

The village's only store supplies the needs of the entire area. Intricate designs on woven flaxen walls, buffalo horns and two-tiered roof identify this house as belonging to Karo Batak, a group living between Medan and Lake Toba. Like houses found on Nias, Karo houses are raised off the ground on stilts. The verandahs of these houses are versatile. On this one (top) a mother gives her baby a bath.

A Karo woman, her mouth red from chewing betel nut, wears the traditional Batak ulos or shoulder cloth.

Guests arrive for a Karo wedding bearing gifts. Kampung Lingga's normal population of about two hundred swelled to six times that number as friends and relatives came from all over the province. The bride and groom and their close family members are in the centre. A closer look at the bride (above), who is wearing the Batak head-dress called uis nipes.

Lighting a cigarette, a Karo man watches the wedding go by from a quiet corner. The coffee house where he sits serves as a meeting place for the men of the village. They sip coffee, smoke kretek, *Indonesia's clove-scented cigarettes, and chat. Sometimes silent, more often ringing with heated debate, the coffee house is the Batak equivalent of Britain's neighbourhood pub. Another guest at the wedding (right).*

Lake Toba is the ancestral home of the Batak peoples. Nine hundred metres above sea level, it is also Asia's largest crater lake. Prapat (above), on the shores of Lake Toba; (left) another view of the lake.

36

Toba Batak villages consist of a small number of closely-spaced, multi-family houses bordering one street or yard. The village itself is surrounded by an earthen wall with access at either end. This village on Samosir Island, Lake Toba, has six traditional houses and one of modern design. Like those all over Indonesia, the local barber-shop is simple: a shady tree, a chair, and a reasonably sharp razor.

The Toba Batak did not convert to Islam. Instead the majority are Christian with some animistic practices mixed in. The interior of the Protestant church (far right) on Samosir Island.

A vegetable seller at a market near Padang, West Sumatra. Markets start at dawn while it is still cool and are usually over by 9 or 10 o'clock in the morning.

Wearing a pretty dress and an even prettier smile, this Minangkabau girl stands in front of her family's new house. She is wearing kain songket, *a silk textile with a supplementary weft of metallic thread. At one time these cloths were woven with real gold and silver, but now synthetic yarns are widely used. As old cloths deteriorate, however, the precious thread is picked out and used again. Weaving* songket *is a thriving cottage industry in Sumatra; the same girl (right) weaves her own complicated designs.*

Rice shoots and the view south from Tabek Patoh. The landscape is dominated by hills and valleys with two main lakes—Maninjau and Singkarak.

Minangkabau houses have horn-shaped sway-backed roofs and walls covered with carved and painted panels. This one at Solok has been lived in for several generations and will be used as long as it is comfortable. Well-tended gardens are also a feature of the houses of the Minangkabau.

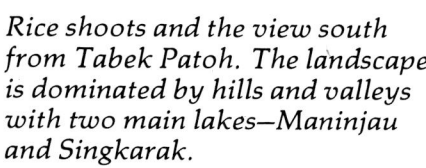

A Pagai girl in a faded cotton dress. Until recently the people of this village wore only grass skirts. Contact with outsiders over the last ten years has led to styles that, although more modern, are perhaps less comfortable and certainly more expensive.

40

A view of the village of Sikakap on North Pagai. This part of the village is new, having sprung up to meet the needs of the nearby timber company. Company workers often marry Pagai women and settle in the village. A ship arrives (below) with supplies. The mountain in the background is Gunung Kerinci.

There are no roads to speak of on the islands of North and South Pagai; the river is the principal means of transport. A Pagai woman (above) paddles to market or perhaps to her household garden. Taro is the staple food, though dry-rice cultivation has been introduced by government groups and missionaries. The mortar and pestle (right) is used for husking rice. Sago, generally used as fodder for pigs and chickens, is used for food in remote areas of South Pagai. Other foods are yams, bananas, sugarcane, durian and some fish. Betel nut is not chewed on Pagai, but the people smoke their own homemade cigars.

42

*A Kubu man from near Jambi. Essentially nomadic
hunter-gatherers, the Kubu are found in the area
between Jambi and Palembang on Sumatra's east coast.*

Because their forests are being destroyed by timber cutting, the government is trying to ease the Kubu into a more settled way of life. A Kubu mother (above) carries her child. The sling, a long rectangular cloth called selendang, is used throughout Indonesia for a multiplicity of carrying purposes. This peaceful looking Kubu woman, with the face of a school headmistress, has only recently moved out of the forest into a resettlement village, as has the young boy (right). His future will be very different from the life his parents lived.

Java

Java. The name conjures images of temple ruins, smoking volcanoes and spectacular terraced rice fields, every imaginable shade of green. Winding down the steepest hillsides and covering every square metre that has the water to support it, rice is the back-bone of Java. Because of its intense fertility, Java is the most crowded of the Indonesian islands, and the most intensely cultivated. More than sixty percent of the entire population of Indonesia lives here. It also has the lion's share of industry and technology.

Long before there was a written history to tell of it, wet-rice cultivation was known here, perhaps brought by migrants from the Dongson culture of mainland Asia. Wet rice requires water to flood the fields, water directed by intricate irrigation systems from the rivers to the dry lands between. A highly-structured and authoritarian society evolved on Java to direct and control the flow of water.

When Indian traders came to Java in the 6th Century, the Javanese kings adopted Hinduism, with its divinely sanctioned rule and caste system. Brahman priests were invited to Java. They taught their religion and ritual in the Javanese courts, beginning a period of Indian influence that lasted until Islam gained a firm foothold in the 15th Century. The most important of the Javanese kingdoms was the Majapahit, whose influence and prestige stretched from mainland Southeast Asia all the way to Irian Jaya. The *kraton*, or royal courts of Central Java, are still Majapahit in spirit, and the old religions lie just under the skin of the Muslim Javanese.

Ethnically the island can be divided several ways, but perhaps most conveniently into four major groups: the Javanese of Central and East Java; the Sundanese of West Java; the Tenggerese from the area in East Java around Mount Bromo; and the Madurese. Of these the Javanese are numerically the largest group and, in terms of cultural influence, the most important, although regional differences can allow for further subgrouping among them.

With their cultural heartland in the *kraton* of Surakarta and Yogyakarta, the Javanese of the principalities are known for exquisite *batik*; for the workmanship and supernatural powers of their sacred blades, or *kris*; and for the extreme sophistication of their dance. The Javanese language is elaborate and reflects a complex social system. There are three basic levels of speech in Javanese: *Kromo* is used when speaking to superiors or elders, *Ngoko* is for inferiors or when speaking to equals. The third, *Kromo inggil*, is used in the palaces. The interplay of these levels allows for endless subtlety of speech, especially in defining the relative status of the speakers.

The Javanese are an extremely polite and refined people. Loud displays of emotion and flamboyant behaviour of any kind are considered bad manners. This reserve, coupled with a real unwillingness to make anyone else feel uncomfortable or ashamed, often makes

A young boy from a village on the Dieng Plateau, Central Java.

47

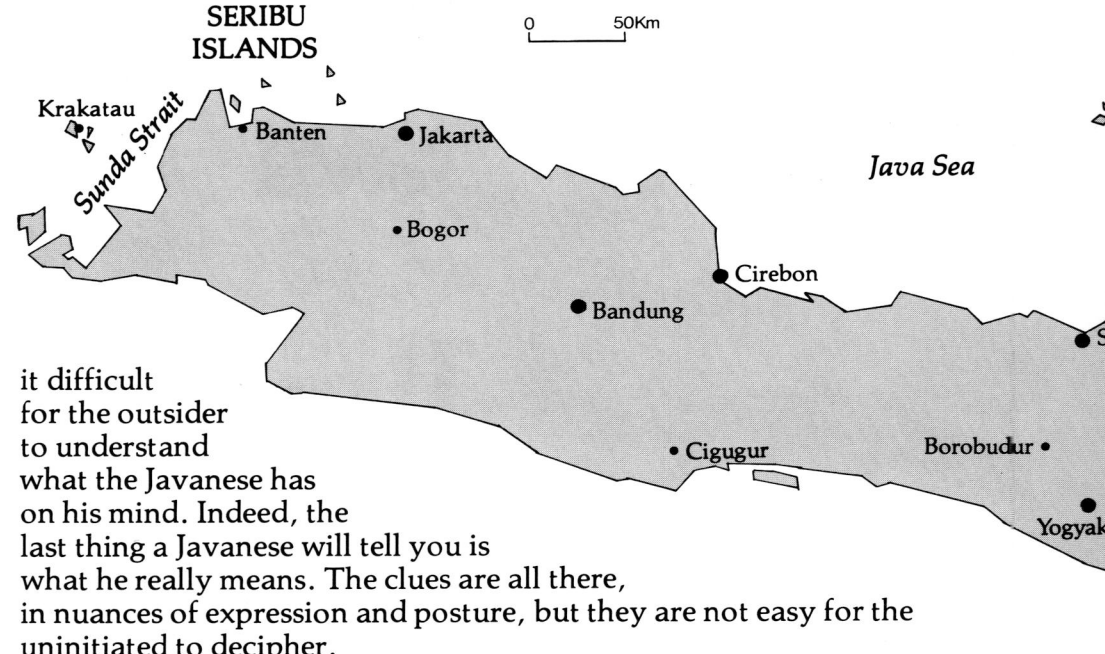

SERIBU
ISLANDS

Krakatau

Sunda Strait

Banten • Jakarta

Java Sea

• Bogor

Cirebon

• Bandung

0   50Km

it difficult
for the outsider
to understand
what the Javanese has
on his mind. Indeed, the
last thing a Javanese will tell you is
what he really means. The clues are all there,
in nuances of expression and posture, but they are not easy for the
uninitiated to decipher.

• Cigugur   Borobudur •

Yogyaka

Se

The people of West Java, the Sundanese, are a little less opaque
to the outsider's eye, a little less ascetic and perhaps livelier, simpler
and less formally structured. If you ask a Sundanese if he is different
from a Javanese, the answer is an emphatic affirmative. If you ask
how he is different, well, it is difficult to say.

The Badui, a small but distinct ethnic group living in the highlands of West Java, are thought to be a remnant of the original
Sundanese people who fled to the mountains and jungles to escape the
rising tide of Islam in Java. They have lived in self-imposed isolation
since the 15th Century.

Most Javanese and Sundanese follow Islam, but under the
surface many old beliefs and traditions persist. The *dukun*, or
specialist in magic ritual, is a valued member of the community. There
are many kinds of *dukun*. Some specialise in fertility rituals, some are
healers of various sorts, some deal with the ghosts and spirits that
abound in Java. Still others perform rituals to avert natural disasters.
The production and sale of *jamu*, traditional herbal medicine, also is a
flourishing business.

The soul of Java is *wayang*, traditional theatre performed with
puppets or with actors, using stories from the Hindu epics
Ramayana or *Mahabharata* to convey a peculiarly Javanese
set of values to its audience. To understand Java one must understand
wayang, but the art form is so subtle, oblique and to the outsider in-
comprehensible, that one must almost be a Javanese to understand it.
There are four basic forms: *wayang kulit* is a shadow play performed
with flat leather puppets behind a lamplit screen. *Wayang golek* uses
three-dimensional wooden puppets; *wayang topeng* is performed by
masked actors; and *wayang orang* or *wong*, the youngest of the
forms, is performed by unmasked actors. The oldest and by far the
most popular are the shadow puppets.

A set of shadow puppets can contain as many as two hundred
pieces, divided into the mostly good characters of the right and the
mostly bad characters of the left. There are no absolutes in *wayang*,
and although "good" usually triumphs, the victory, more often than
not, is ambivalent: a king, for example, who wins a righteous war

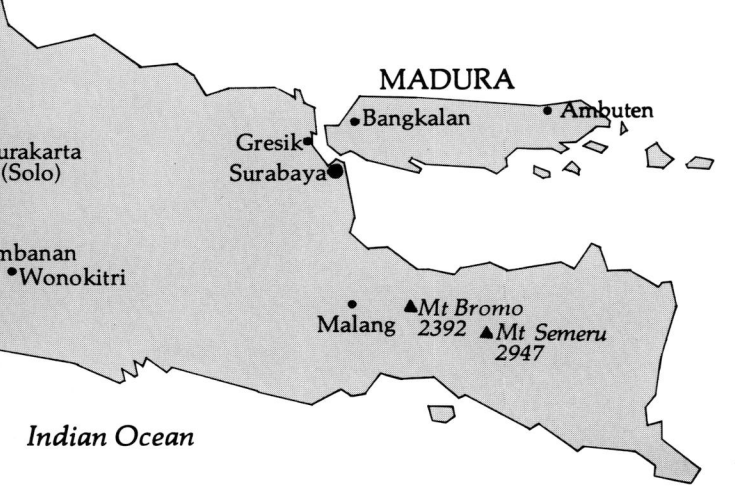

MADURA
•Bangkalan   • Ambuten
Surakarta   Gresik•
(Solo)   Surabaya•
mbanan
•Wonokitri
             •   ▲Mt Bromo
         Malang   2392 ▲Mt Semeru
                            2947
Indian Ocean

loses all his sons in the process. He sets his country to rights, leaves the throne, and retires to a hermitage to spend the rest of life in meditation.

Wayang transmits the values of inner control, dedication and self-sacrifice, and stresses the importance of refined behaviour over the boisterous, violent and crude. The Javanese use shadows to illustrate the invisible world and to place themselves in relation to it. The screen is the world, and the puppets exemplify the different roles that can be played in it. The banana trunk, into which the puppets are thrust when not in use, is the surface of the earth; the lamp that lights the screen and projects the flying shadows is the light of life, and the *dalang* or puppeteer is the spirit of God, breathing life into the puppets. *Wayang* has often been called the "Bible of Java", and it is a powerful tool for indoctrination because it is so pervasive and popular. Usually narrated in Javanese or Sundanese, the dialogue is full of slapstick humour as well as pathos, tragedy and serious philosophy. Children grow up with *wayang*. Everyone attends the all-night puppet shows, and children absorb Javanese values as naturally as they breathe. *Wayang* is often used to transmit information to a broad base of people. It has been used in recent years to urge support of a particular political party, for instance, or to encourage the use of modern fertilisers or family planning programmes.

The Tenggerese, an ethnic group which, like the Badui, has isolated itself from the mainstream of Javanese culture, are found in the area between Mount Bromo and Mount Semeru. Mount Bromo was established as a centre for the worship of Brahma during Majapahit times and was largely ignored in the onslaught of Islam. The Tenggerese, however, unlike the Badui, welcome visitors from outside, and their mountains are a popular destination for both Indonesian and foreign tourists.

According to Tengger mythology, a married couple lived on the edge of a huge plain leading down to the sea. They were childless and prayed to the god of the sea for offspring, promising to sacrifice one of their children to the god should their prayers be answered. Years passed and the couple had twenty-five children, but, as is so often the case, they forgot to fulfil their part of the bargain. A pestilence struck the village and many people died. Then the man had a vision, reminding him of his debt, and he summoned all his children to ask which should be sacrificed. Only the youngest child, whose name was Kusuma, offered himself. His father took him down to the edge of the sand and left him there for the god to claim. Immediately, a volcano erupted and Mount Bromo was born. Every year on the fourteenth day of the tenth month, the Tenggerese climb Mount Bromo and throw offerings into the crater to appease the spirit of the volcano and to honour the memory of the child Kusuma.

On Madura, a beautiful but arid island off the northeast coast of Java, live a people having little in common with the East Javanese. Even though many of them have moved to Java itself, they speak a different language, and, because their island does not support much agriculture, live a very different style of life. The raising of cattle, not an important activity on Java, plays a central role here, and the breed is improved by the competitive bull races for which Madura is famous. Fishing, for which the Madurese use double-outrigger sailing canoes, is a major activity on the island. The Madurese are one of Indonesia's four main sea-faring peoples. Their cargo boats, which in former days brought cattle to East Java from as far away as Roti and Timor in Nusa Tenggara, are now used predominantly in the Sumatra timber industry.

The capital of the Republic, Jakarta, is in West Java, and it is in this sprawling city, where the ultramodern and extremely traditional meet head on, that the challenges of the future are first met. Jakarta is the cutting edge of change in Indonesia, exhibiting the benefits as well as the costs of rapid modernisation. There is great wealth, seen in the tree-lined avenues of the southern suburbs, and the abject poverty of the tarpaper slums on the edges of the city. Because people from all over the country meet here, bringing with them the food, clothing, language and customs of their different cultures, Jakarta can be seen as an Indonesia in microcosm.

Rahwana menacing Sita. Performed on the stage of the Prambanan complex not far from Yogyakarta, this splendid production of the Ramayana tells the story of Rama, whose wife Sita is kidnapped by Rahwana, a rival king. The original epic was brought from India and translated over a thousand years ago. It was adapted for theatre in the 19th Century.

OVERLEAF: *Looking as delicate as a Chinese brush painting, the town of Ngadisari wakes with the early morning sun. Its rays reflect off shiny surfaces — fish ponds and tin roofs.*

Although it is the custom all over the island of Java to refrain from public displays of emotion, after hours of formal ceremony this bride from Cigugur, West Java, shows her relief and happiness. The wedding party then moved to the area's only Catholic church for a short, second ceremony.

54

A Sundanese boy and his grandmother, from Cirebon, West Java.

Members of a musical troupe (above right) from Bandung. Their instruments, called angklung, *are made from differing lengths of bamboo. When shaken, each produces a different note. The* angklung, *an ancient instrument on Java and Bali, had fallen into disuse. It has recently been revived using Western scales and modern tunes.*

Nestling in a valley beside a steadily flowing stream is the village of Naga. Self sufficient in most respects, the people of this small community perfectly exhibit the Indonesian custom of gotong royong, mutual assistance.

If anyone has a need he or she cannot fulfil—anything from house repairs to extra food for a guest— the neighbours help, confident that they too will be helped in their time of need.

Women at a harvest festival, Cigugur, West Java.

In Cigugur, a few hours from Cirebon, the people annually give thanks for the season's harvest in a ceremony unique in the area. Processions of girls, boys, men and women start early in the morning to carry the harvest from four separate villages to a central temple atop a hill. A portion will be used for the ceremony and the rest stored in a granary near the temple. Also carried are elaborate offerings of fruit and woven leaves. Music and dancing, as always in Java, are an integral part of the ceremony.

59

Called Batavia by the Dutch, Jakarta, Indonesia's cpaital, is a bustling, cosmopolitan city. Traffic is always heavy on Jalan Thamrin, a wide modern boulevard crowded with hotels, office buildings and embassies.

Istana Merdeka, Freedom Palace, is the President's official residence. Jalan Gajah Mada, leading down to the harbour, is in the background.

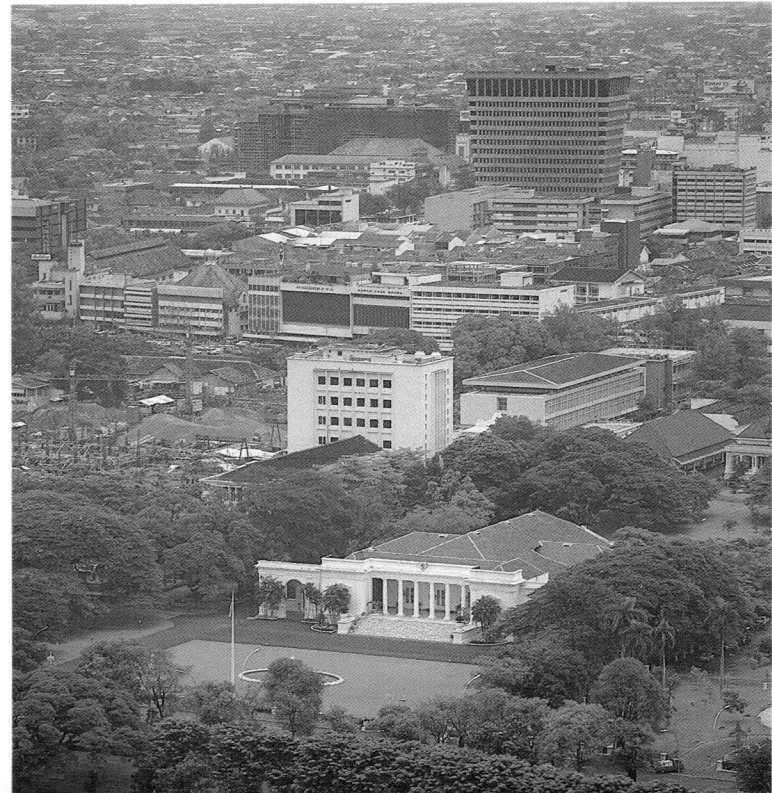

Jakarta's Istiqlal Mosque on the northeast corner of Merdeka Square is one of the world's largest mosques. The city's Roman Catholic cathedral stands close by.

The old port of Sunda Kelapa is the centre of inter-island trade in Jakarta. These elegant prahu pinisi sail all over Indonesia, bringing raw materials into Jakarta and supplying the islands with manufactured goods. Wide hulled and flat bottomed, with only a negligible projecting keel, they can carry an enormous amount of cargo. Although most are now equipped with engines, they generally follow monsoon winds as they sail around the islands.

Figures in a Chinese ancestral temple in Glodok, the city's original commercial centre. The man behind the desk selling oil and incense holders looks after the temple, where some of Jakarta's Chinese Indonesians come to pray.

Two Jakarta street scenes: Young poultry (above) for sale at Glodok market. In the background, the tattered remains of an election campaign poster. A row of becaks (right), Indonesia's omnipresent pedicabs, wait for fares outside a downtown hotel.

Indonesia produces some of the world's best badminton players. The game is incredibly popular, and children practise everywhere. This youngster, here using her front gate as a net, placed second in the all-Jakarta under-ten badminton competition.

Central Java is the heart of Indonesia's batik industry. Batik is made using a resist-dye process in which the design is waxed onto the cloth before it is dyed. Areas covered with wax do not take the dye, and after each dye bath the old wax is removed and different parts of the pattern waxed in. There are two kinds of batik, named for the way the wax is applied: In the finest examples, called batik tulis, designs are drawn by hand with a wax-filled canting or stylus. Batik cap is made with a copper stamp or print block, dipped in molten wax and · pressed onto the fabric. Although princes of the royal courts of Java often created designs for batik, the actual waxing of batik tulis is always carried out by women. Cap, on the other hand, is waxed by men. The finished product (left) is displayed at one of the many hotel fashion shows in Jakarta.

An actress (right) applies make-up before a performance. Small troupes throughout the island perform stories from the Hindu epics and Javanese history, as well as modern Javanese comic operas. These young people help ensure that traditional Javanese theatre remains a living part of Indonesian culture.

OVERLEAF: These two characters are Semar and Gareng, Java's ever-popular equivalent of Laurel and Hardy. They appear to a television audience of millions.

A performance of wayang kulit is a shadow play projected on a lamp-lit screen. The audience may sit on the shadow side or behind the dalang, watching him manipulate his flat leather puppets. Stories told in Javanese are usually from the Ramayana or Mahabharata, in a Javanese setting. Far more than just a puppeteer, the dalang, composes the dialogue and breathes life into the many puppets he controls, while directing the gamelan orchestra seated behind him.

A puppet maker (above) bends and shapes the horn strips that support and move a wayang kulit. Made of goat skin or buffalo hide, the puppets are intricately carved and painted.

From the 7th to the 10th Century, Central Java was the site of intense temple-building activity under the Sailendra Dynasty. For reasons that are still a mystery, power moved to East Java. Temples long buried in earth and undergrowth disappeared from sight and memory. Prambanan (above) was once the god Shiva's principal temple in Java. One of eight restored Shivaite temples (left) on the Dieng Plateau. Built in the early 9th Century, they are among the oldest known Hindu temples in Java.

An uncovered Buddha gazes down from near the top of the Borobudur. This 9th-Century Buddhist hill temple, for centuries hidden by vegetation and volcanic ash, was only rediscovered in 1814. Villagers living nearby knew nothing of its existence except that it was a place of ill-omen. The Borobudur has been saved from collapse by a ten-year restoration programme under the auspices of UNESCO and the Indonesian Government.

A guard at the kraton, or Sultan's palace, in Yogyakarta. These proud quiet men, descendants of the old palace guard, lend dignity to one of Yogyakarta's main tourist attractions and are perhaps the most-often photographed figures in Indonesia. A world in time away, this Surabaya policeman conveys a totally different impression.

Thousands flock each year to a waterfall at Sedudo in the hills southwest of Surabaya. Bathing annually in its cool clear spray is said to cleanse the spirit. The festival begins with visitors from as far away as Jakarta immersing themselves in the waterfall and lasts as long as it takes everyone present to bathe. Pak Wo (top right) presides over Java's Fountain of Youth. When this photograph was taken, he was 103 years old.

Bathing Indonesian style, this young boy uses a bucket to sluice down, then soaps all over and rinses again with water from the bucket.

The wife of the lurah *or mayor of the Tengger village of Wonokitri. Although under Islam men are permitted four wives, the practice of polygamy in Indonesia has been severly curtailed under the 1974 marriage act. In this case, the* lurah *had been a widower for several years before marrying for the second time.*

The mountains Batok in the foreground and Semeru in the distance both overshadow the rather unimpressive but better-known Mount Bromo to the left. One needs to stand on the lip and look into the depths of Bromo crater to feel the power that broods there. Accompanied by his hosts (right) at the unearthly hour of 4 a.m., the photographer views a spectacular sunrise over the mountain.

76

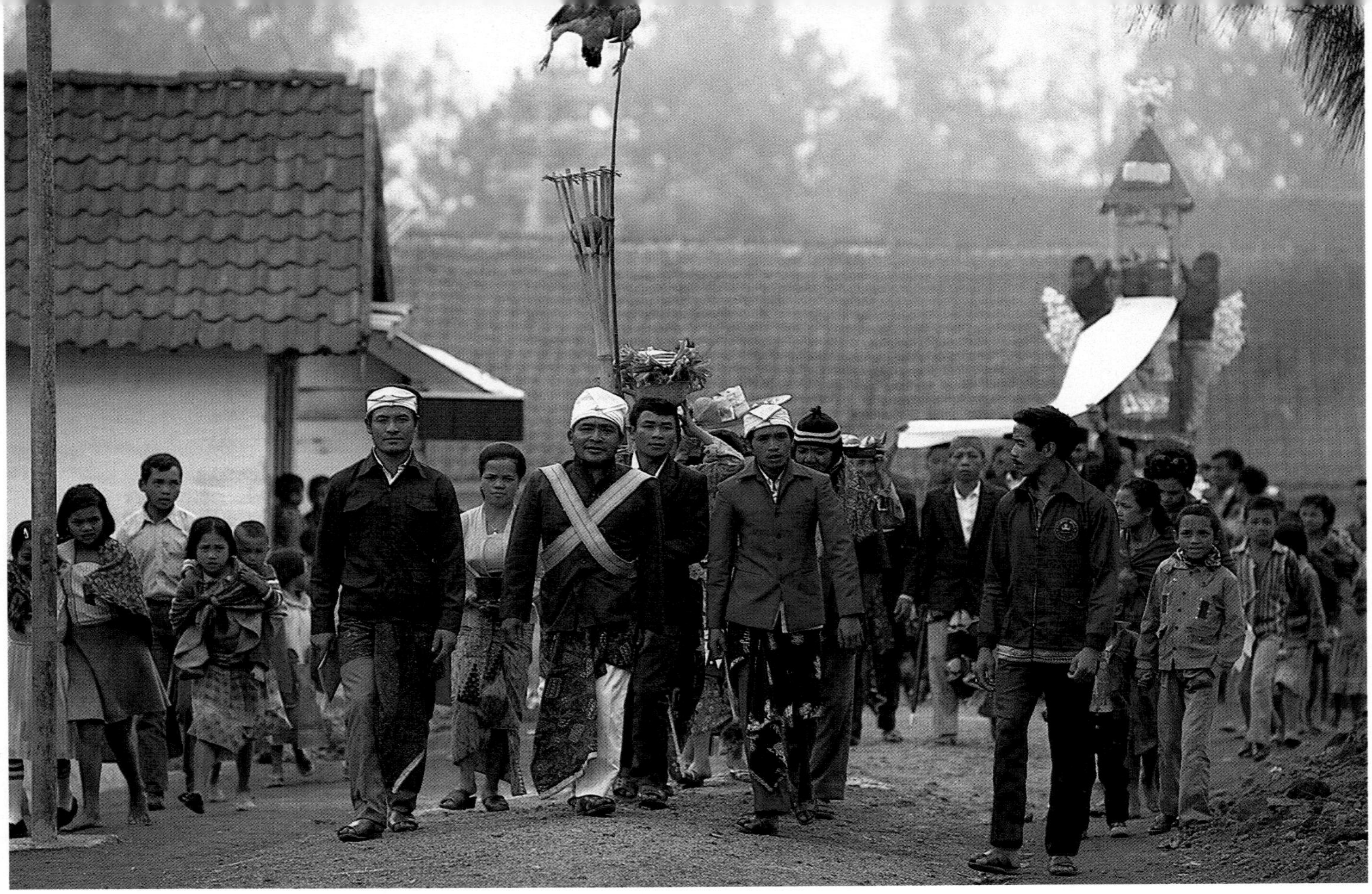

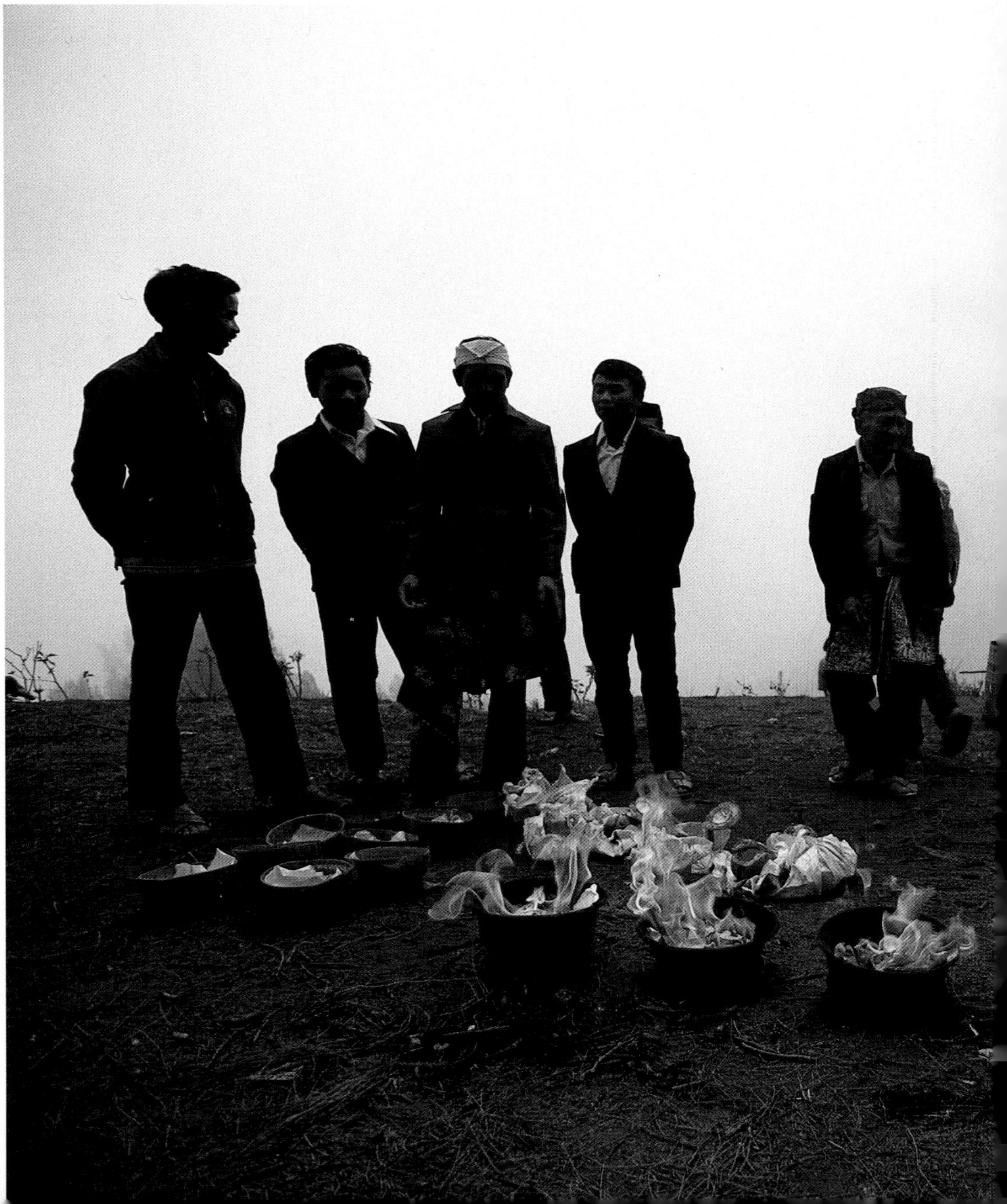

The area around Mt. Bromo is in many ways different from the rest of Java. The Tenggerese people practise their own religion, and some of their ceremonies are unique in Indonesia. In Wonokitri, for instance, one thousand days after the death of a village elder a ceremony takes place to release the spirit of the dead man. Called Entas-Entas, it starts with prayer and fasting. Small effigies, dressed in cloth once worn by the deceased, are then carried in a tower to the top of a sacred hill. Also carried, tied to the top of a pole, is the body of a bird, wings spread, whose soul will help the departed make the long journey. After chanting, and when the people are sure the spirit is ready, the effigies are slid down a chute and disrobed. The clothes are then cut up and placed in small coconut-shell bowls, doused in flammable liquid and set afire; shortly afterwards, the chute is also burned. The spirit is thus freed from all earthly ties and can leave in peace. A village elder later takes the effigies and burns them in private, scattering the ashes in a secret spot. Two young women (below right) watch the ceremony.

A Madurese woman on her way to market. Perhaps trading fish, she will buy rice, corn, vegetables and spices to supplement her family's fish diet.

The aquamarine seas at Telaga Biru in northwest Madura are cool, clear and refreshing. Not yet overwhelmed by tourists, the villagers are hospitable and friendly and show little interest in the hive of activity that exists in Surabaya, just a ferry ride away.

After a long night at sea the boats arrive at Ambunten (right) on the northeast coast of Madura. Nets are emptied and taken in to be washed, dried and repaired.

Not all men in the village go to sea. This village elder (left) tells tales common to fishermen everywhere.

Madura is famous for its bull races, held the first Sunday of every month. The races always start with dancing and a procession of beautifully decorated bulls in racing harness. Fed rice wine and whipped furiously during the race, the bulls are often hard to stop. These races are a source of great prestige to the breeders and their villages. Competition is fierce, and much care and preparation goes into the event. The second-place winner (right) proudly receives his prize.

83

The beaches on the dry south coast of Madura are being stripped. These women take their filled baskets to add to piles at the roadside.

A lone farmer (right) works in his rice field near Madura's south coast as the sun goes down.

Bali

Bali. The jewel at the eastern tip of Java, where the music of the *gamelan* fills the night, and gold-draped children dance the *legong*. A green, green island, where terraced hillsides meet the sky, and everyone is an artist.

The history of Bali has been turbulent, and in some of its episodes only slightly less fantastical than its legends. Ruled by Hindu Balinese kings from the earliest days of Hindu Java, the balance of power fluctuated between the two islands for a thousand years. Sometimes Bali was a vassal state, sometimes an independent kingdom. In the early 11th Century under Erlangga, the son of a Javanese princess and a Balinese prince, Bali even ruled Java for a time.

In 1343 General Gajah Mada of Java conquered Bali, and the island, along with the rest of the archipelago, became subject to Majapahit rule. The Kingdom fell during the reign of Brawijaya V when the ruler was told that in forty days the title of King of Majapahit would cease to exist. He took the prophecy so seriously that he burnt himself alive on the fortieth day. His son fled to Bali and proclaimed himself king. The rulers, priests, intellectuals and artists of the most civilised kingdom in Southeast Asia, along with the cream of Javanese culture, were transplanted in Bali's receptive soil. The art, religion and literature of Hindu Java were absorbed into Balinese culture and have flourished there, almost undisturbed, up to the present day.

In 1597 a fleet of Dutch ships discovered the island. For more than two hundred years the Dutch tried without success to gain control of Bali and her territories. In the mid-19th Century the first Dutch military expedition was sent to Bali over the issue of the ancient rights of the Balinese to salvage cargo from ships wrecked on her shores and by the late 1880's the Dutch had treaty rights with North Bali. By the beginning of the 20th Century they controlled all but the states in the south.

In 1904 a Chinese trading vessel, the *Sri Komala*, was wrecked and looted at Sanur on Bali's south coast. The owners applied for relief to the Dutch government, demanding three thousand silver dollars in damages from the Raja of Badung. After two years' negotiation, the Raja gave his final refusal, and a Dutch punitive expedition was launched against him. Five days later, when defeat was inevitable, the Raja gave his followers leave to return to their homes, inviting them, if they wished, to follow him to an honourable death. His advisors, priests, relations, wives, and many of his slaves and hereditary servants, all dressed in funeral white and carrying *kris* or short spears, prepared to accompany their lord into *puputan*, "the end". They marched in procession to meet the soldiers of the Royal Netherlands Indies Army, carrying the Raja on their shoulders under his gold umbrella of state. The women wore all their jewellery and

An actress takes a break back-stage during a performance of the Barong *dance.*

carried their babies. The Dutch commander begged them to stop, but they kept coming in a white and gold wave. At twenty metres they charged, waving their spears and *kris*. The Dutch had no choice but to fire. The Raja fell under the first volley, but his frenzied followers continued to attack. Men walked among the people, dispatching the wounded; priests sprinkled holy water on the dead and dying. The women of the palace threw their jewellery to the soldiers, stabbed their children and then themselves, falling in heaps over the body of the prince. When one group was killed another came to take its place until everyone was dead. The Dutch lost only one man.

Theirs was, however, a bitter victory that was to have tremendous consequences for the Balinese. The suicidal last stand of the royal house of Badung, although gaining them control over South Bali and the Rajas, was traumatic for the Dutch authorities. Not understanding what caused the Balinese to react so violently in the first place, they did not know what might cause them to react the same way again. Rather than risk a recurrence, the Dutch pursued a hands-off policy on Bali that was unprecedented in their handling of any other Indonesian possessions. The colonial administration was organised along much the same lines as it had been under the Rajas, and life went along virtually unchanged on the island.

In any case, the real life of Bali is in the hamlets and village temples and rice fields, not in the palaces of the great. A simple village in Bali is made of walled family courtyards lining tree-shaded streets. Where the two main streets intersect is the village square, and here are found the important public buildings. The village temple is here, as is the market, the cock-fight pavilion, the palace of the local lord if there is one, and the public assembly hall. There is also a tower where the *kulkul*, wooden slit-gongs used to summon the villagers to meetings or sound the alarm in times of trouble, are hung. Every village square also has its sacred *waringin* tree, under whose shadow many dances and village festivals take place. On the edges of the village are the cemetery and Temple of the Dead where the sacred guardian *barong* is kept, and in a cool shaded spot on the nearby river is the village bathing place.

Religion is a dominating force on Bali and pervades every aspect of life. Hinduism is practised on the island, but, mixed with animism

Bali Sea

0   10   20Km

araja

Lake Batur

Bratan

▲*Gunung Agung*
3142
Besakih

Tenganan

Ubud

Klungkung
Blahbatu
Batubulan

Denpasar

Badung Strait

Sanur

egian

Kuta

PENIDA

and softened by the unique spirit of the Balinese, it is a Hinduism that an orthodox Indian might not recognise. It is impossible to separate the Balinese from his religion. Indeed, anyone who converts to another faith ceases to be Balinese because he has cut himself off from his family's gods. Law and religion are also inseparable on Bali, because it is the proper and harmonious behaviour of the people that brings the supernatural forces abounding on the island under control. Evil deeds and magic of the "left"— that is, black magic — weaken the spiritual force of the village and allow evil influences to run rampant. Temple ceremonies, beautiful offerings, proper ritual, all entice the spirits of ancestors to stay in the village and keep it strong.

Balinese dance and drama are integral parts of religion, and performances are pleasing to the gods. Dancers are trained from the time they are tiny children and are highly valued in the community. A village which can train and support dancers of the *legong*, for instance, is exempt from taxes during the years they dance. Music is supplied by clubs of amateur musicians playing in *gamelan* orchestras. Those who can neither dance nor play may make the costumes or contribute in some other way. Rehearsals are long and arduous and usually take place at night, as do most performances. One wonders when the Balinese ever find the time to sleep.

The temple is the most important institution on Bali. Temples range from the grandeur of Bali's Mother Temple, Besakih, high on the slopes of the holy mountain Gunung Agung, to the small family shrines found in every household. Each household, in connection with the other families in their *banjar* or ward is responsible for its share of village temple maintenance and road building. The members of the *banjar* also pool resources for large temple ceremonies and musical activities. Families may also be members of the *subak*, which comprises all the households whose fields share the same irrigation source. The *subak* apportions the water to each family, guards the irrigation ditches and repairs the dikes.

The Balinese belongs to his family, his *banjar*, his *subak*, his temple and his village, living a communal and corporate life that has no counterpart in the West. But life is changing on Bali, as it is all over the developing world. As Indonesia's most important tourist attraction, this small island is inundated with thousands of visitors every year, and the resilient, unchanging Balinese culture is beginning to show the strain. The beaches—Sanur, Kuta, Legian—have lost their character and swarm with half-naked tourists and hawkers selling souvenirs and cheap clothing. Bus tours offer tourists the "real" Bali in half-day, whole-day, or two-day packages. There seems not to be a real Balinese in sight, and yet, through all the crush on Kuta's main street, a graceful youngster, ignoring the clamour, quietly sets out the evening offering of sticky rice and incense. Somewhere underneath all the noise and confusion the "real" Bali carries on.

Still, the problems of the outside world impinge on Bali too. Overpopulation is severe on this tiny island, and the overcrowding resulting from a high birthrate and long life make it, in the words of one old Balinese, "hard to breathe". Inflation also is taking its toll. People must work longer hours to meet the rising prices, and there is less time and money for traditional pursuits.

Tourism in Bali is a major foreign-exchange earner and is encouraged by the government. Bali alone attracts more visitors to Indonesia than all the other regions combined. Bali's unique culture and people are changing under the onslaught of foreign visitors. However, Bali has always been subject to foreign influences, and her people have been able to absorb what seemed useful, to change what did not quite fit, and to retain, in spite of everything, their own essential character.

A funeral procession on Kuta Beach. The bearers of these cremation bulls shout, chant and sing as they weave their way along Kuta's main street and turn down Jalan Pantai to the beach. The procession continues along the water's edge to the temple, where a mass cremation will be held. The remains of more than a hundred bodies were to be burned that day, many after waiting years for their families to collect enough money for the ceremony.

OVERLEAF: *Sunset over Tanahlot, a pagoda-like temple on a rock off the southwest coast.*

Time is computed in a special way on Bali, where a "year" has 210 days and a "week" can be anywhere from one to ten days long. The Balinese calender, in which these two cycles intersect, is based on the movements of the seven visible planets. Astrologers use the calender to cast horoscopes, and priests use it to fix the dates for ceremonies and festivals.

Once every Balinese year, each temple holds an odalan *or anniversary festival. As there are hundreds of temples on the island, almost every day at least one ceremony is in progress somewhere. Here at Bukit Djambul the villagers spend the entire night at their temple, high on a hill overlooking Bali's east coast. These festivals ensure that the villagers do not lose contact with one another or with the village itself. Even those who have moved away to find work are expected to return for the ceremony.*

Women wait beside their offerings for the ceremonies to begin. A Pemangku, or non-Brahman subsidiary priest (right), hands out woven-leaf offerings that have been blessed in the temple.

Small offerings like this one (right) are placed on the ground in front of houses, stores and temples all over Bali. Consisting of rice wine, water, rice, fruit, flower petals and incense, they are offered to appease evil spirits.

High on the slopes of Gunung Agung rests Besakih (below), Bali's mother temple. Called by Balinese the "navel of the world", every village on the island has a shrine here. Bits and pieces of this great temple are usually under repair, and the entire complex has been destroyed several times by natural disasters. Besakih's last and most dramatic levelling occurred in 1963 when Gunung Agung erupted during the Eka Dasa Rudra, a purification sacrifice which takes place only once every hundred years. It was the first time the holy mountain had erupted since the 14th Century. The ceremony was repeated in 1979.

Women (left) proudly carry offerings, piled high in silver bowls, to a temple ceremony. Traditionally made at home, there is a growing trend in the larger towns to buy them ready made. This is just one aspect of the changes occurring in Balinese religion in response to modern ideas and the pressure of increasing population.

After one 210-day Balinese year children have their first important contact with the religion and tradition that will guide them through the rest of their lives. Today this little girl will be named, blessed, and allowed to touch the ground for the first time. Three times, actually, once for each of the three deities that influence the lives of the Hindu-Balinese: Brahma, Shiva and Vishnu. The bowl in the foreground is used to bathe the child and to help the priestess at left to tell her future. She will be encouraged to pick up the various pieces of gold and silver jewellery in the water, each of which holds special meaning for her later years.

After a long life spent ministering to family and followers, a priestess is cremated at Blahbatu. Death is not an occasion for grief on Bali, but rather the joyous beginning of the soul's great journey to another life. The tower, representing the cosmos, dips and weaves its way to the cremation site, carrying the corpse high above the crowds of villagers, tourists and followers gathered to pay last respects or simply to watch. The bearers are all family or former students of the priestess.

On the way from the family's gate to the cremation site, the tower is turned three times to confuse evil spirits and prevent the soul of the deceased from trying to return to her former home. Having arrived at the nearby field, the corpse is swiftly transferred to a bull-shaped coffin, mantras are chanted, and the fire starts. Both the bull and tower are yellow and white, the colours of the Brahman caste.

As the heat intensifies, cleansing the bones and incinerating the bull, the arm joints contract, causing the arms slowly and eerily to rise. Later the remaining few bones will be crushed and ground, mixed with cane sugar, and ceremonially spread along the nearby shore.

A woman from Tenganan, East Bali, explains the ancient art of weaving grinsing, the sacred Balinese double-ikat textile. Grinsing, which has the power to protect the wearer from illness and evil, is an important part of many ceremonies on Bali and is woven only in this village. An incredibly complex process, it involves dying the pattern into both the warp and weft threads, and, because various components of the dyes can only be gathered during certain phases of the moon, it can take as long as nine years to dye and weave a single piece of grinsing. The Indonesian government considers grinsing a national treasure; it may not be taken out of the country.

Villagers work in the drained rice fields at harvest time. Threshing the rice stalks frees the grains from the stalk; the grain will later be pounded to separate the husk from the inner kernel. Rice that is consumed locally is husked a little at a time, only enough for one day's cooking. Green rice terraces (below) are a popular image in Balinese paintings.

With bemused expressions on their faces, these muttering, tripping ducks head for home. They spend their days lazing, bathing and growing, never straying from the pole of their owner who returns late every afternoon to take them home. Their lives are a short six months, as they are destined for temple offerings or family ceremonies.

Three dancers rest onstage while the main action continues elsewhere. Balinese dance-dramas are justly famous all over the world.

A seven-year-old girl (below) performs the Sanghyang trance dance. She has dressed and put on her make-up with little help from others and is put into trance by a priest before being conducted to the stage. As the chorus begins to sing and chant, the girls begin to dance. Although never taught to dance, no one is surprised at their skill; their bodies are occupied by the spirits of female deities who dance for them.

Bells, drums, metallaphones and gongs make up the Balinese gamelan orchestra used here to set the various moods of a Barong dance at Batubulan.

The young man (above) is one of the Barong's followers.

The Barong dance enacts the struggle between the forces of harmony and discord, climaxing with a fight between the Barong (right) , a mythical creature whose magic power is concentrated in his beard, and the witch Rangda (below).

The fight is inconclusive, and the Barong leaves the stage to summon his followers . They attack Rangda, but she rallies and casts a spell, causing them to turn their knives upon themselves. The witch departs in glee, but the young men are protected by the Barong's magic, and the blades do not harm them. They are released from trance by the Barong and a Pemangku.

A group of children take a break from selling souvenirs and fly their kite on Legian beach. Nearby a sun-loving tourist relaxes on the hot sand. The woman to her right, carefully protected from the sun, waits to give her a massage.

106

A village scene comes to life under the hand of one of Bali's many painters. Bali's long tradition of artistic expression provides fertile ground for her many budding artists.

Silverware, necessary for all ceremonies in one form or another, is finely worked and of high quality. Samples from this village suburb of Singaraja, capital of North Bali, include bowls, cups and other containers. Although jewellery and objects of modern design are making their way into tourists' hands, most of this craftman's work will eventually be used in ceremonies by people from surrounding villages.

Wood carving (far right) is a treasured craft on the island. This rendition of Vishnu riding on Garuda is a fine example of the traditional Balinese style.

A girl receiving blessings at a temple ceremony.

Sitting in one of the open houses in the public meeting area, an afternoon is spent making a new cage for a prized fighting cock.

Kalimantan

Kalimantan. The Indonesian two-thirds of Borneo, one of the largest and most mysterious islands in the world. Its dense, often impenetrable forests abound with wildlife, many species of which are not found anywhere else in the world. The deep waters of the Mahakam river, for instance, harbour a rare species of fresh-water dolphin. There are clouded leopards, hundreds of species of exotic birds, reptiles, and insects, and a bewildering variety of monkeys and apes, including the rare proboscis monkey and the orangutan. The most important creature of the forest, from a symbolic point of view, is the black hornbill, soul carrier of the Dayaks. Since prehistoric times the hornbill has played a major role in Dayak culture, but, hunted for its feathers and huge beak, the hornbill was in danger of extinction. Now a protected species, its numbers are increasing. The durian, Southeast Asia's notorious "smelly fruit", flourishes in the jungles, and Kalimantan's durian *lai* is considered the most delicious of all varieties. Durian smells like a combination of sour milk, onions and over-ripe mangoes. It tastes, to those who appreciate its flavour, like heaven; to those who don't, durian tastes the way it smells.

Although its area is huge, the population is sparse, and the island's incredibly rough terrain makes communication and travel difficult. Life in Kalimantan centres on the many rivers that serve as the main channels of communication throughout the island. Roads are few, and where there are no navigable rivers travel is virtually impossible.

Like Sumatra and Java, the island was a cultural crossroad in prehistoric and early historic times. In the Neolithic period, migrants moving south from China brought with them artifacts and technology from the Chou Dynasty and the Sino-Vietnamese Dongson culture that has been influential all over western Indonesia. Sanskrit inscriptions dating from around 400 A.D. give evidence of Hindu influence in East Kalimantan, and it is likely that the area was a trade centre on the much-travelled route between China, the Philippines, and the Javanese Majapahit Kingdom. Many bronzes and porcelains in the style of the Chou Dynasty have been found in Kalimantan, and in inland areas Chinese-style bronze gongs are important items of currency, used especially to pay the bride price when a couple marries.

There are three basic ethnic groupings in Kalimantan: coastal Malays, relatively recent arrivals who follow Islam and live in towns and cities and small settlements at the mouths of the rivers; ethnic Chinese, who have controlled trade in Kalimantan for centuries; and the island's original inhabitants, the Dayaks. Dayak is a comprehensive term used to describe more than two hundred inland tribal groups. Originally coastal dwellers, they have been driven farther and farther inland by successive migrations of Malays. They

inhabit the river banks and highlands deep in the jungle and live a life not very different from that of their Neolithic forebears. Dayak culture varies from tribe to tribe, but most of it centres around the *lamin* or longhouse. A Dayak village may consist of one large *lamin* — some in East Kalimantan are nearly 300 metres long—or several smaller ones. *Lamin* are built on ironwood piles often three metres high to offer protection from enemies, wild animals and flooding. Notched ironwood logs, sometimes beautifully carved, serve as ladders which can be pulled up into the longhouse at need.

The area below the house is used to stable domestic animals, usually pigs and chickens. Above, longhouses are divided lengthwise. Most have a communal verandah running the length of one side and private family quarters running the length of the other side. In some groups, however, private quarters line both sides of a central verandah. The verandah is the main street and communal area of the *lamin*. Here the women pound the rice and mend the fishing nets. Villagers meet here, and here the traditional, songs, dances and ceremonies are performed. In one Dayak group there is a sunken square built on springy poles in the middle of the verandah. It is used for jumping dances, and acts much like a trampoline. Fish traps, paddles, blowpipes and clothing are stored on the verandah, and the unmarried men sleep there. The space under the roof is used to store rice, baskets, mats, fishing nets and other valuables.

Until quite recently head-hunting was an important activity among many Dayak tribes. Heads were needed to keep a village strong and for ceremonial functions, such as the building of a new *lamin*. They were useful in warding off plague and famine and in keeping evil spirits at bay. The continual threat of head-hunting raids from neighbouring villages turned longhouses into well-fortified bastions of defense. In some places, the verandahs were made of loosely-tied lengths of bamboo which rattle when walked upon, to

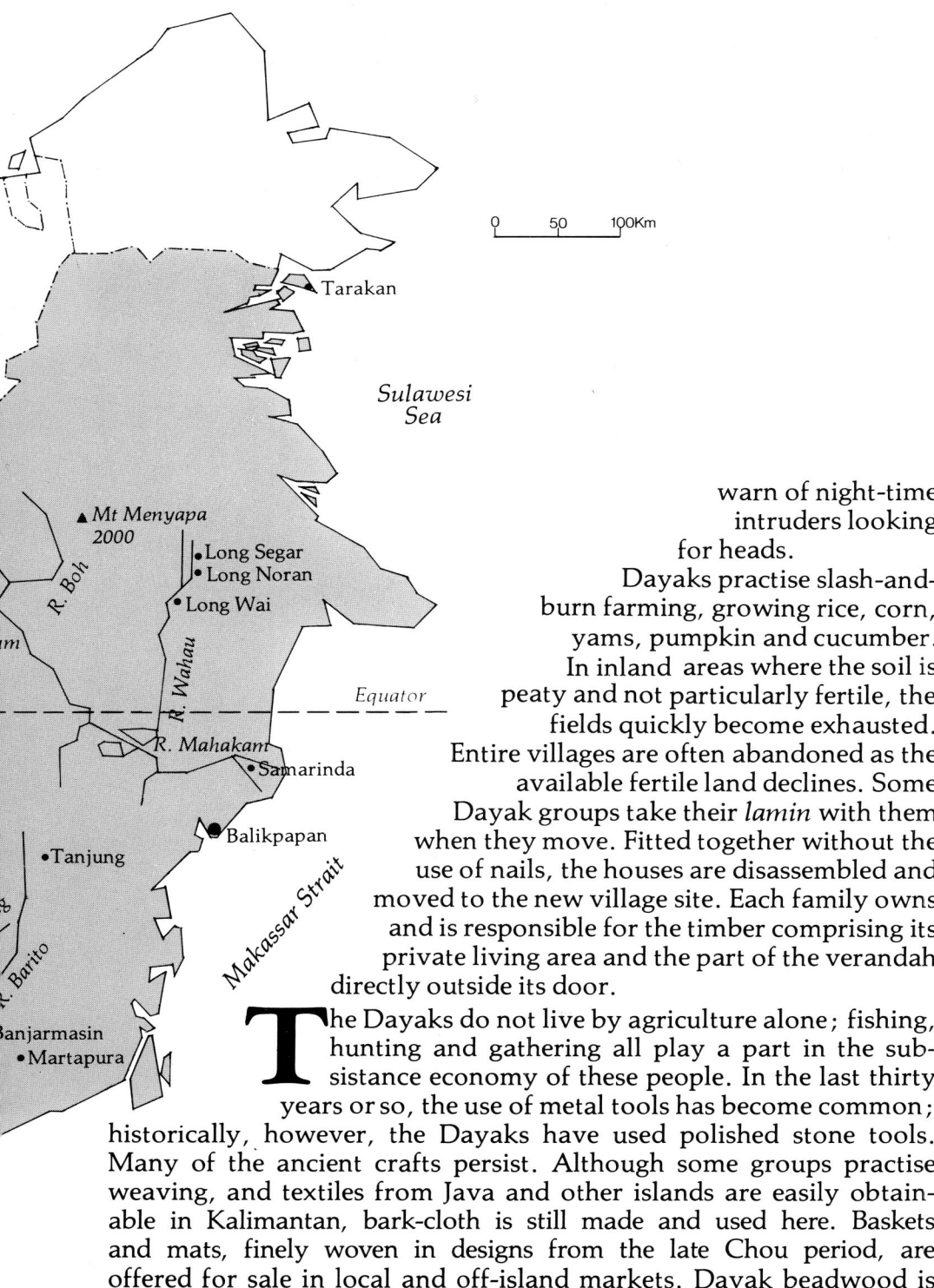

warn of night-time intruders looking for heads.

Dayaks practise slash-and-burn farming, growing rice, corn, yams, pumpkin and cucumber. In inland areas where the soil is peaty and not particularly fertile, the fields quickly become exhausted. Entire villages are often abandoned as the available fertile land declines. Some Dayak groups take their *lamin* with them when they move. Fitted together without the use of nails, the houses are disassembled and moved to the new village site. Each family owns and is responsible for the timber comprising its private living area and the part of the verandah directly outside its door.

The Dayaks do not live by agriculture alone; fishing, hunting and gathering all play a part in the subsistence economy of these people. In the last thirty years or so, the use of metal tools has become common; historically, however, the Dayaks have used polished stone tools. Many of the ancient crafts persist. Although some groups practise weaving, and textiles from Java and other islands are easily obtainable in Kalimantan, bark-cloth is still made and used here. Baskets and mats, finely woven in designs from the late Chou period, are offered for sale in local and off-island markets. Dayak beadwood is excellent. Some of the beads still in circulation came to Kalimantan from Italy in the time of Marco Polo.

Not all Dayaks live in settled villages. One group, the Punan, live in a much more primitive style than their relatively sophisticated neighbours. They are classic hunters and gatherers and wander through the forests at will. Although the government is encouraging them to live in villages and cultivate rice, most Punan are not interested in settling down. They may live in a village for a few weeks or even months, but the houses are often abandoned in the pursuit of their traditional nomadic ways.

Kalimantan has greatly changed since the turn of the century, especially in the last forty years or so, and much the old Dayak culture has gone or is fast disappearing. Head-hunting, as elsewhere in Indonesia, is a thing of the past. Ceremonial life is in decline, and the rule of *adat*, tradition, has been broken by the conversion of many Dayaks to either Christianity or Islam. *Tuak*, a kind of palm wine drunk at many ceremonies and dances, has been forbidden by the

Protestant missionaries; without it, the ceremonies and dances do not take place. Longhouse living has been discouraged both by missionaries and by the Indonesian government on the grounds that it is unsanitary and spreads disease. Conventional Javanese-style villages are replacing them, but the longhouse-centred communal Dayak culture does not survive in these villages.

Timber is big business in Kalimantan, and the island's wealth of natural hardwoods is proving to be a mixed blessing. Indiscriminate tree-felling has led to serious erosion in some areas, and, although reforestation projects have been undertaken, it will take decades to repair the damage. Timbering has also disturbed the breeding patterns and destroyed the habitat of many species of wildlife already rare in the world's forests. The government has lately taken steps to restrict timbering and protect the forests and their inhabitants, but poaching of both trees and animals is easy and, given the size of the jungle, almost impossible to prevent.

In the vicinity of Balikpapan, locally known as *Kota Minyak* or "Oil City", is an immense field of natural gas. Thousands of foreigners and Indonesians from other islands have come to work in Balikpapan and nearby Badak, where a huge liquefaction plant has been built. The contrast between the lives of these outsiders and the local inhabitants is staggering. The influx of coastal peoples and traders upriver has had an eroding effect on Dayak culture. As always, when faced with pressure from outside, the Dayaks retreat farther inland to parts of Kalimantan as yet inaccessible to outsiders.

The Dayaks are, of course, only one part of Kalimantan's story. The coastal people and those who live in the increasingly modern and prosperous cities and towns are more in the mainstream of Indonesian life than they have been since the great days of the Majapahit Empire. People flock to Kalimantan from all over Indonesia, especially Java, looking for work, and the modern world is fast encroaching on the jungle. Although the days of the "wild man of Borneo" are fading fast, the jungles of Kalimantan are still the custodians of precious cultural and natural treasures.

A man and woman chat at a floating market in Banjarmasin on the Barito River, South Kalimantan. The market consists of a group of boats, large and small, to which buyers and sellers come in their simple dugout canoes. Trading begins soon after sunrise and lasts until mid-morning. At nine or ten o'clock people begin their journeys home, disappearing up the many small tributaries of the river.

OVERLEAF: *A father and son fish for prawns on the Mahakam River, East Kalimantan. Some of the rattan baskets on board are used to trap the shellfish; others are used to store the catch.*

A woman bathes her child on one of her village's several floating tempat mandi. These platforms tied to the bank serve as wash-houses, jetties, entrances to the village and gathering places for the village women.

Like children everywhere, the young in Kalimantan are quick to invent games in their spare time. Stilts, hopscotch and bicycle riding are popular, and in the hot weather a quick plunge in the river is always welcome.

118

A Kenyah Dayak woman cheerfully mixes the old and new. Wearing Western clothes and smoking a cigarette, she also bears the traditional tatoos of a Dayak lady. Her earlobes, though pierced to hold heavy gold or brass rings, are modern and empty.

An old woman (right), quietly watching the world go by from her house on the river, has decorated one lobe with a safety pin. Almost a hundred years old, she has seen enormous changes since the days when she and her family wandered deep in the forests. The tatoos on her forearms and calves, intricate curvilinear designs of birds and spirits, are a legacy of the time when all Dayak women thought them beautiful and necessary.

The village head of Neheslah Bing on the Mahakam River. A Modang Dayak, his ears are pierced for ornaments only. Had be been a headhunter in bygone days, his upper ears would have been pierced to display trophies.

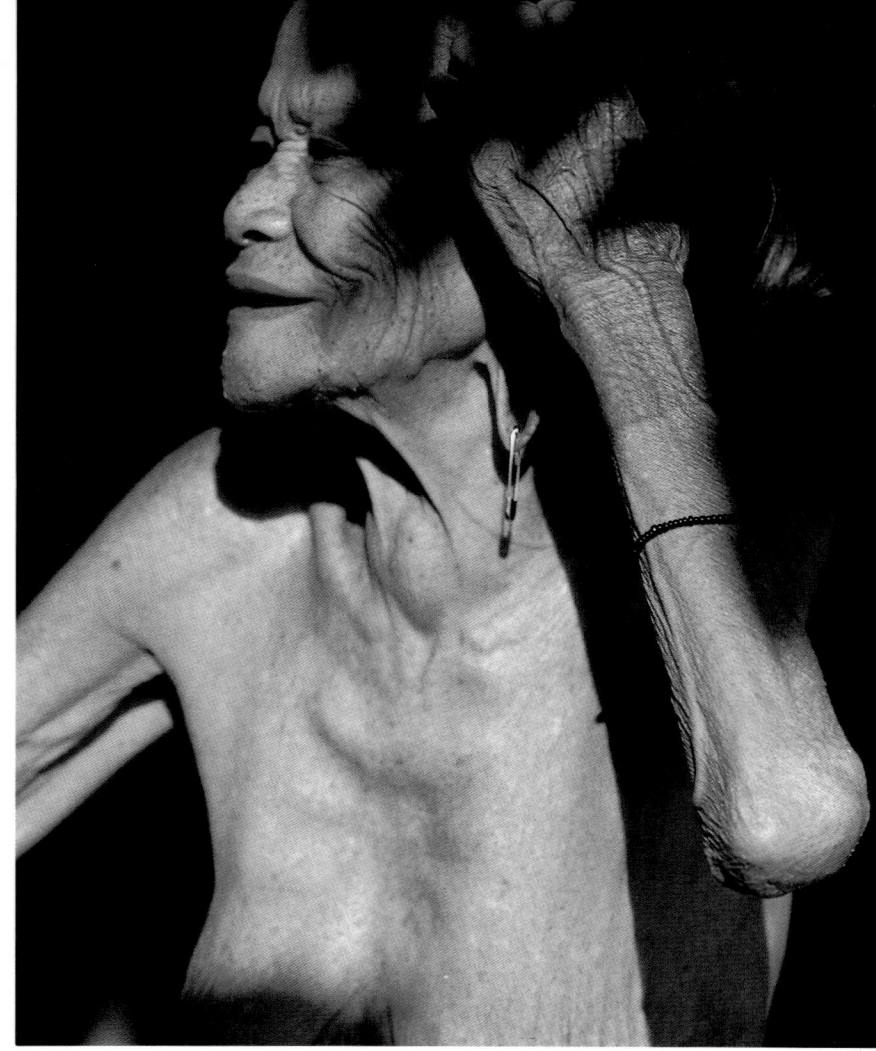

The rain forests are the home of many primates, including macaque monkeys (left), proboscis monkeys (above) and orangutans like Rico (right), an adolescent male seen here prowling around the orangutan rehabilitation centre in Tanjung Puting, a wildlife reserve in Central Kalimantan. This centre helps orangutans which have been kept as pets return to their native forests. Orangutans are a protected species in Indonesia, but their future is still at risk. Although the indiscriminate deforestation which destroyed huge areas of their habitat has ended, the controlled timbering which continues is enough to disrupt their breeding patterns. Orangutans are shy creatures, easily frightened, and when under stress their fertility rate drops drastically. Sumatra and Borneo are the only places in the world where these rare primates can be found. If the areas where they can live undisturbed continue to shrink, they could face extinction in the wild.

Cocks in a training fight in Central Kalimantan. In real matches they wear poisoned spurs, and death occurs within seconds after a wound is inflicted.

In many parts of Indonesia, babies are carried in selendangs, long strips of fabric looped under one arm and fastened on the opposite shoulder. Dayak babies, however, ride in beautifully decorated wooden or rattan carriers on their mothers' chests or backs. Baby carriers may be painted, beaded, carved or hung with coins, ribbons and pieces of ivory. The coloured ones are most commonly black with yellow designs, as are the two shown here. The Dayaks are famous for their beadwork, and many of the glass beads still in circulation are Italian, having come to Kalimantan from China in the time of Marco Polo.

The Kenyah Dayaks are splendid dancers. This swift and skillful mock attack (far right) is performed with traditional Dayak swords called mandau. The mandau is as important to the Dayaks as the Kris is to the Javanese, and as much care goes into its making. The carved handles (right) are especially beautiful. Unlike Kris, which can only be used in battle or ritual, mandau are often put to practical use.

The central pole in the meeting house at Long Noran, East Kalimantan. Interpretations vary, but the village chief tells of an ancient king and the burung enggang or black hornbill, soul-carrier of the dead. These as well as flowing water, mandau and other symbols can clearly be seen on the pole. There is also a martavan, a Chinese storage vessel made of porcelain or earthenware decorated with dragons and floral designs. Many martavan are truly old, dating back to the Ming Dynasty, but their desirability as collectors' pieces has led to a flourishing trade in forgeries.

125

Kalimantan is mainly jungle, penetrated by numerous rivers which are the main lines of communication on the island. Small outboard and inboard engines are being used more and more, but dugouts, paddled with the single carved Dayak oar, are still a common sight. Thick vegetation cloaks both sides of the river, broken only by occasional houses and timber concessions.

A man empties a sack of rice (left) onto a woven mat. The flower tatoos on his shoulders and chest identify him as Punan, one of the original inhabitants of the island whose ancesters moved inland as waves of migration forced them away from the coast. Like the Kubu of South Sumatra, the Punan are nomadic hunters and gatherers, roaming the forests of East Kalimantan. Occasional contact with river dwellers has brought with it stories of the outside world, and with encouragement from the government, some Punan are beginning to live a more settled life.

The Dayaks practise dry-rice cultivation, rather than the wet-field method practised in Java and Bali. These fields, called ladang, are in Long Segar, East Kalimantan. This family works for a few hours each morning, and then everyone settles down for the mid-morning meal. They return to the village by noon to rest and prepare the evening meal of rice, vegetables and the occasional fish.

127

In a village on the upper reaches of the Mahakam river, a woman weaves a fishing net on the verandah of her lamin *or longhouse.*

In any small village a death in the community is a major event and a time of mourning for all. In this new Punan village, comprised exclusively of one large extended family, the dead woman (above) was the oldest member to arrive at this isolated shallow tributary of the Mahakam river; now she is the first to leave it.

South Kalimantan is one of Indonesia's major diamond-producing provinces. A large variety of precious and semi-precious stones find their way from mines here to market places around the country. Jakarta in particular has a number of markets frequented by shabby-looking but eloquent salesmen who tell of magic gems from mines in distant Kalimantan. The mines themselves, however, silt-filled waterlogged holes and pits dug along the mouths of ancient streams, are not nearly so romantic. A miner, up to his waist in water, works at a diamond mine near Martapura.

At Tanjung market a woman sells dried fish, a dietary staple all over Indonesia.

130

South and East Kalimantan are famous through Indonesia for their high-quality mat and basket weaving. Intricately designed, they are prized for their beauty as well as for durability and strength.

131

Early morning on the Barito River, near Banjarmasin, South Kalimantan.

A young girl from Anjir Serapat (right), a small village in South Kalimantan, is being dressed for her most untraditional-looking wedding. Wearing a curled black wig and a white dress with a Paris label, she awaits the arrival of the groom from a village down river. One hundred and eighty guests were present to witness the formal meeting of the young couple. The bride was third in her family to wear this spectacular outfit, which is at least two generations old. Nearly as elegant as she, the groom wore a black and grey pinstriped suit.

Sulawesi

ulawesi. An odd orchid-shaped island in the middle of Indonesia, with three long petals topped by a curving stem. Each peninsula is ridged with central mountains and surrounded by coral reefs. The northernmost part of the island was once linked to the Philippines. When the land bridge was broken, many plants and animals were isolated and the island evolved into a zone of wildlife unique in Indonesia. Sulawesi is the home of the *babi rusa*, a pig-like animal with curving tusks; the *anoa*, a fierce pygmy buffalo living in the mountains of the north central part of the island; and the black-crested baboon. Away from the coastal fringe, the land is covered with rain forests and rugged unarable highlands.

In prehistoric times, from about 12,000 to 4,000 years ago, Sulawesi was an entrepot for many races and cultures. As new waves of migration moved onto the coasts, the older inhabitants moved inland. The mountainous interior makes communication and travel difficult. Rivers are narrow and for the most part unnavigable, and until the Spanish brought horses in the 17th Century, the only mode of transportation inland was on foot. Communities out of reach of the sea had to be self sufficient if they were to survive. The resulting pattern of inland settlement was one of isolated ethnic groups with very different cultural patterns, until recently having little contact with each other or the outside world. The largest and perhaps oldest of these groups is the Toraja, the people of the mountains. Tana Toraja (Torajaland) is located in the centre of the orchid, in an area that comprises parts of the provinces of Central and South Sulawesi . Until Christian missionaries entered their lands in the early 19th Century, the Toraja lived in almost total seclusion from the foreign influences that had been flooding coastal Sulawesi for hundreds of years. All outside trade occured through the mediation of the Bajau sea nomads from northeast Kalimantan who were the only people the Toraja would tolerate. Now, however, because of the uniqueness of the culture and its interest for tourists, the number of outsiders passing through the area every year has dramatically increased.

he first thing that strikes a visitor to Tana Toraja are the houses. A traditional Toraja house or *tongkonan*, is built according to unchanging ancient requirements. It must stand facing north, the source of felicity, and its entrance must face the east, which is associated with life. Built without nails and sitting on top of thick octagonal posts, it must be made in such a way that it can be moved without falling apart. Rice barns, smaller versions of the *tongkonan*, are built in a row in front of the house. The number of barns indicates the wealth of the family. Only women may enter the upper part of the barn where the rice is stored. Underneath is an open platform where guests are received. The most striking feature of the house is its sweeping boat-shaped roof, thatched with split bamboo.

A guest at a death feast in Tana Toraja, South Sulawesi.

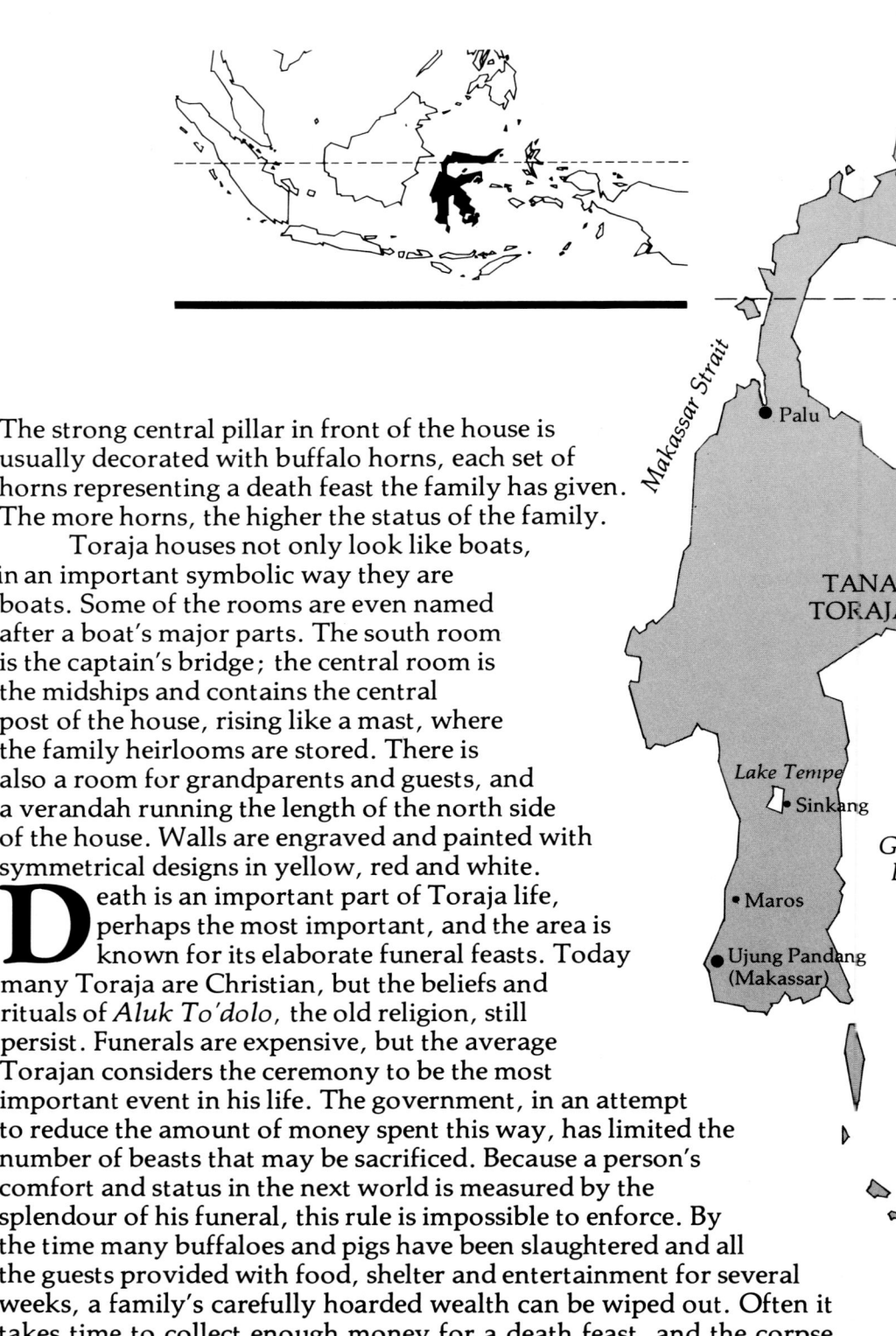

The strong central pillar in front of the house is usually decorated with buffalo horns, each set of horns representing a death feast the family has given. The more horns, the higher the status of the family.

Toraja houses not only look like boats, in an important symbolic way they are boats. Some of the rooms are even named after a boat's major parts. The south room is the captain's bridge; the central room is the midships and contains the central post of the house, rising like a mast, where the family heirlooms are stored. There is also a room for grandparents and guests, and a verandah running the length of the north side of the house. Walls are engraved and painted with symmetrical designs in yellow, red and white.

Death is an important part of Toraja life, perhaps the most important, and the area is known for its elaborate funeral feasts. Today many Toraja are Christian, but the beliefs and rituals of *Aluk To'dolo*, the old religion, still persist. Funerals are expensive, but the average Torajan considers the ceremony to be the most important event in his life. The government, in an attempt to reduce the amount of money spent this way, has limited the number of beasts that may be sacrificed. Because a person's comfort and status in the next world is measured by the splendour of his funeral, this rule is impossible to enforce. By the time many buffaloes and pigs have been slaughtered and all the guests provided with food, shelter and entertainment for several weeks, a family's carefully hoarded wealth can be wiped out. Often it takes time to collect enough money for a death feast, and the corpse sometimes waits years before burial is possible. During the interim the deceased is thought to be "ill". He or she is visited daily, offered food and cigarettes, and treated with great love and respect.

A death feast in Tana Toraja only lasts a few days, but it cannot begin until all the relatives have assembled. There is often a wait of several weeks before everyone has arrived. When everything is ready, the coffin is carried in procession to the *rante*, a field where tall stones stand. Special houses, called *lantang*, have been built there for the relatives of the deceased, as well as a special pavilion where the coffin lies in state. As soon as the coffin has been placed in the pavilion, buffalo fights are held. The second day is a day of rest. On the third day, groups of guests enter the *rante*, proceeded by their gifts of buffalo, pigs and palm wine. They file past all the *lantang* and are finally

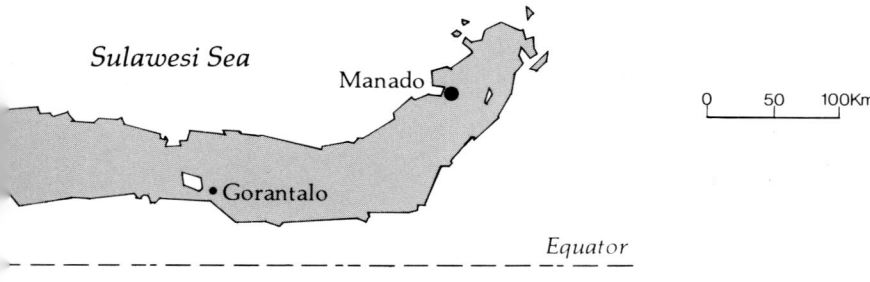

Sulawesi Sea

Manado

0   50   100Km

Gorantalo

Equator

Gulf of Tolo

wuti

Kendari

WOWONI

BUTON

MUNA

Bau Bau

TUKANG BESI ISLES

A

Sea

welcomed in the guest pavilion when they are offered coffee and cake. The group then moves into one of the *lantang* and another group takes its place. On the following day buffaloes are fastened to the megaliths in the open space of the *rante* and slaughtered, and the meat is distributed to family members and villagers.That night the *ma'badong* is danced, recounting the life cycle of human beings and the story of the deceased in particular. After all these rituals have been carried out, the Protestant minister or Catholic priest conducts a Christian funeral service. After the funeral the corpse is interred in a cave or hollowed-out cliff face. Wooden effigies, dressed in clothing similar to that worn by the dead person, look out over the cliffs, waiting to provide a comfortable resting place for the spirit should it wish to return for a visit. The effect on the Toraja landscape is eerie. Wooden figures, coffins, skulls and bones litter the rocky hills in areas suitable for cliff burial. Children often play with old skulls, setting them up in rows to glare emptily at the passersby. But in Tana Toraja death is not morbid or particularly unwelcome. It is a happy transition in the spirit's journey to a better life.

Minahasa, in the province of North Sulawesi, provides the greatest possible contrast to Tana Toraja. Not much is known about the original Minahasa culture because North Sulawesi, with its capital city of Manado, came under such strong European influence in the 17th Century that most indigenous traditions were lost. Most Minahasans are Christian as a result of education in Dutch mission schools, and Western dress is common throughout the area.

The most important crop is cloves, used to make *kretek*, Indonesian cigarettes. North Sulawesi is also Indonesia's biggest producer of copra, or dried coconut kernels, and every family seems to have at least a small stand of coconut palms. The Minahasa people are great traders, and the per capita income in this area is one of the highest in the entire country.

South Sulawesi is also a relatively wealthy area. For years it was the Dutch rice granary, supplying possessions in Maluku. The provincial capital, Ujung Pandang (formerly called Makassar), is the major trading port. Ujung Pandang is the home of the Makassar people, who, with the Bugis of the east coast of the peninsula, form the major ethnic groups in South Sulawesi.

Many Makassarese make their living on the sea. They, along with the Bugis people, are among the most influential of the sea-faring groups of Indonesia. Once feared throughout Asian waters as their pirate ships preyed on weaker vessels, these two groups dominate Indonesia's inter-island trade. For thousands of years they have followed the monsoons in their black-sailed *prahu*, trading sophisticated consumer goods from the cities for jungle products, raw materials and delicacies from the sea. The Bugis and Makassarese traditionally voyaged north to the Philippines and eastward to the Kai and Aru islands to collect sandalwood, mother-of-pearl, bird nests, shark fins, and plumes from the bird of paradise, all for the Chinese market. *Trepang*, or sea cucumber, was also an important item, and Bugis *prahu* went as far as the northwest coast of Australia to find it. They also traded with the Australian Aborigines for tortoise shell. Today they dominate the timber and general cargo trade on the Surabaya–Banjarmasin and the Surabaya–Ujung Pandang routes. Their boats have scarcely changed in centuries. Although they now use diesel engines and are built with iron nails, the two tall masts still carry huge areas of canvas. And, as they have always done, they sail without insurance, loaded to the plimsoll line with everything from rice and onions to motor-cycles and bicycle tyres for the outer islands of the archipelago.

A chorus of singers on Tomea Island, Southeast Sulawesi, wait for the dancing to begin.

OVERLEAF: *Boats on a beach west of Manado, North Sulawesi. They are covered with leaves to protect them from the sun.*

Toraja houses are typically boat shaped, with sweeping roofs. Buffalo horns, symbols of prosperity, often grace the gables and entrances. As is the case with traditional houses all over Indonesia, corrugated iron roofs are fast replacing the cooler and more serviceable thatch. Awnings have been set up in front of the verandahs to accommodate guests at a death feast.

A group of men play cards in the shade under the house while waiting for festivities to begin.

142

As brightly dressed girls sing and chant a welcome,
guests arrive in procession to be greeted by family
members of the deceased. Women hosts greet lines of
women guests, offer betel nut, and show them to their
seats. Men are similarly greeted, but with cigarettes
instead of betel.
For the Toraja, the "people of the mountains" of south
Central Sulawesi, death is a happy state. A corpse is
given two feasts: one shortly after death, and a second
some time later when conditions are right and the
family has accumulated the wealth it needs to perform

144

A funeral is both a solemn and a joyous occasion, as it signals the soul's release from the body and the beginning of its journey to another life. But funerals can be staggeringly expensive. A person's stature is measured in terms of the size and grandeur of his funeral, and wealth accumulated during a lifetime of hard work is often dissipated at this time. Many animals, especially buffaloes and pigs, are slaughtered and distributed to the guests. It is customary for friends and neighbours to contribute food or animals, and a careful tally is kept. The contributions are reciprocated and sometimes increased when someone in the donor's family dies. Guests watch with interest as this magnificent bull is slaughtered and cut up for distribution.

145

While waiting for burial, the corpse, drained of fluids, has spent the interim in the house of his family or in a temporary grave nearby. Should the wait be long, the bones will be exhumed and cleaned; otherwise the body will remain in the casket until after the feast when it is taken to its resting place high in a rock cliff. For poorer families any large rock will do, even one by the side of the road.

A wall of tombs (left) looms eerily at Lemo Lemo, near Rantepao in South Sulawesi. The figures looking out from ledges in the rock are about a metre tall and wear clothing similar to that once worn by the deceased. Should any of the dead wish to come back for a look at the world they have left behind, he or she will have the use of eyes and a well-dressed body.

Figures and rotting coffins (left below) where a rock face, honey-combed with graves, has collapsed. The cult of death is so pervasive in Tana Toraja that the landscape seems, at times, to be fairly littered with skulls. This row was probably set up by local children as a joke.

The province of North Sulawesi is as different from Tana Toraja as can be imagined. Strongly influenced by Western traders and missionaries from as early as the 16th Century, the indigenous Minahasa culture has virtually disappeared. This man, with his sparkling white shirt and well-worn hat, is from the mountain town of Tomohon, near Manado.

146

These small Minahasa villages are amazingly prosperous. Heavily wooded areas give way to wide suburban streets lined with brick and tile houses. North Sulawesi is one of Indonesia's wealthiest provinces, and its wealth comes from cloves. All the cloves grown here are used in the manufacture of kretek cigarettes, more than 50 million of which are produced and smoked every year. Cloves are picked by hand and dried in the sun. Few people have gardens in clove-growing country. Every available square inch of flat ground is covered with concrete and used to dry the crop.

Minahasa food can be quite exotic. Dry-roasted rats (top right) are considered a delicacy.

A hazy Makassar landscape, western South Sulawesi.

148

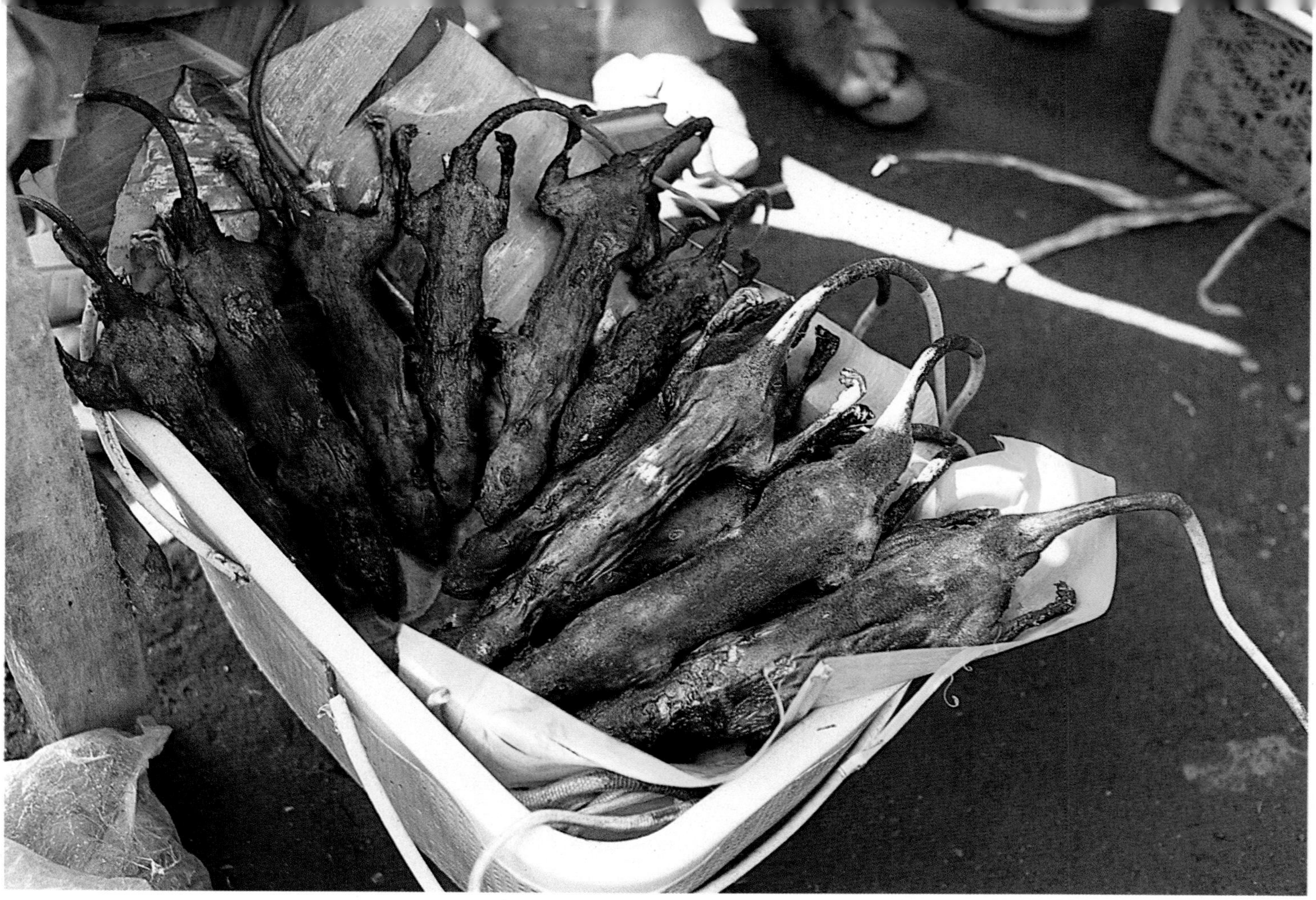

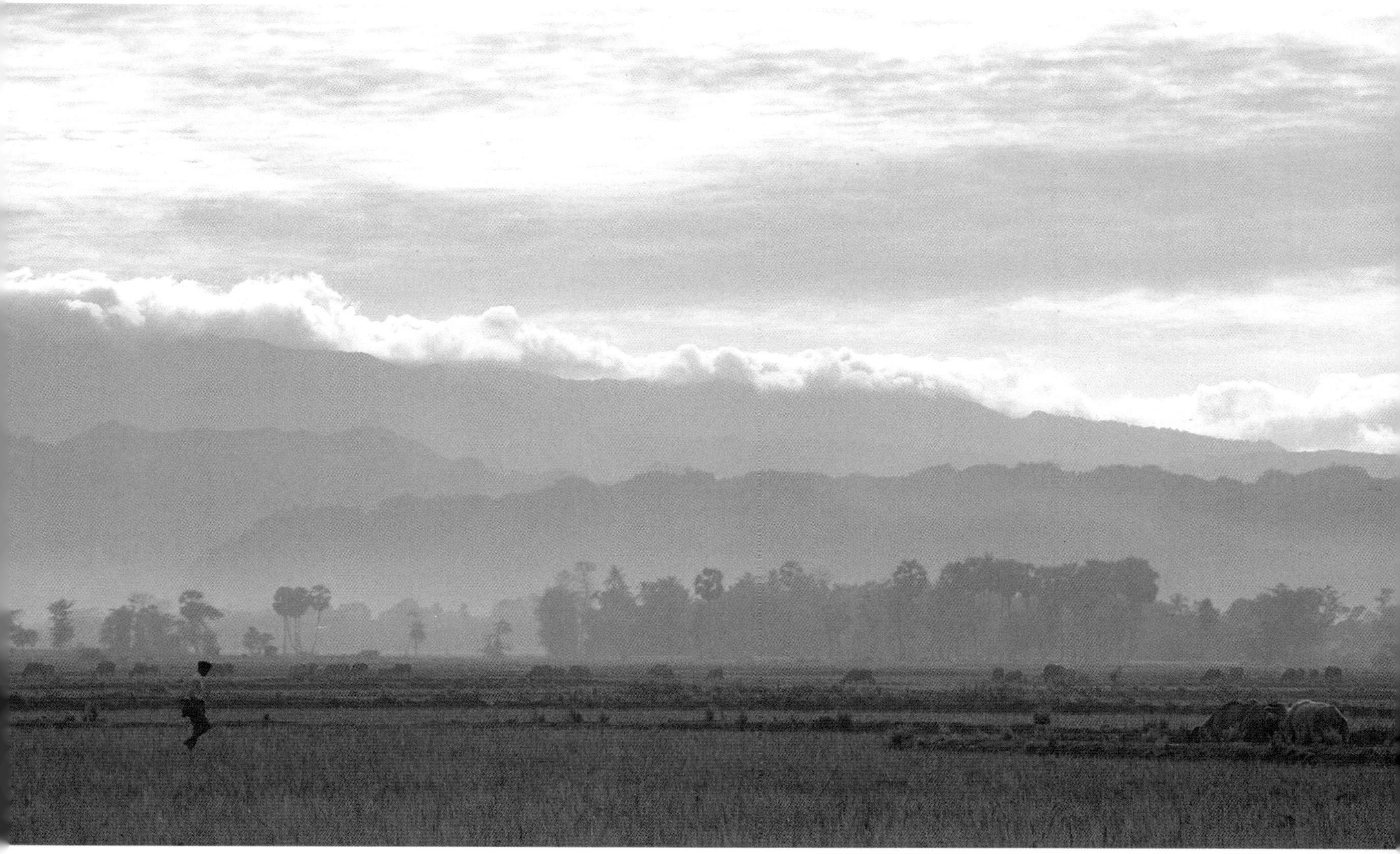

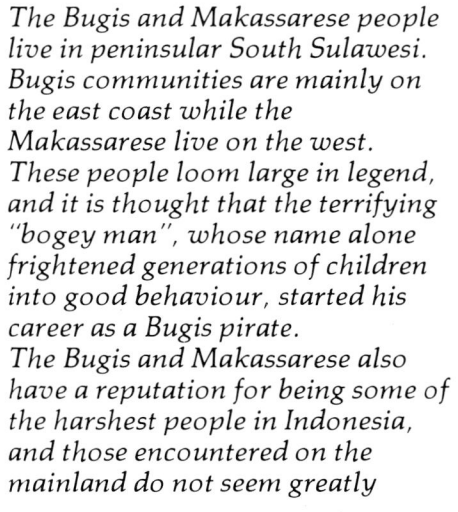

The Bugis and Makassarese people live in peninsular South Sulawesi. Bugis communities are mainly on the east coast while the Makassarese live on the west. These people loom large in legend, and it is thought that the terrifying "bogey man", whose name alone frightened generations of children into good behaviour, started his career as a Bugis pirate. The Bugis and Makassarese also have a reputation for being some of the harshest people in Indonesia, and those encountered on the mainland do not seem greatly enamoured of foreigners. On the islands southeast of the peninsula, however, people are softer and more amenable to strangers. A Bugis woman from the island of Kalao Toa looks into the camera, her head modestly covered with a towel. Another flashes a shy gold-toothed smile. Bugis traders are famous throughout Indonesia as boat-builders, sailors and pirates, and ships feature in all aspects of life. The roof ornament (top left) is a copy of the carved prow of a Bugis sailing ship. A villager (above) hitches a ride as he stands beside his banana-filled canoe. Friendly and hospitable, the people of this little island show none of the fearsome aggression that gave Bugis sailors the title "Scourge of the Java Seas".

The Bugis village on Kalao Toa is built on the beach, with one steep winding track leading to family settlements and farms inland. Horses are the only form of transport on the island. The islanders hold horse races in their spare time, and, to keep them as tough and wiry as their owners, stallions are encouraged to fight. Blood is often drawn, but the horses are separated before serious injuries occur.

152

Peninsular South Sulawesi has been settled for a very long time. Remnants of prehistoric culture there go back to at least the Middle Stone Age. These negative hand prints (right) were made about 5000 years ago by placing the hands against the rock and spitting a mixture of red ocher and water around them. They are part of a group of cave paintings found at Leang-Leang near Masor, 35 kilometres north of Ujung Pandang.

A child (above) plays in the water at Sinkang, South Sulawesi. The houses in her kampung sit on stilts over the water. Another Bugis village (left) nestles at the foot of a huge rock on the way up the peninsula toward Tana Toraja.

A young Bugis woman (right) lights up the morning with her smile.

A Tolaki man from Kendari, the provincial capital of Southeast Sulawesi.
Twin-sailed, twin-hulled sailing vessels, quite different in appearance from the Bugis prahu pinisi, are common in this area.

Volleyball, one of the most popular sports in Indonesia, is played here in a small Tolaki village. The "spiker"—the boy about to hit the ball—is wearing his father's Haji hat.

Pepper (below) is one of a dozen different crops grown on this fertile peninsula, but the area is best known for its large and tasty cashew nuts.

A woman grinds coffee beans (left) in a small Tolaki village north of Kendari. To and Toh are prefixes used throughout Sulawesi; they mean "person" or "man". Tolaki means "big man" in the local language, and probably refers to this group's prowess as headhunters in days gone by. Today the Tolaki are predominantly Muslim.

This modern young woman favours short hair and her father's shirts worn over baggy jeans, but carefully follows her mother's teachings on Tolaki dress and behaviour for formal occasions. The required jewellery includes dozens of heavy gold bangles.

159

A wedding guest, Kendari, Southeast Sulawesi. At Kendari weddings it is customary for the families of the bride and groom to engage speakers who extol the virtues of the individuals they represent. These two splendidly-dressed men spoke on behalf of the bride several weeks before the wedding at a ceremony to commemorate the symbolic payment of the bride price. The payment consisted of simple jewellery, lengths of cloth, a porcelain bowl and two young coconut trees. The bride and groom did not meet in public until the wedding itself.

160

The peoples of the islands off the southeast coast of Southeast Sulawesi, Buton, Muna, Tomea and the Tukangbesi Islands, all speak closely related languages and share a common culture. Their strongest affinities are with the Tolaki on the mainland. A silent family (above), not a smile among them, waits for the ship that will bring their son and brother back to Muna from the island of Buton. A somewhat friendlier figure (left) waits his turn during communal bath time on Tomea. Men and women share bathing facilities, everyone modestly covered in towels or sarongs.

162

The Sultan of Wolio ruled the island of Buton until the Dutch took over direct rule in 1908. This men's dance, held on the grounds of the Sultan's fort at Bau Bau on the southwest coast, depicts the defeat of an invading force. A closer view (far left) of a dancer's head-dress. Though only spectators, the women all wear ceremonial dress.

A traditional women's dance (above) is performed on the island of Tomea.

Low tide, Tomea. These boats have been made in the same manner for centuries. The use of nails instead of wooden dowels has only recently become common.

A smiling mother and child after their afternoon bath.

Nusa Tenggara

Nusa Tenggara. The forgotten islands, a necklace archipelago stretching from Lombok all the way to Timor. Although taken all together these islands comprise less than four percent of Indonesia's land area, they contain such ethnic, cultural and linguistic variety that it is difficult to speak of them as a group. On the tiny island of Roti, for instance, there are nine distinct dialects spoken, and each of the island's eighteen states has a different culture. A few things can, however, be said of Nusa Tenggara in general. The majority of the people in this part of Indonesia are Christian rather than Muslim. The islands are all hot and dry, heavily influenced by the dessicating east monsoon which sucks moisture out of the land and air. Every year, between the planting of crops and their harvesting, many people endure what they call *lapar biasa*, the "usual hunger". When the west monsoon fails, as it does too often for anyone's comfort, the people endure a situation bordering on famine.

The people of Nusa Tenggara, especially those on the large islands of Sumbawa, Sumba, Flores and Timor, practice shifting-field slash-and-burn agriculture. As the fields become exhausted more land must be farmed to gain a sufficient crop for survival. On Sumba and Timor the situation has been aggravated by the raising of horses and cattle for export, which has resulted in the need to spend long, expensive, unproductive hours fencing the cropland to protect it from livestock. Erosion, a serious problem all through these islands, has been made worse by over-grazing. The major crops are corn and rice, grown by the dry-field method in most places because water is scarce. So much effort is needed to fence, work and protect the fields that there is little time to engage in other food-production activities, such as fishing. And because the cattle raised here are not, for the most part, consumed locally, they do not significantly improve the diet of the common people, which is often poor in protein and only barely sustaining.

On two small islands of the outer arc of Nusa Tenggara, however, the economic situation is considerably better. Savu and Roti, called by one ethnographic wit "the islands of non-eating people", depend heavily on the products of the lontar palm for their subsistance. Obvious uses for the leaves and wood of this tree include houses, furniture, musical instruments, mats, baskets and even cigarette papers. But the people of Savu and Roti take their exploitation of the lontar palm a giant step farther. They tap the sweet juice of the palm and drink it, either fresh or boiled into a syrup and diluted with water. The juice can be further reduced by boiling into palm sugar. The froth from the boiling juice is fed to the pigs, thus directly converting palm sap to protein. The consequences of their dependence on the lontar have been sweeping. First, and perhaps most important, there is no annual period of hunger on Roti and Savu. Any

A fisherman from Endeh, Flores, resting on one of the smaller islands of West Nusa Tenggara.

167

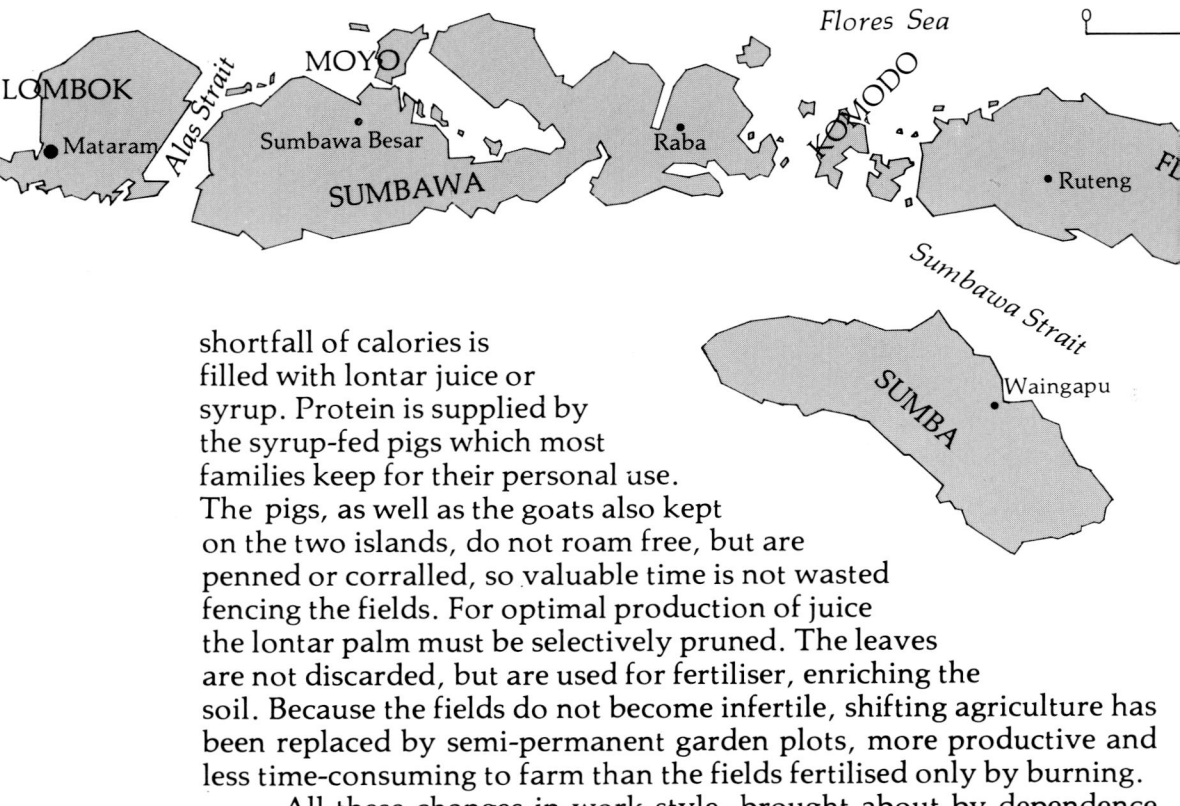

shortfall of calories is
filled with lontar juice or
syrup. Protein is supplied by
the syrup-fed pigs which most
families keep for their personal use.
The pigs, as well as the goats also kept
on the two islands, do not roam free, but are
penned or corralled, so valuable time is not wasted
fencing the fields. For optimal production of juice
the lontar palm must be selectively pruned. The leaves
are not discarded, but are used for fertiliser, enriching the
soil. Because the fields do not become infertile, shifting agriculture has
been replaced by semi-permanent garden plots, more productive and
less time-consuming to farm than the fields fertilised only by burning.

All these changes in work style, brought about by dependence on the lontar palm, have had a further consequence on Roti and Savu that has reverberated through the nearby islands. Palm-tapping, although labour intensive for two to three months each year, does not require much labour through the rest of the year. As much of the garden work and weaving of lontar leaves is done by women, the men have whole blocks of leisure time during the year which they can devote to non-agricultural, non-subsistence activities. They also, because the lontar palms never fail as a source of food, have the resources to take economic risks. The men of Savu and Roti, therefore have become the entrepreneurs of the East Nusa Tenggara islands, especially on Sumba and Timor.

Lontar is a drought-and fire-resistant tree that springs up on fields already exhausted by slash-and-burn farming. It is thought that the small islands of the outer arc, more exposed to forces of erosion than are Sumba and Timor, became infertile sooner. The people gradually learned to use the palms that colonised their exhausted farmland. As erosion and soil-exhaustion take their toll on the large islands, lontar palms are growing there, too, in some places nearly as densely as they grow on Roti and Savu. But there is little opportunity for the people of Timor and Sumba to gradually move towards exploitation of the palm, because migrants from Savu and Roti have filled that niche in the economy. The two sets of islands are already in economic conflict, and the resolution is not yet clear.

Although life can be difficult in Nusa Tenggara, there is a richness of culture here found in few places on earth. One of the area's most striking cultural characteristics is the prevalence of traditional hand-woven textiles using a technique called *ikat*. Unlike supplementary weft, a more widespread and probably newer technique in which extra weft threads are woven in patterns, in *ikat* the threads themselves are dyed in patterns before being tied on the loom to form

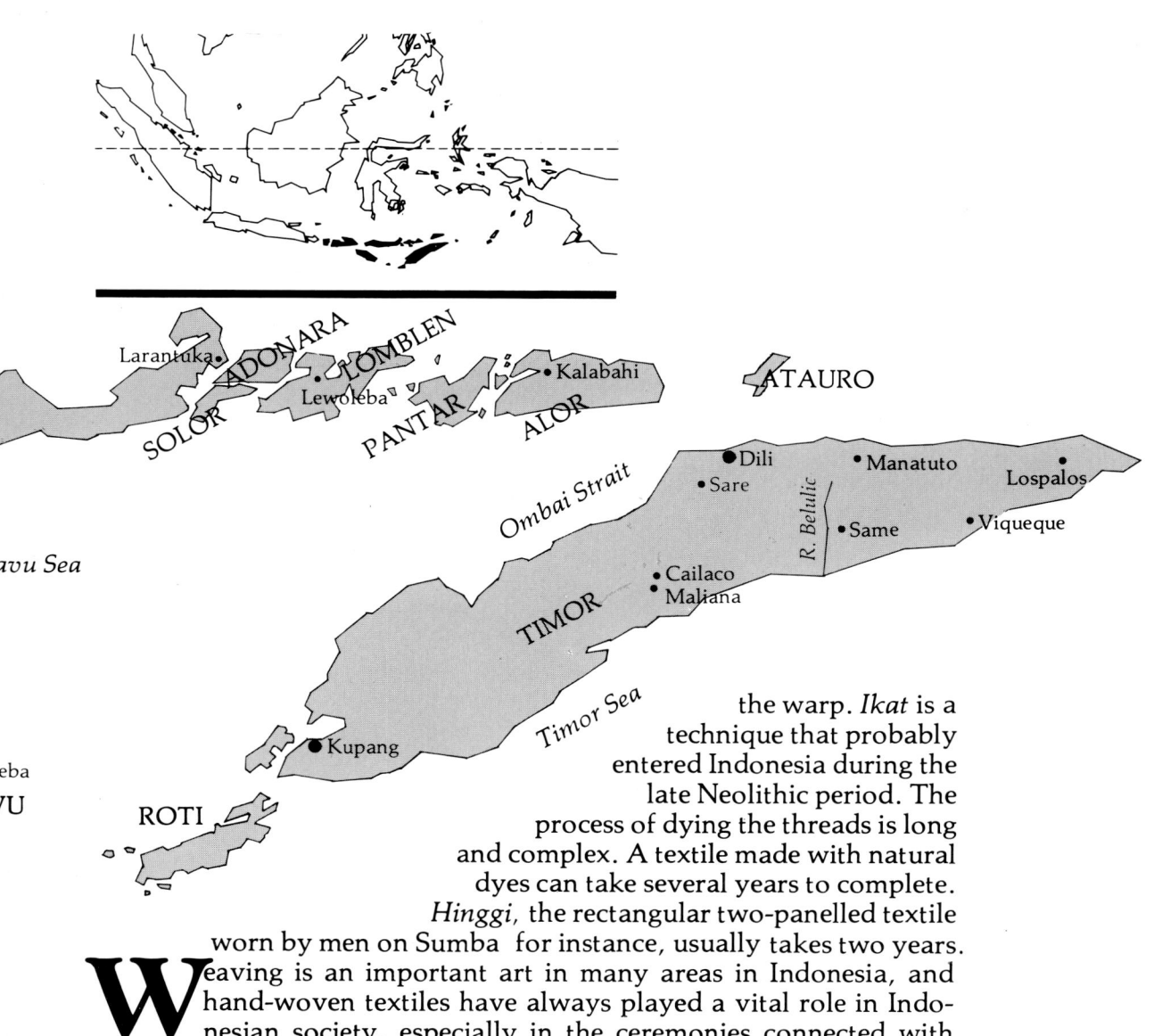

the warp. *Ikat* is a technique that probably entered Indonesia during the late Neolithic period. The process of dying the threads is long and complex. A textile made with natural dyes can take several years to complete. *Hinggi*, the rectangular two-panelled textile worn by men on Sumba for instance, usually takes two years.

Weaving is an important art in many areas in Indonesia, and hand-woven textiles have always played a vital role in Indonesian society, especially in the ceremonies connected with rites of passage—birth, puberty, marriage and death. Textiles are intimately connected with the forming of marriage ties and are part of a girl's dowry in most parts of the archipelago. They circulate as gifts during the negotiations between families and at the wedding itself. Most Timorese textiles, for instance, are used in gift exchanges between bride-givers and bride-takers. A wealthy bride's family would be expected to give more than a hundred pieces of weaving. In some parts of Timor textiles are hung before the doors leading to the bride's room; as the groom moves through the house he has to "buy" his way through the cloth barriers between him and his bride. Equally important is the use of textiles at funerals. On Timor warp *ikat* cloths are used to cover the coffin before burial; on Flores traditional shawls are buried with the dead. On Sumba the dead are often buried with large quantities of *hinggi*.

Cloths are important symbols of status and prestige in the Eastern Islands. The number and quality of textiles owned tends to indicate social rank. To some extent this can be explained purely in economic terms: The weaving of *ikat* textiles, exclusively the task of women, is a time-consuming occupation. The better the textile, the longer the time needed to make it. Although most women weave, only families with sufficient resources to allow much time at the loom can accumulate large stores of fine-quality textiles.

Designs are often indicative of status, and in former times only the rulers could wear cloths with particular designs. The lion and stag motifs on cloths from Sumba were worn only by the elite. *Hinggi* with a broad white centre band were reserved for the raja. In the Lio area of Flores, the size, colour and pattern of the complicated *ikat* shawls worn on ceremonial occasions denoted the status of the wearer. As well as status, design and colour sometimes reflect the wearer's place in society. On Timor, among the Atoni, where many different techniques of weaving are practised, the designs and manner in which they are arranged on the cloth are distinctive to the ten princedoms that once divided the area. To the Timorese, local textiles are a clear indication of one's area of birth and traditional allegiance. On Savu, each person belongs to the father's clan and to one of two other groups determined by the mother. These are called the greater blossom and the lesser blossom. It was once possible to know merely by looking at the colour of a ceremonial textile which blossom affiliation a person had. Today ordinary and ceremonial patterns are mixed together and no longer reflect social division.

Culture in Nusa Tenggara is by no means restricted to weaving; traditional ceremonies and ways of life still flourish almost unchanged. Because this part of Indonesia is resource-poor and industrially still underdeveloped, the modern world has encroached here less than perhaps anywhere else in the archipelago, but progress, with all its blessings and problems, is slowly making itself felt throughout these eastern islands.

A group of musicians on the island of Savu wait for the dancing to begin. The people here are justifiably proud of their musical traditions; all instruments and costumes are locally made.

OVERLEAF: *Komodo village on Komodo, a tiny island between Sumbawa and Flores. Originally settled by convicts from Flores, this is the dry desolate home of Indonesia's famous Komodo dragon. Because the island's rainfall is too sparse for rice cultivation, the staple diet of the villagers is fish.*

Sailing boats enter the sheltered waters near the island of Komodo. Fishermen are not the only visitors, however. The island is becoming a popular stop for tour boats from Bali. A Komodo mother covers her face in laughter as her two daughters, one a lovely teenager and the other a toddler, stand by. Having recovered her poise but with her smile intact, the same woman (right) exemplifies the island's recent prosperity.

Komodo island is literally crawling with dragons, giant reptiles related to monitor lizards. A young dragon (left) still shows the colours it was born with; older dragons are dark green. In olden days, goats were used to appease the dragons and keep them away from the village, where they occasionally raided the local livestock. Today interested tourists can watch as they devour their prey. Altogether thirteen dragons, some nearly four metres long, turned up to feast on this single goat. A villager, by now accustomed to the sight of strangers, offers a carved dragon for sale. He tells the tale of a huge beast living in the hills whose likeness he has carved.

176

Flores is known for the high quality of its textiles, especially warp ikat*, in which the pattern is dyed into the warp threads before they are woven. Although synthetic dyes and machine-spun imported cotton are making inroads here, locally-grown cotton, cleaned and spun by hand, is still in use. A woman uses a small hand-operated "gin" (right) to remove the seeds from raw cotton prior to spinning. The spun cotton will be bundled, tightly tied and then dyed before being wound onto the loom. The weaver uses a plain weave with unpatterned thread to complete the textile. As is the case with many Indonesian textiles, good Flores cloths are becoming rare.*

Lewo Leba, in the hills near Larantuka, East Flores, offers a spectacular welcome to guests of the village. First comes an aggressive war-like dance and an exchange of greetings. Then all guests file past a welcome line (left). Betel nut and lime are offered, but one may politely refuse by touching the carved container and continuing down the line. A distinguished-looking man wearing a large wristwatch waits for his entrance in a dance; and a girl takes part in a dance performed by women on ceremonial occasions.

Horses play an important part in the life and culture of Savu. These are being ridden in the Perhere Jara, *a dance which enacts the use of horses to chase away grasshoppers during the rainy season. Horses are also ridden down to the beach to welcome guests arriving by boat.*

Savu is not merely an island, it is an island kingdom. The Queen (left) is escorted to a place of honour in the shade.

A Savu girl (right), with a fighting cock under her arm, takes part in a local dance-drama. Cock fighting is also used to cast omens on Savu. One cock represents land, the other sea. If sea wins, the omen is bad; if land wins, the omen is good.

Perhaps because of its inaccessibility, the inhabitants of Savu still enjoy a rich ceremonial life. The Pedoa dance (above) is usually danced in moonlight between March and May. This is a harvest dance, and unhusked rice is in the baskets tied to the dancers' ankles. In the Dabba, or blessing ceremony for a child (far left), the parents place betel nut and flowers on the child's head and "hope that he will grow".

A young man (left) takes part in a dance-ceremony which tells the story of the end of war on Savu: fighting between men with swords gave way to cock-fighting with fowl owned by opposing villages. Cock-fights gave way in turn to a peaceful, enlightened time when only dances performed by girls with feathers serve as a remainder of Savu's fierce and warlike past.

A Savu-style "Joe Cool" lounges on a street in Seba, the island's main village.

Thatched huts in the village of Taraka, near Kupang, West Timor.

East Timor, Indonesia's 27th province, is an unknown area to most tourists and to many Indonesians as well. A woman (far left) from the village of Sare pounds corn in a hollow tree trunk to separate the kernels from the cob. The kernels will be placed in the small baskets at her feet and tossed in the air to remove the chaff. She is sitting in front of a palm-frond shed used to store seed corn. Men (bottom left) carry beef ribs to market at the town of Maliana.

Because there is no farmland on the tiny island of Atauro, the government is encouraging families to move to Timor. One hundred families totaling nearly seven hundred people have been resettled in the new village of Cailaco. Upon arrival each family receives one-half hectare of land on which to grow corn, and a one-room house. Another half-hectare will be added later, along with government assistance in growing rice. This family arrived in the resettlement village only three weeks before the photograph was taken. The young girl is the only member of her family to speak Bahasa Indonesia. Her parents, grandmother and little brother speak only the dialect of their former home.

Maluku

Maluku. The legendary Spice Islands, fought over for centuries by a Europe desperate for the cloves and nutmeg needed to preserve their meat. The islands that make up this province cover an immense amount of water, but, taken all together, make up only a tiny fraction of Indonesia's land mass. They stretch from Halmahera in the north, shaped like Sulawesi in miniature, to the eastern tip of Timor in Nusa Tenggara. Historically the most important islands in the province are Ambon, the tiny island of Ternate just west of central Halmahera, and the Banda Islands in Central Maluku south of the island of Seram. These three, along with Tidore, Ternate's rival power in North Maluku, bore the brunt of European contact—first Portuguese and Spanish, then Dutch—that started in the 15th Century and continued into the 20th. Before that time, Maluku was well known to Indian, Chinese and Arab traders who, like the Europeans, valued the spices grown there.

Maluku lies squarely within the "Ring of Fire"; volcanic eruptions and earthquakes are common. Its wildlife, studied by A.R. Wallace, an influential in forming his theory of evolution in the 19th Century, is more similar to that of New Guinea and Australia than of western Indonesia. The crops that made the area famous, cloves and nutmeg, along with cocoa, and coffee, are still major crops. Although rice is grown on some islands, notably Seram, the staple diet of most people is sago, reduced to flour and then boiled into a viscous paste. Fish is also an important item, and some of the world's richest fishing grounds surround these islands.

Very little is known about Maluku prior to the 15th Century. The Muslim empire of Ternate, which dominated the spice trade before the arrival of the Portuguese, reduced the incidence of headhunting and introduced political rather than tribal social organisation on some of the islands, especially the island of Ambon. There was, however, nothing approaching political unity. When the Portuguese conquered Goa and Malacca in the first decade of the 16th Century, Maluku was known as *Jazirat-al-Muluk*, the "land of many kings".

Ambon, which at that time grew neither cloves nor nutmeg, had long been an important way-station in the spice traffic between the Banda Islands and Ternate. With the establishment of a Javanese colony centuries earlier in the town of Hitu on the northern coast of Ambon, a pattern developed that was to be repeated all over Maluku: sailors and traders, usually from off-island, settled on the coasts, while the indigenous peoples moved inland. Their lives were unchanged by the passage of time as they followed their own traditions in the interior. They were called *Alifuro* by the newcomers, a contemptuous term meaning uncouth, uncultured and uncivilised. This attitude has changed little during the intervening years. Now,

A man from the forested regions of the island of Seram, Central Maluku.

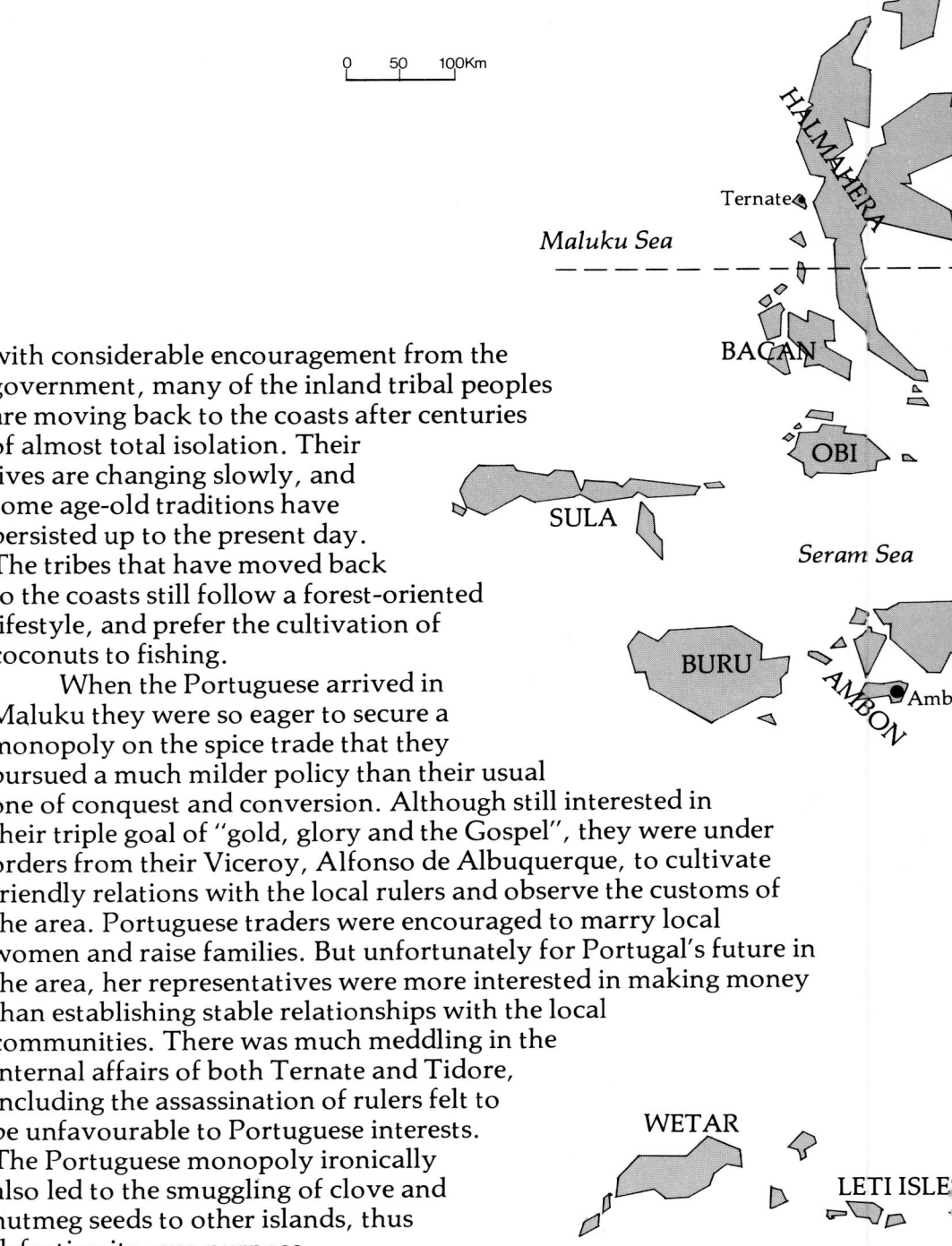

with considerable encouragement from the government, many of the inland tribal peoples are moving back to the coasts after centuries of almost total isolation. Their lives are changing slowly, and some age-old traditions have persisted up to the present day. The tribes that have moved back to the coasts still follow a forest-oriented lifestyle, and prefer the cultivation of coconuts to fishing.

When the Portuguese arrived in Maluku they were so eager to secure a monopoly on the spice trade that they pursued a much milder policy than their usual one of conquest and conversion. Although still interested in their triple goal of "gold, glory and the Gospel", they were under orders from their Viceroy, Alfonso de Albuquerque, to cultivate friendly relations with the local rulers and observe the customs of the area. Portuguese traders were encouraged to marry local women and raise families. But unfortunately for Portugal's future in the area, her representatives were more interested in making money than establishing stable relationships with the local communities. There was much meddling in the internal affairs of both Ternate and Tidore, including the assassination of rulers felt to be unfavourable to Portuguese interests. The Portuguese monopoly ironically also led to the smuggling of clove and nutmeg seeds to other islands, thus defeating its own purpose.

The rulers of the various islands under Portuguese influence grew more and more resentful, until in 1570, they united to proclaim a holy war against the European traders. The Portuguese were forced out of their fortress on Ambon and fled to Tidore, while the ruler of Ternate, a Muslim, consolidated his growing territory and pursued a strong anti-Christian and anti-Portuguese policy.

The Portuguese never recovered their power, and their missionary activities, which had flourished under the influence of the charismatic Jesuit St. Francis Xavier, declined. Other European nations began to arrive in the area. Sir Francis Drake stopped at Ternate in 1579 and the first Dutch fleet come to Ambon in 1599. In 1605 the Portuguese surrendered their interests to the Dutch, after making what provision they could for the protection of Catholic

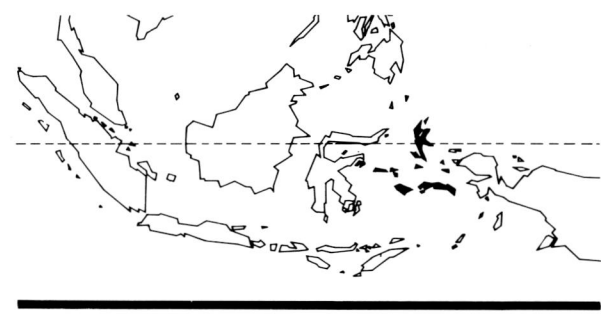

Equator

nera Sea

converts on the islands. The English returned, to the great aggravation of the Dutch, and set up a factory on the Island of Run in the tiny Banda islands. This group's largest island, Banda Neira, was to be the scene of one of the bloodiest chapters in the history of Dutch colonial rule in Indonesia.

When the Dutch first came to Banda Neira, the local population had for centuries been selling spices to regional Bugis, Chinese and Arab traders in return for batik, porcelains, rice, calico and medicine. The Dutch, unaware of local preferences, brought velvets, damasks and heavy woollens, as well as gunpowder, mirrors and other trinkets not particularly valuable or interesting to the people of Banda. They refused to indulge in the age-old practice of bargaining and, in return for their inappropriate and unwanted trade goods, demanded the island's entire crop of nutmeg, mace and cloves. Finally, to compound what must have appeared to the Banda rulers an already mind-boggling piece of idiocy, they insisted on putting their demands in writing to be signed by the Banda village chiefs. What followed was a classic case of culture clash, with neither side at all understanding what the other was about. For the people of Banda the results were tragic in the extreme.

The village chiefs first signed the Dutch agreements out of an embarrassed sense of courtesy in the face of ill-mannered insistance. They clearly had no intention of selling their entire crop at low and non-negotiable prices to be paid for in undesirable goods. They did not know that to the Dutch the documents had the weight of law behind them and could be enforced. Such a notion of law was inconceivable on Banda, where people lived in close-knit village communities presided over by *orang kaya*, "rich men", according to rules made by concensus and backed by centuries of tradition. The rich men politely and perhaps a little nervously signed the treaties, and then went on as they had always done, selling spices to their traditional buyers and adding to their clients the British on Run Island.

AM

WATUBELA ISLES

Neira

BANDA ISLES

Banda Sea

TOYANDU

KAI ISLES

ARU ISLES

TANIMBAR ISLES

Sea

189

The Dutch threatened reprisals, and forced on the Bandanese a series of increasingly harsh and restrictive agreements, which the Banda nutmeg growers virtually ignored. In 1609 the Dutch East India Company sent a fleet and 750 soldiers to build a massive fort on Banda Neira which still stands today. The rich men and their families retreated to the hills, from whence they attempted to negotiate with the Dutch. They asked for hostages to guarantee Dutch good faith and arranged a meeting with the Admiral of the fleet. The Admiral agreed and, with most of his men, was killed in a Bandanese ambush. The consequences were catastrophic. In 1621 the Company Governor General in Batavia Jan Pieterszoon Coen sailed for Banda, determined to secure once and for all the monopoly on the Maluku spice trade. On his instructions, the rich men who had violated Dutch agreements along with most of the Bandanese population were murdered or transported as slaves. Nutmeg groves on all but the two main islands were destroyed in order to keep the supply down and prices up. Villages were razed and burned, and the few people who survived died of starvation or exposure in the hills. Of the Banda Islands original 15,000 inhabitants, a mere thousand remained.

In order to work the nutmeg trees on this now unpopulated archipelago, Coen divided the groves into concessions and offered free land grants to anyone who would, using imported slave-labour, tend the trees and process the nutmeg and mace, delivering the crop to the Company at fixed prices. Thus, after several stormy generations, Banda returned to a state of relative peace and affluence which lasted up to the mid-19th Century. By that time the nutmeg seeds which the British had shipped to plantations in Ceylon, Sumatra, Africa and Malaya reached maturity, and the Dutch monopoly was broken. Finally the advent of refrigeration, which provided a means of keeping meat edible without the heavy use of cloves and nutmeg, greatly reduced the world's demand for spices and ended forever the importance of Banda in the international arena. Ironically, although the Spice Islands are famous the world over, today they form a quiet backwater, neglected by the rest of the world, where the large and gracious mansions of the colonial Dutch crumble into ruin.

Women from a village near the south coast of Seram returning from their gardens. Common belief has it that these people, who call themselves Naulu, were the original inhabitants of the island. They were pushed inland by successive arrivals of outsiders.

OVERLEAF: *The sunsets over the eastern islands of Indonesia have a character all their own. This one is on the island of Tayandu, southeast Maluku.*

At lunchtime in a market on the island of Ambon, this woman does a brisk trade in snacks of rice and vegetables. The food is heated on the spot and wrapped in a banana leaf. Men about town idle on an Ambon street corner. The language may differ, but graffiti is the same the world over.

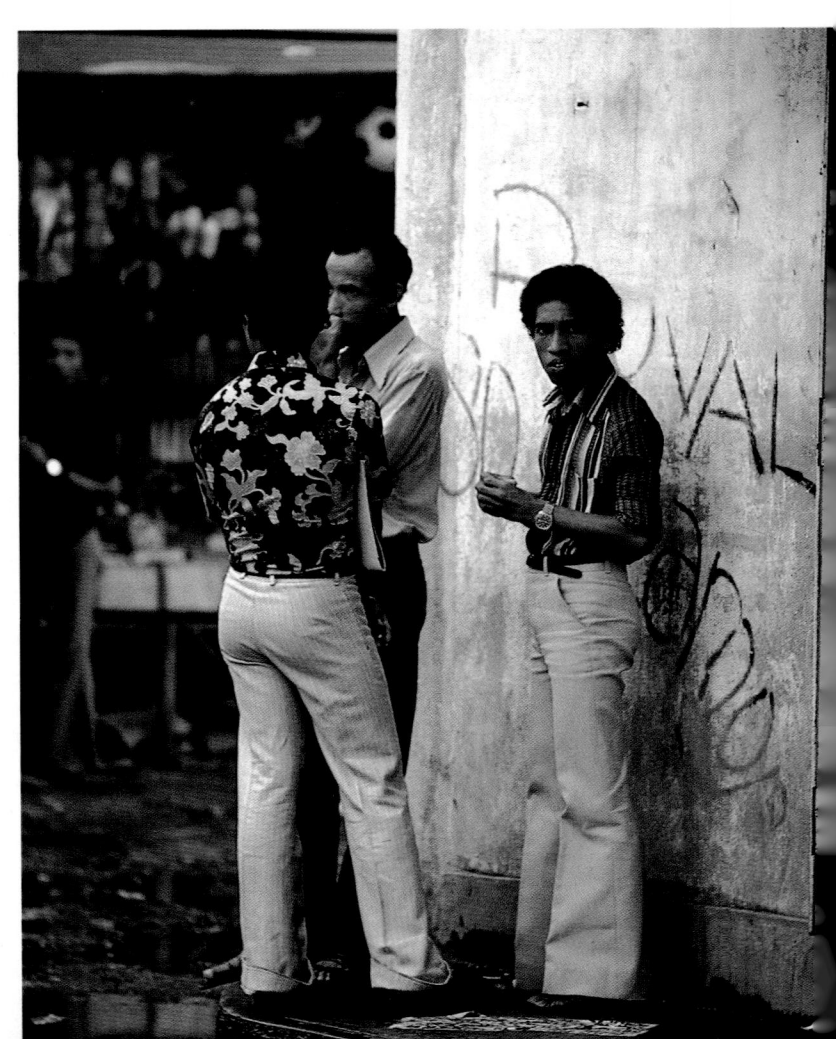

*A fisherman mending his nets,
Ambon island, and a view along
Ambon's peaceful north-coast
shoreline.*

A group of men from a Naulu village in south central Seram. Others of their village were building a new village near the beach. Because their original home was deep inland, the villagers pursue a living in the forest rather than on the waves, cultivating coconut and roots of various types. These men were quite happy to have their pictures taken, but the older and generally more conservative people back at the village were reluctant and did not permit any women to be photographed.

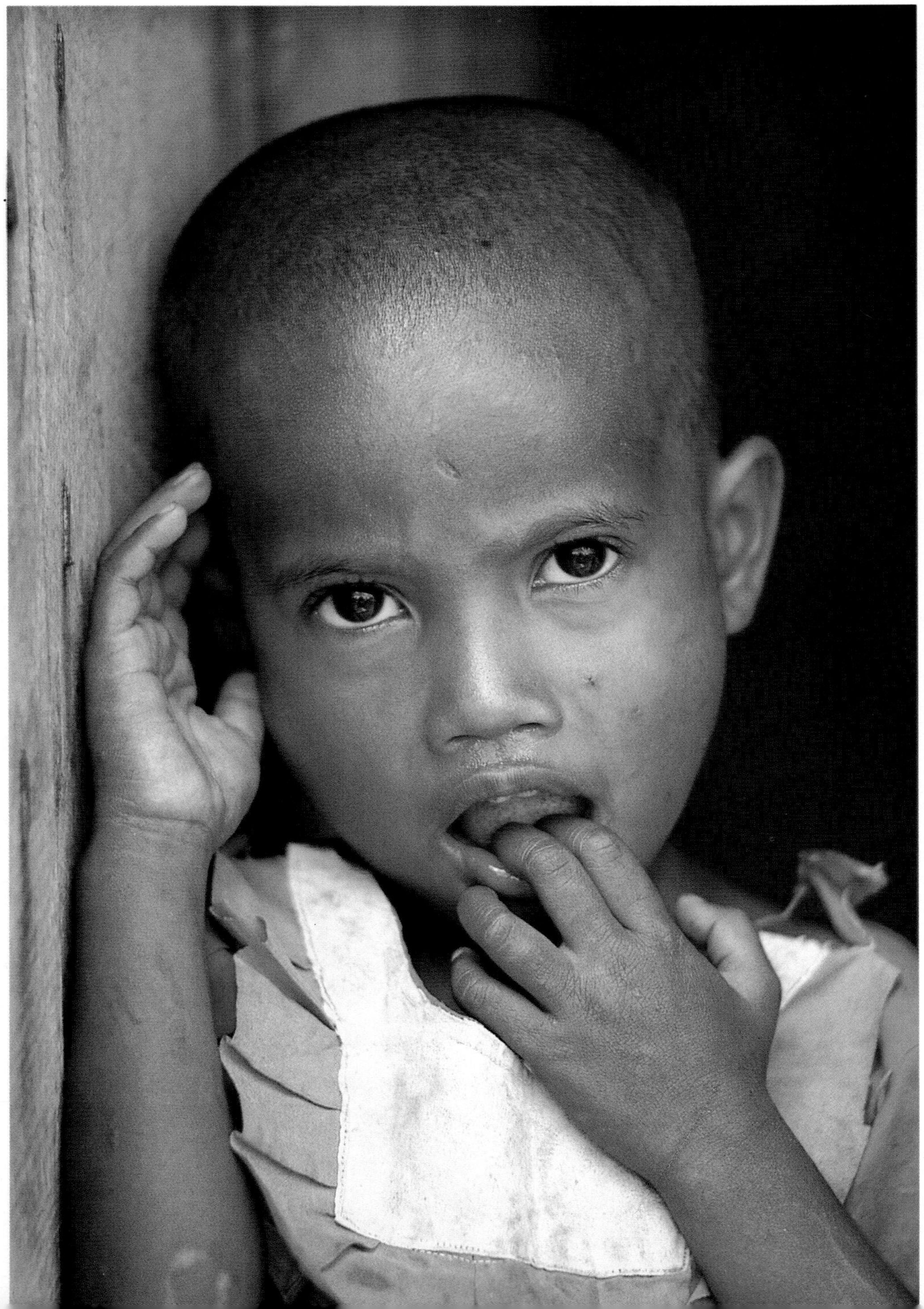

Following a practice common throughout much of Indonesia, this shy little girl has her head shaved to keep it clean and to ensure that when hair does grow it will be strong and healthy.

In a town on the south coast of Ambon (right), a man is on his way to market to pick up some vegetables, which he will carry on either end of the pole over his shoulder.

*A Seram woman from a group who
call themselves Naulu Nuelu. Their
village is near the centre of the
island, now more easily accessible
by means of the trans-Seram
highway which will aid
development on the north coast.*

An Ambonese becak *driver,
stylishly if unseasonably dressed in
a bright plaid scarf, waits at the
mini-bus station at Makariki on
Seram. He has come because there
is less competition here than on
Ambon, where a great oversupply
of* becaks *has led to the use of a
rota system. In Kota Ambon*
becaks *are colour-coded red,
yellow, green or blue and only
allowed to carry passengers on the
days designated for each colour.*

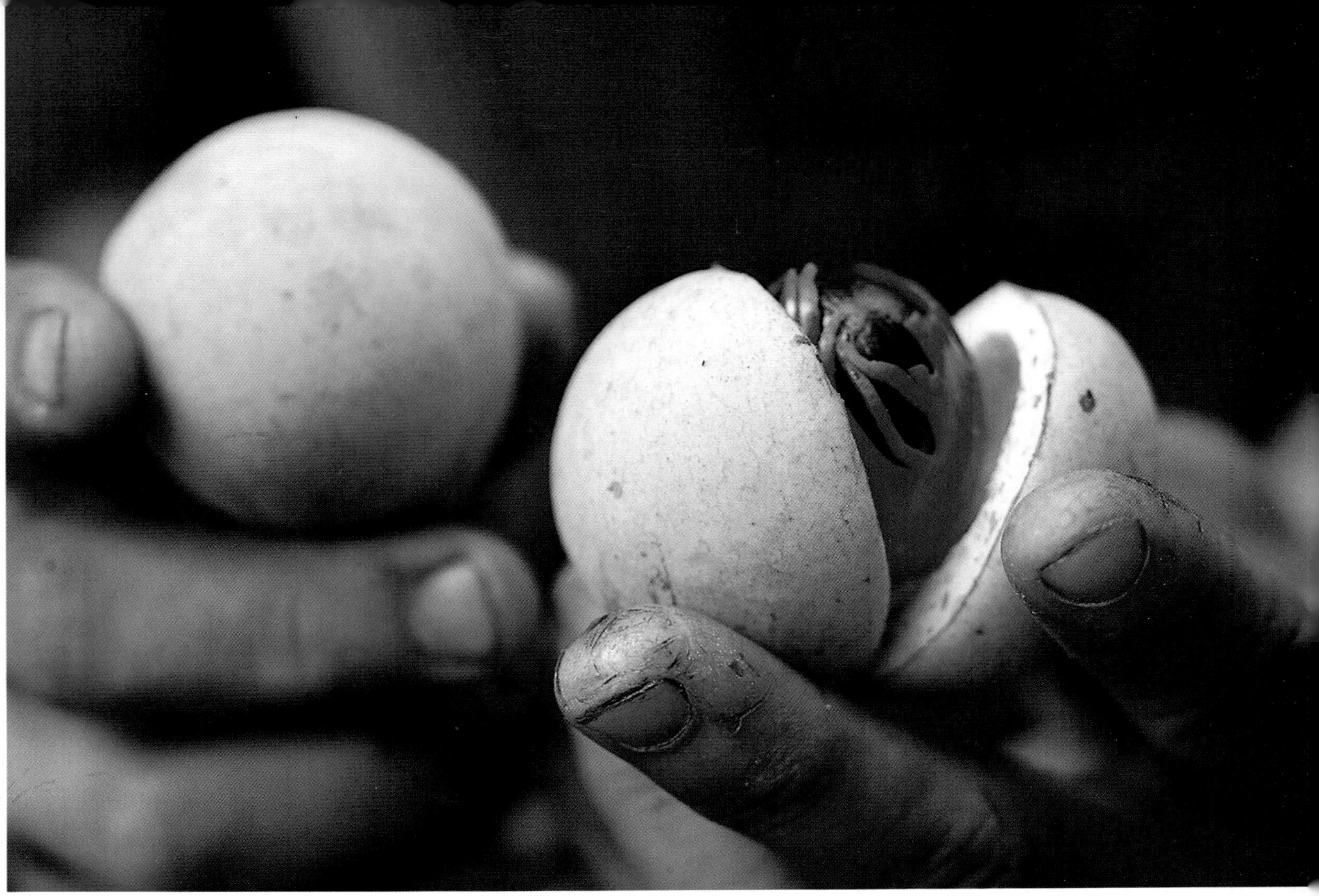

Cloves and nutmeg made the islands of Maluku famous and gave them the name Spice Islands. Nutmeg trees are dioecious—there are both male and female trees — and grow to a height of twelve to fifteen metres. The ripe fruit (far left) has been broken open to reveal the hypocotyl of scarlet mace wrapped around the shiny chestnut-coloured nutmeg seed.

The Dutch fort was built on the ruins of a 16th-Century Portuguese fort on the island of Banda Neira. When the Dutch took control of Banda in the early 17th Century, the Governor ordered the death of many of the influential people on the islands in order to gain control of the nutmeg trade. The Banda islands are still the world's major supplier of nutmeg.

The brown booby (below) a common sight in Maluku.

When the Dutch finally evicted the Portuguese from Banda, they had been there for nearly a century, and the local dances show a distinct Portuguese influence. The helmets, shields shaped like blunderbusses, even the costumes reflect the island's past. By contrast, this rather odd presentation of a tale about a mythical beast bears some resemblance to a Chinese dragon dance. The dancers are for the most part children dressed in sackcloth and wearing papier-maché masks, as does the beast. At night, village men dance around a large bronze drum decorated with leaf offerings.

On Tayandu, a tiny island in the Kai archipelago near Irian Jaya, there is a thriving pottery industry. Both the clay and vegetable colouring used in these pots are locally produced. The potter's wheel is unknown here. Pots are hand built, then dried and fired in small wooden ovens on the blisteringly hot beach. Sold cheaply to passing boats, they are a fine example of village craft.

Traders seeking spices in Southeast Maluku brought their religion with them. On Pulau Kasiui, Watubela Islands, the people are all Muslim. This old man wears a white hat, indicating that he has made the pilgrimage to Mecca and may use the title Haji.

On the verandah of the island's only mosque, a drum summons the faithful to prayer before the voice of the Muezzin calls from the minaret. In cities the Muezzin's call is often taped and broadcast by loudspeaker.

Irian Jaya

I rian Jaya. Not only a different place from the rest of Indonesia, but a different time as well. An enigmatic and difficult land that doesn't yield its secrets easily, virtually nothing about Irian Jaya is well understood. Like its other half, Papua New Guinea, Irian is geographically varied and scenically spectacular. Coastal swampland, broad highland river valleys, soaring mountains—even a glacier high in the central mountains. Except for the glacier, the island shares these features and an abundance of wildlife, much of it rare, with other parts of Indonesia.

What is strikingly different are the people. Culturally and ethnically, the Irian peoples are classified as Papuan, related to the Melanesoids of the South Pacific rather than the basically Malay people of island Southeast Asia. They are dark-skinned and heavily bearded, with facial features reminiscent of Australian Aborigines. This resemblance is not surprising as Australia and New Guinea were once a single land mass.

Because the terrain is so rugged, communities tend to live in isolation from one another, and there is little cross-communication. War is common in Irian Jaya, but it tends to be war between people in the same ethnic group rather than with outsiders. There is some outside trade, but mainly groups tend to keep to themselves. The rugged terrain also makes entry from outside extremely difficult, and not much is known about many of the Irian groups. Two that are relatively accessible, however, are the Dani of the Baliem Valley in the Central Highlands, and the Asmat of the southwest coast.

T he Dani culture is in many ways incredibly primitive. The people have almost nothing in the way of technology— ten years ago all the tools were of polished wood, stone, bone or sharpened bamboo—and produce no art. They have a number system that goes from one to three; anything higher is "many". Their only domestic animal is the pig, which is valued at least as highly as the Dani woman. Pigs and shells are the two media of exchange in Dani society, and circulate freely at funerals, weddings and feasts. Examined closely, however, Dani technology and agriculture are more complex than they first appear. Although sweet potatoes are cultivated with only a digging stick, they are grown on raised plots surrounded by elaborate irrigation ditches. The ditches are also used as compost pits, and each new crop is started on well-fertilized soil. Tobacco and other garden crops are also grown on a small scale. Pigs are bred selectively; all but the best are castrated to increase their size.

The climate in the Baliem valley is temperate, but because the elevation is high it can get cold at night. Dani men's houses are divided into a lower level, with a fire pit, and an upstairs sleeping loft kept comfortably warm by the fire below. What smoke doesn't escape through the gaps in the bamboo and plank walls is useful in keeping

A grim-faced Asmat villager from southwest Irian Jaya.

207

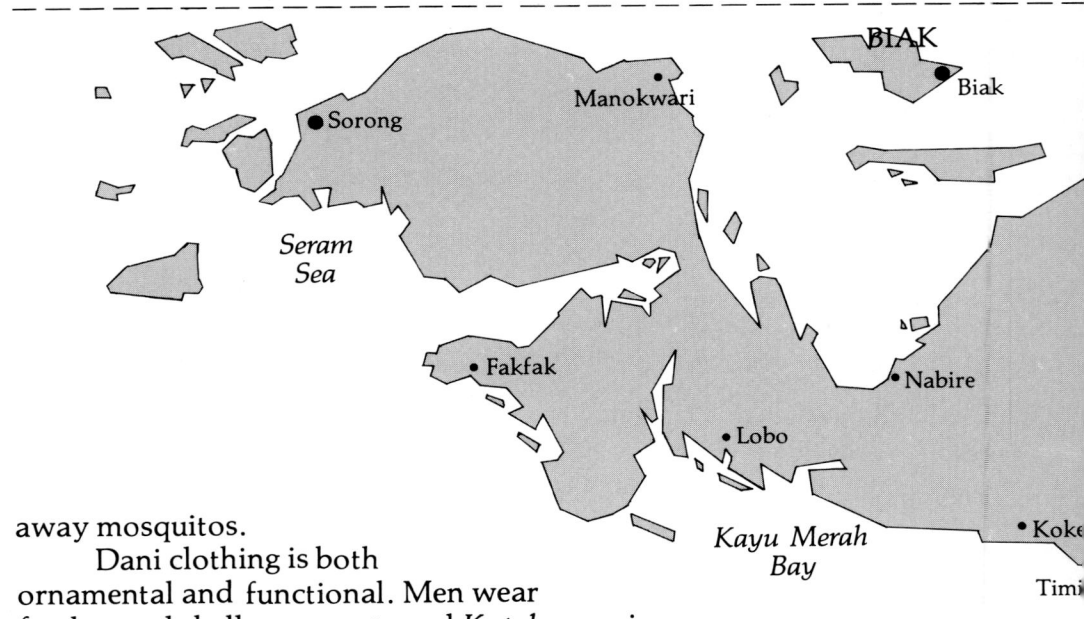

away mosquitos.

Dani clothing is both ornamental and functional. Men wear feather and shell ornaments and *Koteka*, penis sheaths made from gourds of various shapes and lengths, cultivated in gardens. Women wear rolled grass or reed skirts, and hang knotted string bags down their backs. These bags are used to carry everything from pigs and sweet potatoes to babies, and also protect the women's vulnerable backs from attack by ghosts which are likely to enter the body through the anus or the base of the throat. Necks are protected by shell ornaments or a kind of bib made of pigskin, worn fat side down. As protection against the cold, the Dani grease their bodies with a thick layer of pig fat.

Men and women in Dani society live very separate lives. The activities of men centre around the men's house and tend to be communal. Women spend their time in the sweet potato gardens and the cookhouse, working alone or with their young daughters. Although husbands and wives often have affectionate and harmonious relationships, interaction between the sexes is low key. One custom peculiar to the Dani is a five-year sexual abstinance after the birth of a child. No one seems very bothered by this practice, and it seems to be unfailingly observed. When asked why, the reply is usually that the "ghosts" demand it.

Although the Baliem Valley Dani have been exposed to increasing contact with outsiders, both Indonesian and foreign, their way of life has not changed a great deal. Police posts in the valley have helped diminish the incessant tribal wars, but war has turned out to be less central to Dani culture than was previously thought. The polished stone tools used for thousands of years in the Baliem valley are still being used and made, but steel axes and blades are increasingly popular. The Dani have little cash income to pay for such things. Self-sufficient in sweet potatoes and pigs, and trading salt and pigs to other tribes for forest products, they produce little extra that can be traded for currency. It is perhaps to their advantage that the Baliem valley has no easily exploitable natural resources bringing hoards of other Indonesians and foreigners to the area. The same cannot be said for the Asmat.

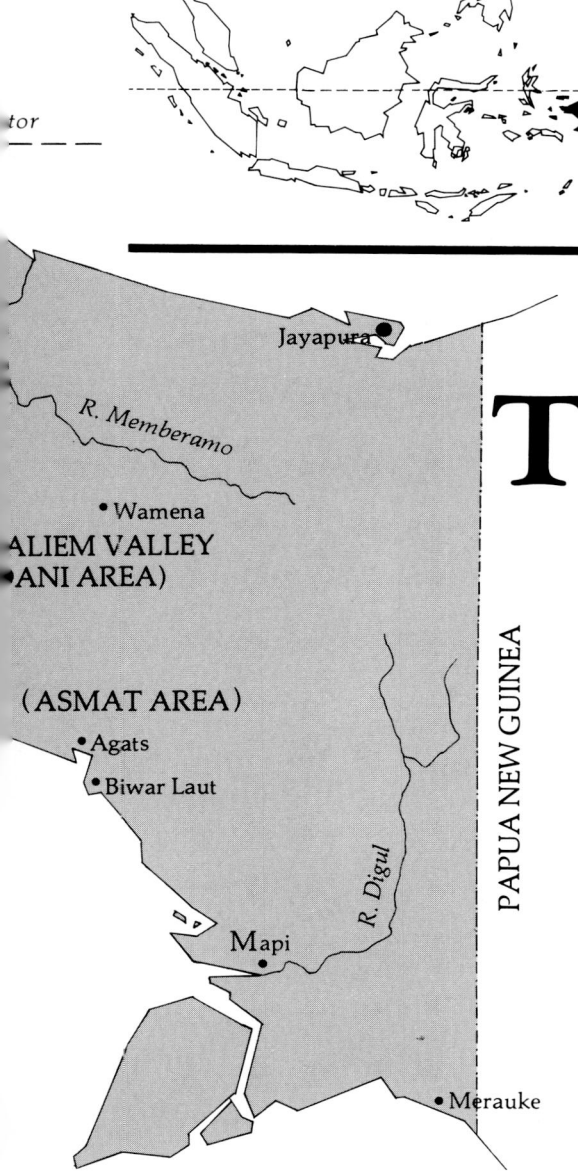

The Asmat live in lowland swamps, in a world that is half land, half water. More than six metres of rain falls on Asmat territory each year, and the swamps, stretching 70 kilometres inland, are inundated twice every day by the rising tide. When the waters receed, they expose a nighmarish tangle of tree roots to trap the unwary foot. Reptiles of every sort abound, and crocodiles are an ever-present menace. Travel is on foot or by canoe, paddled standing, with long, carved and decorated paddles. Since 1969, when what is now called Irian Jaya became a province of the Republic of Indonesia, many changes have taken place in Asmat culture. The most obvious is the banning of headhunting and inter-tribal warfare in the area, which has struck deep at the roots of Asmat tradition and way of life. Another subtler change, has been the development of permanent Asmat villages. Historically, temporary houses made of palm-leaf were the rule, used for about three months, then abandoned as food in an area was depleted. This practice still continues, but the Asmat are now required to visit their "villages" one or two days each week. Schools, hospitals and churches are all found in the villages, as are the men's ceremonial houses. The Asmat are pure hunter-gatherers, planting no crops, but roaming the tidal forests in search of sago, wild pig, lizards, insects, grubs, wild hen's eggs and edible plants. Sago is the staple, made into a flour and then roasted. Every four or five days a family fells a sago palm and spends the day processing the pith. Occasionally palms are felled and left in the forest for about six weeks to develop a good crop of capricorn beetle larvae, a great delicacy for the Asmat.

Like their Creator, who fashioned them from ironwood and brought them to life with the beat of a drum, the Asmat are master carvers. Their tribal art is considered some of the best in Oceania. Best known for two to three metre tall *Bisj* poles—tree trunks carved with crouching interlocked phallic figures—their ceremonial shields, paddles, sago bowls, and intricately carved prows for dugout war canoes are prized by collectors all over the world.

Under ordinary circumstances, Asmat men and women have little to do with one another. Women gather food, repair the houses, fish, cook and prepare sago. Men build the houses, hunt wild pig and, in former times, fought enemies and took heads. During the cycle of ceremonies that revolve around the carving of *bisj* poles, however, there is much stylised but cathartic contact between the sexes. During this time the men spend a lot of time in the forest choosing trees for carving, felling and decorating them. Each time they return to camp they are repulsed by the women, who attack them with stones, untipped arrows, and slung earth. These are mock battles, but a great deal of pent-up emotion is released.

Occasionally the Asmat practise a kind of ritual wife exchange for the purpose of tribal solidarity, creating pacts between men that last their whole lives. The men first agree to the exchange; then they pursuade their wives to agree. The women exchange houses for the night, cook the evening and morning meals for their new families, and then return to their original homes laden with gifts. In times of extreme stress—if, for instance, foreigners are seen in the village for the first time—or during *bisj* ceremonies an entire village may exchange wives, welding the village into single intimate unit.

Unlike the Dani, for whom tribal war was not irreplaceable, without war the Asmat have little motivation for art and cultural tradition. With luck and help from the authorities and missionaries in the area they may find another way to organise their lives that makes sense in their particular cultural context. In the meantime, their reaction to the outsiders who come into southwest Irian to exploit the timber, coal and copper is one of passivity. Although increasing sensitivity to their needs on the part of government officials in the area is mitigating to some extent their sense of cultural dislocation, the Asmat situation is still extremely difficult. Only the future will reveal if their cultural and artistic traditions, unique even in a country rich with such traditions, can adapt to the modern world.

Curious children gather on a jetty at Kayu Merah Bay to watch the arrival of visitors.

OVERLEAF: *The main street of the Asmat village of Biwar Laut, one of the villages visited by Michael Rockefeller shortly before his disappearance in 1961.*

These children live with their grandparents on a small island in the Triton Bay waterway just north of Kayu Merah Bay. Their parents work in Desa Lobo, a day's journey away by dugout canoe. Every fortnight the grandfather paddles to Desa Lobo to trade yams, fish and coconuts for supplies.

In the Triton Bay area the use of Western clothing is more common than in places less subject to outside contact. Some people, however, still prefer the older styles. This man was visiting the village for a day, perhaps to trade, perhaps only to look around. Despite pressure from missionaries and government personnel, he shows no inclination to change his ways.

Desa Lobo sits at the foot of Gunung Lobo, a sheer cliff face more than a thousand metres high. The whole Kayu Merah Bay area is alive with birds. Along with the crested tern shown here, birds spotted in a single afternoon include Blythe's hornbill, white-bellied sea eagle, sulphur-crested cockatoo, reef heron, black-naped tern, common sandpiper, whimbrel, Australian pelican, frigate bird and Brahminy kite.

Confronted by what is probably the largest vessel he has seen in his life, this lone boatman exhibits remarkable sang-froid. The contrast between their stone-age culture and the modern world is so shattering that many Irian natives, especially those of the older generation, respond to new wonders with a kind of not seeing, a refusal to integrate the unbelievable sights around them.

215

The Dani people inhabit the Baliem Valley in rian Jaya's central highlands. In accordance with Dani mourning rituals, this old woman is missing several fingers. When a man dies, his close female relatives have one or more fingers amputated at the knuckle as a sign of grief. A Dani mother (right) with her child.

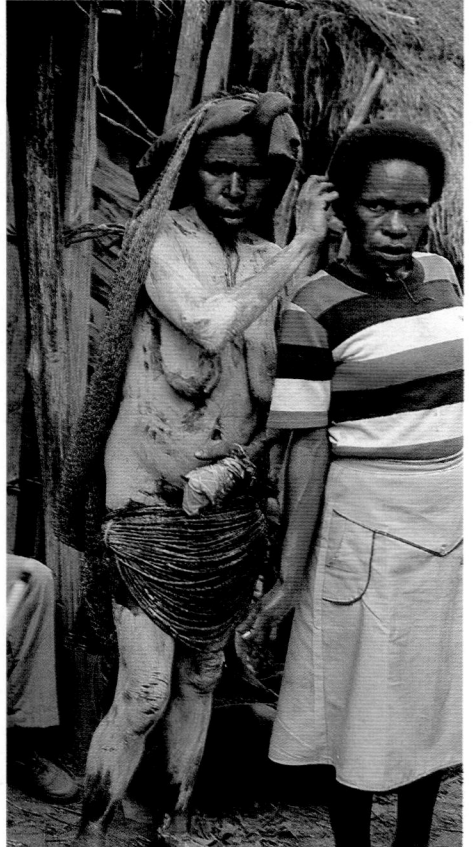

The dances of the Dani are quite elaborate. Villagers (above) enact the "Siege of the Chief's Pole"

A grieving widow (left) shortly after having one of her fingers amputated. The operation is performed with a sharp stone chopper, and the stump is dressed with a mixture of clay and ashes and a wrapping of husks and banana leaves. The widow, like all the female relatives of the deceased, has smeared her body with mud. When the mud dries it turns bluish white, giving her a ghostly pallor. She is accompanied by the chief's wife, who is also missing several fingers. Although ritual mutilation is now forbidden, the practice continues in remote areas.

The village chief wears only a hat, necklace and three-foot-long kote- ka. Made of hollow gourds and supported at the waist with twine, penis sheaths are standard dress for men in the Baliem Valley.

An Asmat woman (right) from the village of Biwar Laut. Classic hunter-gatherers, the Asmat live in the mangrove swamps of the south-west coast. They are taller and more angular than the highland Dani.

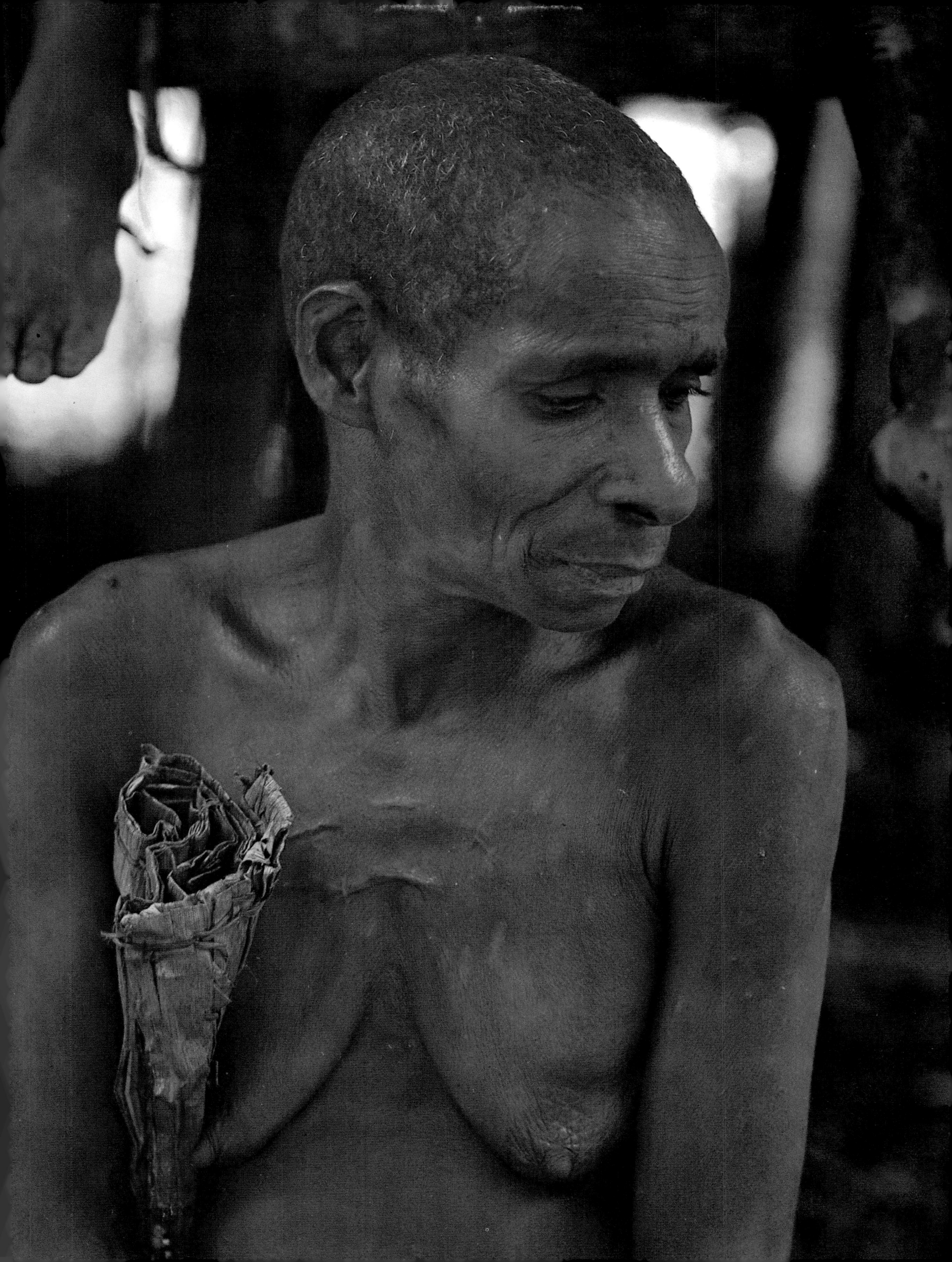

The traditional Asmat greeting at the mouth of the river for guests arriving by sea. All the men of Biwar Laut take part, and, should the visitors be unfriendly, their spears and perhaps the sharp ends of their paddles can be put to lethal use. The carved prow of the boat (below) typifies the care that the Asmat take in the things they make.

An Asmat adat *chief studies his unexpected visitors with dark piercing eyes. Another man turns up in full ceremonial regalia, including a shell nose ornament. Bone and bamboo nose ornaments are popular, as are headbands made from* kus-kus *fur and trimmed with cowrie shells, though these are generally worn only by men. Cowrie shells had the same history of use as currency here as in many other areas, notably East Africa and Polynesia. Now, however, they are only used as ornaments and for payment of the bride price.*

Head-on exposure to modern technology: listening to music on a borrowed tape player. This smiling mother wears a kus-kus *headband, which she would not do for a serious occasion.*

223

A Bisj *pole, elaborately carved and dressed.
The* Bisj *ceremony is part of a cycle of rituals performed on behalf of a dead man. Because its use promoted tribal warfare, the ceremony was once banned by the government. It has recently been revived in a more peaceful context, as a purely commemorative ritual.*

An artist displays his shield. Used both ceremonially and for war, these weapons are highly prized. Today, however, many beautiful old pieces have left family lineages to grace the shelves of collectors. In areas where visitors are common, the standard of workmanship is dropping in a bid to increase production.

A village elder (right) sits on the welcome porch of the men's house.

Three men wave a cheerful farewell from their dugout canoe. The pride and optimism of these people will stand them in good stead as they go through the changes ahead.

PHOTOGRAPHER'S NOTES

What started as an after-dinner conversation in 1980 has finally, after three years, eight thousand photos, two bouts of cholera, and who knows how many miles, become a finished product. It wasn't easy, but neither has it been dull. Indonesia is a fascinating, if often frustrating country to visit. Few people realise how vast it is until, as I did, they try to cross it from one end to the other.

Travelling in planes of all sizes, boats ditto, jeeps, mini-buses, on horseback and on foot, carrying my never-failing Hasselblads and Nikons, I gradually came to understand this vast country where I had spent so much time as a child.

For those readers who are camera buffs, I have included a list of equipment used in taking the photographs for this book:

Hasselblads, both the 500 C/M and the SWC/M, with lenses from the 38mm Biogon to the 250mm Sonnar. I also used the Nikon F3, F2AS and FE, all with motor drives to minimise missed shots and save time, with Nikkor lenses from the 20mm f3.5 to the 500mm f8 mirror. My favourite combination for people is the Nikon F3 with the 105mm f4 Micro-Nikkor lens.

PRODUCTION NOTES

The efforts of many people combined to produce this book, and much thought and care has been invested in it. For those who are interested a list of technical details follows:

The typeface used is Paladium T, set by Computype on a Compugraphic ACM 9000 Keyboard. Colour separations were by Colourscan made with a Hell Chromagraph DC 350 ER Laser Scanner. The book was printed by Tien Wah Press in fine screen (175 line per inch) lithographic process on a Heidelberg Speedmaster Press.

ACKNOWLEDGEMENTS

In a book of this nature it is never possible to acknowledge everyone who helped bring it to fruition.

Special gratitude, however is due to Ibu Dra. Cri Murthi Adi, Director of Marketing at the Directorate General of Tourism; Garuda Indonesian Airways; Lindblad Travel; and Mrs. Nora Suryanti, retired from the Ministry of Information. We would also like to thank P. Ngr. Ardika; Dr. Jacques Delmon; The Ganesha Volunteers; Linda Go; Mrs Lucy Lawalata; Karen Longeteig ; Drs. Wahyono Martowikrido; Natour Hotels Indonesia; Nyoman S. Pendit; Ronald Shaw; Soedarmadji J.H. Damais; Dea Sudarman; Dr. Parsudi Suparlan; Sylvia The; and Drs. I.G.M. Wismaya.

The photographer would like to thank his parents for their faith and encouragement in his work.

Indonesians : Portraits from an Archipelago has been published under the auspices of the Indonesian foundation *Yayasan Bhakti Putra*. Established by the Mahendra family, this foundation will provide scholarships to promising Indonesians, at the high school or university level, for study within Indonesia or abroad. The photography in this book was funded by the foundation and forms the core of its photo-archives. The photographs are accessible to the public.

BIBLIOGRAPHY

The following books were used in the preparation of this book and may prove interesting to the general reader.

Abdurachman, Paramita R. "Moluccan Responses to the First Intrusions of the West". In *Dynamics of Indonesian History* edited by Haryati Soebadio and Carine A. du Marchie Servaas. Amsterdam: North-Holland Publishing Company, 1978.

Barnes, R.H. *Kedang: A Study of the Collective Thought of an Eastern Indonesian People.* Oxford: Clarendon Press, Oxford, 1974. Monographs on Social Anthropology.

Bartlett, Joe C.; Cale, Roggie; and George A. Fowler, Jr. *Java: A Garden Continuum.* Singapore, Amerasian, 1974.

Baum, Vicki. *A Tale From Bali.* 1937 Reprint. Kuala Lumpur: Oxford University Press, 1973.

Black, Star, and Stuart-Fox, David. *Bali.* Hong Kong: Apa Productions, 1980.

Caldwell, Malcolm, and Utrecht, Ernst. *Indonesia: An Alternative History.* Sydney: Alternative Publishing Cooperative, 1979.

Covarrubias, Miguel. *Bali.* 1937. Reprint. Kuala Lumpur: Oxford University Press, Oxford in Asia Paperbacks, 1972, 1981.

Dalton, Bill. *Indonesia Handbook.* Franklin Village, Mich.: Moon Publication, 1977.

dePanthou, Patrick, and Muller, Kal. *Bali.* Papeete: The Two Continents Publishing Group, 1978.

Duly, Colin. *The Houses of Mankind.* London: Thames and Hudson, 1979.

Fischer, Joseph. *Threads of Tradition: Textiles of Indonesia and Sarawak.* Berkeley: University of California & Fidelity Savings and Loan Association, 1979.

Fox, James J. *Harvest of the Palm: Ecological Changes in Eastern Indonesia.* Cambridge: Harvard University Press, 1977.

Geertz, Clifford. *The Religion of Java.* Chicago: The University of Chicago Press, 1960.

Gittenger, Matiebelle. *Splendid Symbols: Textiles and Tradition in Indonesia.* Washington, D.C.: The Textile Museum, 1979.

Hanna, Willard A. *Indonesian Banda: Colonialism and its Aftermath in the Nutmeg Islands.* Philadelphia: Institute for the Study of Human Issues, 1978.

Heider, Karl G. *Grand Valley Dani: Peaceful Warriors.* Case Studies in Cultural Anthropology, edited by George and Louise Spindler. New York: Holt, Reinhart & Winston, 1979.

Horne, Lee. "Rural Habitats and Habitations: A Survey of Dwellings in the Rural Islamic World". In *The Changing Rural Habitat*, Vol. II. (Proceedings of a seminar held by the Aga Khan Award for Architecture.) Singapore: Concept Media, 1982.

Horridge, Adrian. *The Prahu: Traditional Sailing Boat of Indonesia.* Kuala Lumpur: Oxford University Press, 1981.

Hutton, Peter. *Java.* Third Edition. Hong Kong: Apa Productions, 1978.

Koentjaraningrat, Ed. *Villages in Indonesia*, Ithaca: Cornell University Press, 1967.

Lebar, Frank, M, ed. *Ethnic Groups of Insular Southeast Asia. Vol. 1: Indonesia, Andaman Islands and Madagascar.* New Haven: Human Relations Area Files Press, 1972.

Lee Khoon Choy. *Indonesia: Between Myth and Reality.* Singapore: Federal Publications, 1977.

Loeb, Edwin M. *Sumatra: Its History and People.* 1935 Reprint. Kuala Lumpur: Oxford University Press, Oxford in Asia Paperbacks, 1972, 1982.

McPhee, Colin. *A House in Bali.* 1944 Reprint. Kuala Lumpur: Oxford University Press, 1979.

Pelzer, Dorothy W. *Trek Across Indonesia.* Singapore: Graham Brash, 1982.

Powell, Hickman. *The Last Paradise.* 1930 Reprint. Kuala Lumpur: Oxford University Press, Oxford in Asia Paperbacks, 1982.

Smithies, Michael. *A Javanese Boyhood: An Ethnographic Biography.* Singapore: Federal Publication, Federal Asian Library 1982.

Van Ness, Edward C. and Shita Prawirohardjo. *Javanese Wayang Kulit: An Introduction.* Kuala Lumpur: Oxford University Press, Oxford in Asia Paperbacks, 1980.

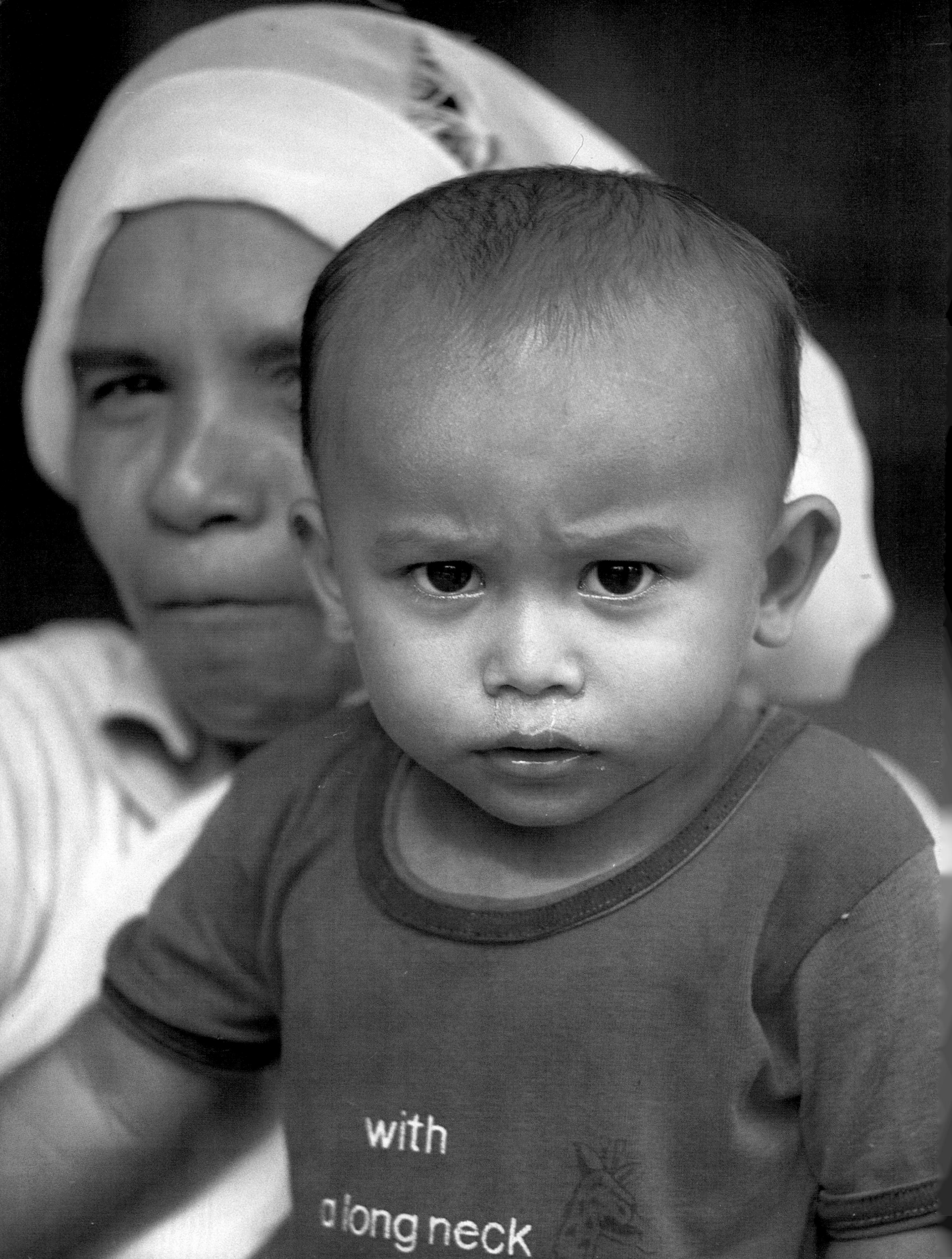

GOLDEN WINGS

A Pictorial History of the United States Navy
and Marine Corps in the Air

Books by
MARTIN CAIDIN

GOLDEN WINGS
AIR FORCE
BLACK THURSDAY
THUNDERBIRDS!
LET'S GO FLYING!
PROJECT MERCURY
VANGUARD
BOEING 707
WORLDS IN SPACE
SPACEPORT U.S.A.
WAR FOR THE MOON
THE LONG NIGHT
ZERO!
SAMURAI!
THUNDERBOLT!
THE ZERO FIGHTER
COUNTDOWN FOR TOMORROW
THE NIGHT HAMBURG DIED
THE NIGHT TOKYO DIED
TEST PILOT
ROCKETS BEYOND THE EARTH
ROCKETS AND MISSILES
JETS, ROCKETS & GUIDED MISSILES

GOLDEN WINGS

A Pictorial History of the United States Navy and Marine Corps in the Air

by MARTIN CAIDIN

IN CO-OPERATION WITH THE U.S. NAVY

BRAMHALL HOUSE, NEW YORK

for

ED MACK MILLER

(C)

This edition is published by Bramhall House,
a division of Clarkson N. Potter, Inc.
by arrangement with Random House.

Library of Congress Catalog Card Number: 60–12150
Manufactured in the United States of America
Layout by MARTIN CAIDIN and FRED L. WOLFF

FOREWORD

GOLDEN WINGS is a unique pictorial documentation of the evolution of airpower within the United States Navy and its smaller but highly distinctive Marine Corps. It is a history of America in the air that has up to now not been told in full. It is a story of both men and machines, rich in tradition, and exemplifying man's ability and courage. It has long needed telling; the writer hopes that in GOLDEN WINGS justice is done to this brilliant page in the air.

Many of the historical photographs reproduced in this book the reader will see for the first time. These pictures bring to life vital moments in Naval aviation history. Many of these photographs are not of machines, but of men who flew, who served on the ground, and aboard those artificial islands—the aircraft carriers. In the history of our Navy and Marine Corps, these men have labored not only on the earth, but far at sea and deep within the bowels of mighty ships.

The writer personally searched through many tens of thousands of photographs in the Still Picture Section of the Naval Photographic Center, Anacostia Naval Air Station, and I am grateful for the outstanding assistance provided me by the personnel of this Section. Many other sources were, of course, researched for the book, including the historical files of the Institute of Aeronautical Sciences, and several private collections of truly rare photographs. The aircraft companies that have produced the long lineage of Naval and Marine aircraft were more than generous in their assistance.

Thus GOLDEN WINGS represents the combined work of many people in many organizations. In this respect there were many contributors to the text contents of this book: official records and documents, many interviews, and private diaries—all were utilized to assemble the story in its proper continuity. Naval officials have studied the manuscript with the greatest possible care to assure absolute authenticity.

No book of this scope, obviously, can be created without the labors of many people, and I am indebted to many more individuals than it is possible to list on this page. I would be remiss, however, if I did not take special pains to express my gratitude to Commander Herbert J. Gimpel, USN, with whom this book received its initial planning. Without the efforts of Commander Russ L. Bufkins, USN, Chief, Magazine and Book Branch, this book would have been impossible to assemble in its present form, and I am especially indebted to him. My thanks to Lieutenant Commanders A.E. Atkinson, USN, Ray Robinson, USN, and an old and good friend, Commander Bart Slattery, USN, a walking encyclopedia on Naval aviation; and to Adrian Van Wyen, Naval Aviation Historian, for technical research and checking.

And my personal thanks to Fred L. Wolff, who worked long into many nights laying out this book; and above all to my editor, Robert D. Loomis, with whom the idea, the planning, and the work of GOLDEN WINGS were nurtured.

MARTIN CAIDIN

Contents

THE BEGINNING

OF NAVAL AVIATION

Curtiss pusher takes off from USS *Pennsylvania* at 11:58 A.M., January 18, 1911, in San Francisco Bay; the landing was made 57 minutes before.

ONE-PILOT AIR FORCE

But no airplanes . . .

In the field of military aviation, the United States Navy was a tardy arrival. The Army stepped into the flying business first on August 1, 1907, when the Signal Corps established on paper an Aeronautical Division and began shopping around for a machine that was both airworthy and practicable for military reconnaissance purposes. Two years later the Army was in business, with a rickety Wright biplane that blistered the air with the astonishing speed of 42.583 miles per hour.

In September, 1908, Army Lt. Thomas E. Selfridge became the nation's first military air fatality in the crash of a Wright airplane during demonstrations at Fort Meyer, Virginia. Only by a twist of fate was young Selfridge the victim of this crash; the "potential" victim of the fatal accident was Navy Lt. George C. Sweet.

Lt. Sweet attended the Wright demonstrations as an official Navy observer. On September 17, 1908, Sweet was scheduled to fly as a passenger with Orville Wright. Sweet was a large, heavy man; to compensate for his weight, Wright fitted the airplane with oversize propellers. Just before the flight, Lt. Selfridge asked Sweet if he would give up his turn that day for the flight. Sweet consented, and this was the step that saved his life. In the ensuing flight, one of the oversize propellers struck a rudder brace wire. Before Sweet's horrified eyes, the airplane smashed to the ground; several hours later Selfridge was dead.

Despite the tragedy—and his narrow escape—the potential of the flying machine as a Naval weapon deeply impressed Lt. Sweet. In his official account he reported with enthusiasm: "The Navy must have that! It will be

The Wright B-1, an early airplane purchased by the Navy, "at anchor" in Baltimore Harbor, Maryland. The Navy's first $25,000 for aviation purchased the *Triad,* a landplane, and Wright B-1. In 1911, Navy set up first air station on Severn River, Annapolis, Md.

Helpful civilians:
Curtiss and Ely

important to us!" One year later, Lt. Sweet became the first U.S. Naval officer—and perhaps the first naval officer in the world—to fly.

Unhappily for the Navy's few far-sighted exponents of the flying machine for military purposes, there existed no official support for air activities. Long before the Wrights achieved their epochal success on December 17, 1903, both the Navy and Army had exhibited a grudging but official recognition of the possibilities of using the flying machine. Some five years earlier, when political oration against Spanish activities in Cuba was at its loudest, Theodore Roosevelt, Assistant Secretary of the Navy, wrote of the experiments of Professor Samuel Langley with his steam-powered aerodrome that: "It seems to me worth while for this government to try whether it will not work on a large enough scale to be of use in the event of war. . . ."

The Board of Construction of the Navy maintained, however, that the airplane "pertains strictly to the land service and not to the Navy." Ap-

parently the Army agreed, and with a handsome subsidy of fifty thousand Army dollars, the good professor did his best to make history. On October 7, 1903, he launched his aerodrome from a houseboat on the Potomac River. History was stalled as five years of labor splashed awkwardly into the

Langley's aerodrome (*above*)—also called a gas-driven man carrier—just before its first "flight" on October 7, 1903, from a houseboat on the Potomac River. The machine failed to fly, and plunged into the water. (*Below*) Curtiss's North Field, San Diego, as it appeared in 1911. Glenn Curtiss trained Navy's first aviators, demonstrated uses of airplanes with warships. North Field is now sprawling San Diego Naval Air Station.

One of early Navy Curtiss amphibians *(left)* during training flight. The 50-hp machines were slow, unstable, difficult to fly, but established the foundation of future Naval aviation. They flew from land and water, from ship decks, and were catapulted into the air. *(Center)* Lt. T. G. Ellyson, Naval Aviator No. 1, who received his training from Glenn Curtiss at North Field, San Diego. On April 12, 1911, Curtiss wrote the Secretary of the Navy that: "Mr. Ellyson is a hard worker and has acquired considerable knowledge of the art of aviation. He has been especially successful in operating the machine and is easily capable of qualifying for a pilot's license. . . ." On September 7, 1911, Ellyson made the first successful "launching device" take-off for the Navy, running down an inclined wire on the beach at Hammondsport, N.Y. On November 12, 1912, Ellyson made the first successful launch of an airplane by catapult in the AH-3 at Washington Navy Yard. *(Below)* on January 26, 1911, Glenn Curtiss made the first successful flight with a hydro-airplane by taking off from and landing on the water in San Diego harbor. On February 17, he taxied out to the USS *Pennsylvania*, maneuvered under the boat crane and was hoisted aboard. Lowered to the water, he took off and then flew back to his own field; it was the first seaplane operation aboard a ship.

$5500 BIRTHDAY CAKE

river. A second attempt one month later brought another failure, a stream of curses from the floundering pilot, and an abrupt end to military financial support. The official Army report stated simply that: ". . . The claim that an engine-driven, man-carrying aerodrome has been constructed lacks the proof which actual flight alone can give."

The Wright Brothers met subsequent success in their ventures with the Army, but except for official observations, received only the Navy cold shoulder. On December 2, 1908, Rear Admiral William S. Cowles, Chief of the Bureau of Equipment, recommended to the Secretary of the Navy that "a number of aeroplanes" be purchased to operate from a ship's deck, carry a wireless telegraph, operate in weather other than a dead calm, maintain a high rate of speed and, among other things, "be of such design as to permit convenient stowage on board ship."

On August 2, 1909, the Signal Corps of the Army cheered weakly the acceptance of its first flying machine; fourteen days later a Navy Bureau of Equipment request for authority to advertise for the construction of "two heavier than air flying machines" was disapproved with the comment that: "The Department does not consider that the development of an aeroplane has progressed sufficiently at this time for use in the Navy." Watchful waiting best described official policy toward flying machines.

One year later, in September, 1910, aviation began to sneak into the Navy through a back door; Captain W.I. Chambers was assigned the task of replying to correspondence of civilian flying enthusiasts. Spurred on by his associates, he made plans to fly an airplane from a battleship—a civilian airplane, since the Navy had none—and ordered an 83-foot platform built over the forecastle of the cruiser USS *Birmingham*. Searching around for an airplane and pilot, he was almost thrown out by the Wright Brothers, but met success with Eugene Ely, a pilot who worked for aviation pioneer Glenn Curtiss. And on November 14, 1910, the Navy focused sharp attention on Ely's feat of flying the 50-horsepower Curtiss pusher from the *Birmingham* in the first successful launching of an aircraft from a ship.

Events moved faster from this point on. Glenn Curtiss at his own expense offered "to instruct an officer of the Navy in the operation and construction of the Curtiss aeroplane." On December 23, 1910, Lt. T.G. Ellyson was ordered to report to North Island, San Diego; four months later he was "graduated" by Curtiss, who wrote the Secretary of the Navy that Lt. Ellyson "is now competent to care for and operate Curtiss aeroplanes" and stated further that ". . . Mr. Ellyson [is] a man who will make success in aviation."

On March 4, 1911, the Naval Appropriations Act, 1912, provided $25,000 for developing Naval aviation. Two months later the Navy wrote its first aircraft requisition: a wooden, canvas, and bamboo aircraft that could fly at 45 miles per hour.

This is the "birth day of Naval aviation," when, for a

November 14, 1910: Loading Curtiss pusher on 83-foot sloping deck of Cruiser USS *Birmingham;* here Eugene Ely made first ship take-off. On January 18, 1911, Ely landed on 120-foot deck built on USS *Pennsylvania,* took off (see page 1) again 57 minutes later.

price of $5,500, the Navy ordered from Glenn Curtiss an eight-cylinder "hydro-terra-aeroplane" (named the *Triad* by Curtiss) and designated A-1, that could (and did) operate on land or water and fly at 45 miles per hour. The Navy was on its belated way in the air.

Lt. Commander R.P. Brewer of the carrier USS *Intrepid* explains that "the good old days were not without their pitfalls and pratfalls; there's a surprising similarity in the pattern of bang and prang down through the years. When spruce and glue and linen were replaced by titanium and flush riveting, the prangs merely became noisier, and the repairs got awfully expensive. . . ." Pictured here are the five proud builders of the Navy's first Skimmer, a contraption that just skimmed over the water—but didn't fly.

Ground crew—attired in bathing suits and rain slickers—drag ashore a Curtiss amphibian pusher at the training school on the banks of the Severn River at Greenbury Point, near Annapolis, Maryland. Hangars for maintenance work were large tents into which the Navy's first three airplanes were pushed and pulled. Although the Navy's first airfield, which began operations in September, 1911, was essentially a training base, it was also the Navy's *only* airfield, and many experiments were carried out there. One such test brought the small Navy air group international acclaim; on October 6, 1912, Lt. J.H. Towers in the Curtiss A-2 took off from the river at 6:30 A.M., and remained in the air for 6 hours, 10 minutes and 35 seconds, a new record for hydroplanes.

MORE SWIMMING THAN FLYING

Flying the Navy's airplanes—sans seat belts—in the early days was an occupation that more often than not led to a severe meeting with the brine and a thorough dunking. One incident best illustrating the hazardous flight duty in the "old days" befell a young lieutenant named John H. Towers. The pusher airplane in which he flew had no cockpit, no seat, no safety belt, yielding fabric, and propellers that whirled perilously close to the passengers. At 1,600 feet a violent downdraft threw the airplane out of control. The sudden maneuver hurled the pilot through space; Towers clung grimly to a strut, whirling and spinning into the water. A nearby ship pulled him out and rushed him to a hospital; four months later he was back on duty.

Not only did Towers survive his wild descent—he went on to become Admiral Towers, and Commander, Air Force, Pacific, during World War II.

The Navy managed to avoid the circus stunts that killed many civilian pilots, and watched in distress as accidents claimed the lives of seven Army pilots. But no matter what precautions might be taken, flying was still learn-as-you-go—as proved by Ellyson's first catapult attempt. The plane left the ramp with its nose straight up. Naval Aviator No. 1 swam away from the wreckage—wet, but unhurt.

Curtiss pusher was a widely used trainer; it provided first experience with units of fleet.

Commander Wick and Lt. Rounds, early aviators, making dual-control take-off in AH-8. *(Below)* Wreck of Lt. V.D. Herbster's (Aviator No. 4) plane at North Island; he escaped.

MARINES ADD DRAMATIC PAGE TO NAVY LOG

"I called her everything in God's name to go up. I pleaded with her. I caressed her, I prayed to her, and I cursed that flighty old maid to lift up her skirts and hike, but she never would."

This is how 1st Lt. Alfred A. Cunningham, USMC, described his first attempts to fly, when stationed at the Philadelphia Navy Yard in 1911. The unco-operative female he refers to was a civilian's homemade machine called *Noisy Nan* that Cunningham had rented and that, despite his efforts, never really made it into the air.

Cunningham—who was to the Marines what Mitchell and Arnold were to the Air Force—served as a sixteen-year-old Army corporal in the Spanish-American War. In 1909 he was commissioned a Marine Corps officer; two years later he found himself at the Philadelphia Navy Yard, where he squandered part of his $166.67 monthly pay to try and coax *Noisy Nan* into the air.

Although these efforts failed, the new lieutenant did get into plenty of hot water. As a member of the Aero Club of Pennsylvania, he talked club members into dunning Congress to build a Marine flying field in Philadelphia. Cunningham was thoroughly chewed out by his superiors, but emerged partially triumphant and with orders to report on May 22, 1912, to the Naval Academy "for duty in connection with aviation."

That day marks the beginning of Marine Corps aviation, but birth was little more than a querulous whisper. Cunningham went to the Burgess-Curtiss air factory at Marblehead, Mass., for instruction; on August 1, 1912, after exactly 2 hours 40 minutes of training, he made his first solo flight.

1st Lt. Alfred A. Cunningham, USMC (left), first Marine aviator and Naval Aviator No. 5, with Belgian flier V.D. Yoncheere, Philadelphia Navy Yard in 1912. Cunningham was guiding spirit for early Corps aviation.

Trial, error, practice and new ideas

Cunningham was duly listed as Naval Aviator No. 5.

Six weeks later, Lt. B.L. Smith (who became Naval Aviator No. 6) reported to the Naval Aviation Camp at Annapolis for flight training. Between Cunningham's solo flight and the American entry into World War I, a total of five Marines joined Cunningham as fliers. These included Smith, William M. McIlvain, Francis T. Evans, Roy S. Geiger, and David L.S. Brewster. The first Corps warrant officer to become a pilot was Walter E. McCaughtry; the first enlisted pilot was Sgt. James Maguire.

Even as the new men joined the fledgling aviation group, the Marines suffered from outside interference. Cunningham became engaged; smitten with love, he wavered under the adamant stand of a fiancée who refused to marry any madman who persisted in flitting through the sky. Torn between two desires, Cunningham requested that he be detached from flight duty. This accomplished, he married; eighteen months later, however, not even the wails of his wife availed, and he returned to his beloved flying. Except for this brief period, Cunningham remained the head of Marine aviation from 1912 to 1920.

Cunningham's own words best describe the perils and tribulations of flying in those early days; in writing of his airplane to Captain W.I. Chambers, officer-in-charge of Naval aviation, he made it clear that ingenuity was an essential attribute of the early aviator:

"My Machine, as I told you and Mr. Towers probably told you, is not in my opinion fit for use. I built it from parts of the Burgess F and Wright B, which are not exactly alike and nothing fitted. I had to cut off and patch up parts and bore additional holes in beams in order to make them fit. The engine bed, made by Burgess, was not exactly square with the front beam, so the engine had to be mounted a little out of true (with reference to the engine bed). I have made over 200 flights in this machine and recently, in spite of unusual care of myself and men, something seems to vibrate loose or off a majority of the flights made. One of

the propeller shafts is the same one used with the Cyro motor in the old machine. It is the only left-hand shaft here. While the engine runs smoothly, it does not deliver nearly as much power as when it was newer, and even then, it did not have enough power to fly safely in any but smooth weather. It is impossible to climb over a few hundred feet with a passenger. The whole machine has just about served its usefulness and I would like very much to have a new machine of the single propeller type. Lt. Arnold, of the Army, after seeing the machine run and examining it, said that none of the Army fliers would go up in it. Will you kindly let me know what the prospects are for my getting a new machine."

Despite these problems, the Marines not only sustained themselves, but in a dogged way even flourished. On October 7, 1913, Franklin D. Roosevelt, Acting Secretary of the Navy, set up the Chambers Board to draw up "a comprehensive plan for the organization of a Naval Aeronautic Service." Along with six Naval officers, Cunningham was made a member of the board, assuring the Marines a voice in Naval aviation's growth almost from its infancy, a step that the Marine Corps greeted with a collective sigh of relief.

On January 6, 1914, the Corps received orders establishing Marine aviation as a separate, official organization. A Navy letter ordered: "1st Lieut. B.L. Smith USMC and 2d Lieut. W.M. McIlvain will go by USS *Hancock* from Philadelphia, Pa., direct to Culebra with the Advance Base outfit, including Navy Flying Boat C-3, Navy OWL Boat E-1 . . ." The letter further stipulated that: "This outfit is to be regarded as a Marine Section of the Navy Flying School. . . ."

Smith and McIlvain saw flying duty with the fleet at Culebra, Puerto Rico, and Guantanamo, Cuba, in the ancient Curtiss. Smith reported that he "gathered valuable data on spotting possibilities and on the ease with which a force attempting to land in small boats might be bombed from the air." Those brief weeks in the Caribbean were the first steps in air support practiced by Marines.

Distinction between Marine and Navy fliers was only on paper; they flew all operations together. One of WW II's greatest figures, Admiral Marc A. Mitscher (then lieutenant) flew vintage seaplane at Pensacola, Fla.

Some of Navy's outstanding leaders contributed to birth of Naval aviation. At controls of AH-3 is Naval Constructor H.C. Richardson (later a Captain), who was a pioneer in ship-hull and flying-boat designs.

IDEAS INTO WEAPONS

True military force begins to emerge from experiments

In 1913 the first school for Naval ground officers was designated at the Massachusetts Institute of Technology, where Naval Constructor J.C. Hunsaker went to start a course in aerodynamics. Later in the year Hunsaker made a special European tour to study foreign aerodynamic equipment; his report was not encouraging to the still-struggling American Naval air arm. Although the U.S. Navy was definitely leading the world in some of its experiments, the European nations were far ahead in their naval air forces. Britain was converting the cruiser *Hermes* into the first aircraft carrier; Germany was the authority on airships (already in use with its army and navy); and French seaplanes were world leaders.

In contrast, in that year the U.S. Navy bought only four new airplanes, and authorized but four men to flying duty. The brilliant Captain W.I. Chambers was ordered for retirement; this was a severe blow to Naval aviation, for Chambers had fought lack of funds, skepticism, opposition, and adverse technical opinion to build the embryonic Naval aviation force.

Against this unhappy background, Naval aviators individually made brilliant experiments, showing the way toward effective weapon use of the airplane. Then came the outbreak of war in Europe. The Naval Appropriations Act of 1915 afforded Naval aviation its first million dollars, and created the National Advisory Committee for Aeronautics; NACA contributed more to aeronautical science than any other organization in the world. With its first sizable funds, Navy engineers turned with new enthusiasm to the problems of aviation.

Navy's first tests of airborne radio; checking out equipment prior to flight. On July 26, 1912, tests were made at Annapolis under Ensign C.H. Maddox. In first flight, Lt. John Rodgers sent letter "D" at short intervals which were "easily received" by the USS *Stringham* about a mile away. Two years later, Lt. P.N.L. Bellinger worked with Army forces in developing airborne artillery spotting.

A combination of strange designs is illustrated in this photograph. The plane is a Burgess-Dunne AH-7 seaplane which, 47 years ago, was a flying wing—and sweptback at that! Demonstrating one of the Navy's test bombs is a "Mr. Capehart." The bomb is a long, tubular affair, and represented one of a series of missiles to be thrown by hand from the airplane in flight (picture taken on November 11, 1915). Armament tests at this time were well behind developments in Europe, where the airplane was being applied effectively as a weapon; Navy planes were regarded worthy only for reconnaissance.

The Navy owed much to efforts of Glenn H. Curtiss (left), who helped build embryonic Naval air arm. Curtiss trained many Navy fliers, including Lt. John H. Towers, seated with him in this 1910 Curtiss pusher; Towers received his flight training at the Curtiss School, Hammondsport, N.Y. Later, Towers fell 1,600 feet in a hydroplane that plunged out of control; injured in the crash, he returned to flying several months later. Towers became an outstanding pilot, and at one time held world's altitude record. In 1939 he headed the Navy's Bureau of Aeronautics; in WW II commanded the Pacific Air Forces.

On January 10, 1914, the Secretary of the Navy, Hon. Josephus Daniels, announced that: ". . . The science of aerial navigation has reached the point where aircraft must form a large part of our Naval force for offensive and defensive operation." Navy hopes for a major scouting and reconnaissance airborne force sparked development of aerial reconnaissance techniques and equipment. The first Naval aerial photographer was W.L. Richardson (left; pilot unidentified), seated in an AH-14 at Pensacola, 1914. Handling the heavy Graflex camera on open wing was a tricky, hazardous feat.

On November 5, 1915, Lt. Commander H.C. Mustin, at the controls of the AB-2 flying boat, made the first catapult launching from a moving vessel. The USS *North Carolina* was under sternway—moving stern first. Later, he made first launching from *North Carolina* while ship was under headway.

Lt. P.N.L. Bellinger (right) and Machinist Adams, as they returned the AH-3 pusher seaplane to the USS *Mississippi*, standing off Vera Cruz, in late April, 1914. Scouting over enemy positions in the Vera Cruz Incident, Bellinger's plane was later hit by rifle fire—Navy's first plane damaged in battle.

Operations with early seaplanes aboard Navy ships were often hazardous affairs. Highly inflammable dope and fabric, exposed fuel tanks presented dangerous fire risks. In a rare historical action photo, Martin-Thomas seaplane on a shipboard catapult (June 7, 1917) explodes into flames.

RECORDS AND FIRST DEATH

The first world's record went to the Navy for Towers' October 6, 1912, endurance flight in the Curtiss A-2; soon after, standing records fell to the ill-equipped but intrepid Naval pilots. On November 12, 1912, Lt. T.G. Ellyson in the AH-3 made the first successful launch of an airplane by catapult. On June 13, 1913, Lt. P.N. Bellinger in the A-3 set an American altitude record for seaplanes, at 6,200 feet over Annapolis. The next year a different type of record was listed. During the Vera Cruz Incident, when the Navy moved to occupy the Mexican port, Lt. Bellinger and his machinist, Adams, had their AH-3 airplane struck by enemy rifle fire during a reconnaissance flight over the port; it was the first mark of combat on a Navy plane.

In 1915 the Navy made the first catapult launching from a ship under way. On April 2, 1916, Lt. R.C. Saufley flew a Curtiss to 16,072 feet, for a new Navy record. Then came February 13, 1917, when Marine Captain F.T. Evans looped and spun a Jenny N-9 floatplane, ignoring predictions that to do so would be suicidal.

Less in the headlines but far more important were technical developments. In March, 1912, Captain W.I. Chambers designed a speed indicator combined with an electric stabilizer—the first automatic pilot. Rear Admiral Bradley A. Fiske was granted Patent 1032394 for a method of directing and delivering an attack by a self-propelled torpedo launched from an airplane.

Up until June 20, 1913, all Naval flying had been performed without a single fatality. On that day, however, turbulent air threw Ensign W.D. Billingsley, Naval Aviator No. 9 from his plane; he fell 1,600 feet to his death. One reaction to this first fatal accident—the Navy ordered safety belts installed on all its planes.

AB-3 flying boat launched from USS *North Carolina* at Pensacola, July, 1916. Early catapults interfered with the gun batteries, and were taken off ships while engineers designed new equipment.

An early model seaplane at Pensacola, February, 1917. This tractor-type seaplane —and other tractor designs—came into Navy use after two fatal accidents. Lt. M.L. Stolz was killed in a pusher seaplane crash in 1915, when the motor crushed his head. In June, 1916, Lt. R.C. Saufley died in a similar accident. The Army had already shifted to tractor types and Curtiss had produced a tractor biplane. Developed to take the Curtiss OXX engine, this became the JN, forerunner of the famous Jenny. The Navy worked with Curtiss and produced the N-9. This plane was so successful a trainer that, with higher-powered engines, it was used for training purposes at Pensacola air station as a seaplane through the year 1927.

S PROMISE, STRENGTH

Marines patrolled for subs:
A few men saw combat

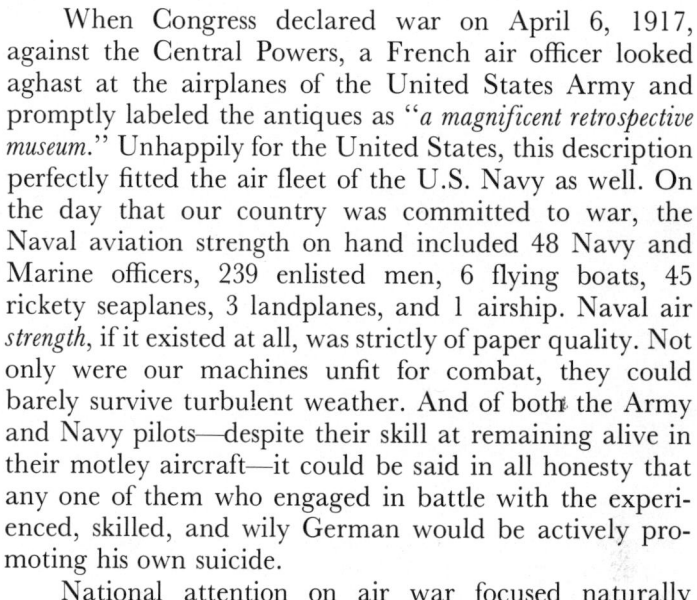

When Congress declared war on April 6, 1917, against the Central Powers, a French air officer looked aghast at the airplanes of the United States Army and promptly labeled the antiques as "*a magnificent retrospective museum.*" Unhappily for the United States, this description perfectly fitted the air fleet of the U.S. Navy as well. On the day that our country was committed to war, the Naval aviation strength on hand included 48 Navy and Marine officers, 239 enlisted men, 6 flying boats, 45 rickety seaplanes, 3 landplanes, and 1 airship. Naval air *strength*, if it existed at all, was strictly of paper quality. Not only were our machines unfit for combat, they could barely survive turbulent weather. And of both the Army and Navy pilots—despite their skill at remaining alive in their motley aircraft—it could be said in all honesty that any one of them who engaged in battle with the experienced, skilled, and wily German would be actively promoting his own suicide.

National attention on air war focused naturally enough on the daring and frenzied antics of the single-seater pursuits—the Camels, Fokkers, Spads, Nieuports, and other whirling dervishes. Completely beyond the glare of this spotlight, the Navy faced more prosaic, but no less demanding, problems. The major task at hand (accentuated by a coastal populace screaming for "protection") was to stop the German submarine force.

Flying from hastily prepared bases on the Atlantic Coast and the Gulf of Mexico, Naval aviators struggled against the elements and lack of proper equipment, and the history of antisub operations is essentially a tale of a grim and bloody struggle merely to stay alive.

Overseas, both the Army and Navy, and the few Marines who were rushed to the combat theater, suffered what has been aptly described as ". . . moral and mental disintegration and disarrangement." Disdained by our Allies, shunted to outlying camps, and subjected to exasperating disappointments, delays in receiving equipment, and plain "raw deals," theirs was a record of utter frustration. In the Mediterranean, the Army and Navy fought over control of equipment. Later in France, where Naval aviators flew foreign Donnet-Donkauts, Telliers, and Le Peus planes, there was sustained action against the enemy. It was a war fought with pistols, rifles, shotguns, hand grenades, and—literally—bricks that were thrown against German submarines.

Curtiss N-9 training seaplanes were most widely used machines for Naval air training during WW I; preliminary training was given at Bay Shore, Long Island; Key West; Miami; and San Diego. Advanced training for planes and blimps was given at Pensacola.

As newer, more powerful engines became available, Curtiss N-9 seaplane was modified into R-9 model, shown here taxiing in to the ramp at Pensacola. More pilots learned in "seaplane Jennies" than any other type.

Flight training of Navy pilots in WW I was often a haphazard affair, carried out with primitive facilities in open areas; a good example of these conditions is shown in this picture of beach seaplane training area at Pensacola.

Burgess-Dunne AH-10 seaplane (*above*) at Pensacola, March, 1916. Once an old clipper ship harbor, Pensacola was opened as Navy Yard in 1914; during WW I became advanced flying school.

Beach crews drag N-9 training plane up the ramp at Pensacola. Tents were used as hangars; wooden ramps built on the beach to facilitate plane handling. Plane accidents were not infrequent.

NAVAL AIRPOWER WAS MOCKERY

Abuses crippled U.S. air industry

Of the Naval air arm's role in World War I, Admiral William S. Sims claimed that this air fleet was "a factor in persuading the enemy to acknowledge defeat." General John J. Pershing reacted to this statement with something less than expected dignity, and snapped that the Navy's planes "possessed no advantages over destroyers, and [their] use was certainly of no immediate aid in meeting the crisis that confronted us on the Western Front . . . the most important consideration."

Pershing's remarks were, sadly, true enough. But the fact is that history has emphasized the lack of accomplishment of our Naval and Marine air units during the war and ignored the superb efforts of the men themselves. From the first day that Navy fliers and crewmen landed in France in June, 1917, through their first flights in July to the close of the war, they flew 22,000 flights and missions, an outstanding record when one considers the scarcity and low performance of the machines that they flew. The bedraggled stepchild of the European air war, despite its shortcomings, managed to patrol over 800,000 nautical miles, and drop more than 100 tons of bombs against German submarines and sub pens. This feat was accomplished by 1,147 officers and 18,308 enlisted men—with but 19 casualties.

Ensign Albert D. Sturtevant was the first Navy pilot to die in combat against the enemy. Fighting against overwhelming numbers of German planes, he was shot down over the North Sea on February 15, 1918. Ensign Kenneth MacLeish shot down an enemy plane, and almost immediately after was blown out of the sky. Ensign Curtis Read died in a seaplane crash. Lt. David Ingalls, who was to become the Assistant Secretary of the Navy for Air, shot down 5 German planes, and was the Navy's sole World War I ace. Artemus L. Gates, who also became an Assistant Secretary of Navy for Air, won not only the stirring cheers of all the Navy, but also a recommendation for the Congressional Medal of Honor for his daring rescue, under fire, of several British aviators shot down off Ostend.

ON THE HOME FRONT

On July 24, 1917, in a grandiose gesture calculated to overcome its long-standing indifference to the needs of American aviation, the Congress appropriated $640,000,000, to create overnight, solely on the strength of the dollar, an overwhelming Army air fleet. To the Navy went an additional sum of $143,000,000—compared to a total previous *expenditure* of $1,000,000.

It was an incredible carnival: a nation engaged in a wild financial thrashing to overcome our military inadequacies. Congress hoped by its unprecedented appropriations to bring to reality its boast of sending to the front 4,500 combat planes by June 30 of the next year. But this was a stupid, futile, and empty promise. The Germans laughed loudly, exhorted their own workers, and dubbed the Reich's aviation effort the *Amerikaprogramm*.

The verbal antics of Congress before an impressed populace helped cover up for a while the chaos and confusion that crippled the American military airplane production program. The Navy had no bombers and no fighters, but early in the war had launched a sound program to build flying boats for antisubmarine warfare. On July 27, 1917, Congress authorized a Naval Aircraft Factory, which began to build H-16 flying boats. By June, 1918, production reached the commendable figure of one airplane per day. But neither the Curtiss company nor the new Naval Aircraft Factory could meet the immediate demands for 874 of these boats, so subcontracts were let throughout the nation; NAF was to serve as an assembly

Curtiss R-9 seaplanes, like this one shown at an Atlantic coast air station early in 1918, served in double roles as trainers and submarine patrol. Armament included one machine gun, hand bombs.

Burgess-Dunne taxiing to beach ramp on Florida coast, March 3, 1916. Navy started war with handful of motley planes; by November 11, 1918, when Germans surrendered, Naval air arm had mushroomed to total of 6,716 officers, 30,693 enlisted men. In air fleet were 2,107 planes and 230 dirigibles and balloons, a force that gave Navy chance to develop new weapons.

plant. Only at this late stage in the war did Naval authorities recognize the superiority of the British F-5 flying boat built at Felixstowe. The H-16 was relegated to secondary status in favor of the F-5L, the British machine with the excellent American Liberty engine.

Army pilots had to fly fighters and bombers which the British and French had discarded as unfit for combat. Great hopes were held for the British-designed and American-built DH-4 bomber, but this shining light of our "massive bombardment campaign from the air" turned out to be one of the worst-built airplanes in our history. The machines that reached France were so inferior in workmanship and defective in their parts that the majority had to be torn down and rebuilt at Romorantin. The airplane was too heavy for its power, wallowed ungracefully through the air, and frightened the bravest of pilots because of its tendency to explode into flames. Yet the Army flew these machines in combat, as did the Marines, even though they knew they were potentially winged coffins.

The United States failed to deliver to the combat front in Europe a single airplane fit to carry a man into battle. Upon investigating the nation's air industry, Justice Charles Evans Hughes damned that industry, and in a blistering indictment regretted that "the provisions of the criminal statutes do not reach inefficiency."

Against this disheartening background, the Marines also performed brilliantly. On January 22, 1918, the 1st Marine Aeronautic Company (12 officers and 133 men) commanded by Captain Francis T. Evans reached Ponta Delgada in the Azores. With them were 10 Curtiss R-6 twin-float seaplanes, 2 Curtiss N-9 seaplanes, and 6 HS-2 flying boats. This was the first American flight unit of any service, completely equipped and trained, to sail overseas to a combat theater. It was a small force, but the men flew convoy lane patrols and, although they never sank, or helped to sink, an enemy submarine, they did provide surveillance of the shipping area—with the result that the German submarines were denied use of the Azores as a refueling base.

Things were much worse with land-based forces. Three months before the end of the war, Assistant Secretary of the Navy F.D. Roosevelt in disgust reported that not a single Naval plane could operate in offensive warfare, and that only eight Navy warplanes could so much as stagger off the ground. For their brief period in the land war, the Marines—flying with the British and for a few weeks with their own DH-4's—dropped 14 tons of bombs, flew some food-dropping missions in the face of heavy German opposition. The records aren't clear, but it appears that the flying leathernecks in their brief forays scrapped hard enough to shoot down 10 German airplanes.

Beaching party moves plane into water "somewhere in England."

American-manned flying boats at Brest, France, in mid-1918. Navy's first group of 7 pilots and 122 mechanics arrived in France in June, 1917, moved into bases at Dunkerque, later into Le Croisic, St. Trojan, and Moutchic. Navy had four sites in Ireland; in England Navy had assembly and repair base at Eastleigh, operating base at Killingholme.

Wet, cold flying

If there was any other group of fliers who suffered a generally more miserable tour of duty than the Navy and Marine pilots on convoy land patrol, no one has yet identified them. The Marines who flew in their antique planes from the Azores fought a wet, miserable, unrewarding, drab war. They flew sometimes when the clouds were thick and the rain heavy, when fog rolled in in an impenetrable mass from the sea and, as their official history has recorded, without benefit of "radio, pigeons, or Very pistols." To say nothing of accurate instruments or reliable compasses. Yet these were the men who flew "routine" missions 70 miles across the ocean from the Azores with but 2 hours' fuel capacity in their machines. Along the English Channel and the North Sea, Navy pilots faced many of the same conditions, but with one added hazard. If they were caught by German fighters, being shot down was almost inevitable.

Curtiss H-16 flying boat, also built by the Naval Aircraft Factory, carried a crew of four, a radio, two 230-pound bombs and four machine guns. It was a vast improvement over the float-equipped seaplanes, and featured a maximum speed of 95 mph and an endurance on patrol of 4 hours. After production was started, Navy concentrated on the F-5 flying boat, best of the war.

HS-2L flying boat sails past the battleship USS *New York;* almost the entire crew lined the decks to see the airplane fly by. HS-2L was an outgrowth of Loughead Brothers' F-1 flying boat; in 1918 Navy ordered the single-engine, pusher-type machine into production. HS-2L carried three men, and a 330-hp Liberty engine pushed the airplane at 91 mph, and a cruise speed of 55 mph.

H-16 flying boat, in rare photo of WWI (*below*) over the Atlantic on anti-submarine patrol. Of flying-boat effectiveness on convoy patrol, Secretary of the Navy Daniels stated that no U.S. convoy protected by Naval aircraft was successfully attacked by a submarine during the last ten months of the war.

NAVY EMPHASIZED SEAPLANES:

Foreign warplanes forged ahead

In 1914 three of the early aviation pioneers—Mustin, Saufley and Bellinger—traveled to Europe aboard the USS *North Carolina,* and had the chance to study Italian and French naval planes. Their report made it all too clear that the Curtiss machines equipping the U.S. Navy were hopelessly antiquated. The Navy probed deeper into the state of aviation in Europe at the outbreak of war, and what it discovered was dismaying.

Britain's F-type flying boat was developed from the H-16 by Porte, and maintained strong British superiority in this field. The British Navy had its own flying service, and was making remarkable strides with carrier development. The *Hermes* was ready in 1913; the *Campania* and *Ark Royal* in 1914 (the *Pegasus* and *Furious* in 1917). Non-rigid airships held an important place in antisub patrols.

Germany was surprisingly ill equipped with naval planes, although by the end of 1915 the German Navy had 15 airships, and Zeppelin raiders over England were manned mostly by navy personnel. In July, 1914, the Imperial Navy had 20 serviceable airplanes, but pilot training was so poor and equipment so bad the air force was worthless. Because the Germans concentrated on building landplanes (the world's best), their navy before the war bought its seaplanes from the U.S. and Britain. *Before* the war, however, a navy Rumpler biplane flew to 25,750 feet, and a navy pilot flew a landplane Albatross for the amazing endurance record of 24 hours 10 minutes!

NAVY USED FRENCH BASES

No naval air fleet held more promise than that of France; the French Navy had the first navy pilots, the first navy planes, and enjoyed huge appropriations. By the time the war came, however, bitter infighting between the army and navy wrecked the value of the naval air force; the army seized all factories and threatened to take over any foreign airplanes purchased by the navy. At the end of the war what had been the brightest star in naval aviation was well tarnished; the French fleet had only one quarter the pilots and men in the U.S. Navy air arm, and only half the planes—most of them small, single-engine types.

Italy had a small, but fairly operational naval air arm; it was, however, generally ineffective, and the Italians concentrated on semi-rigid airships. At the outbreak of the war, the Russians enjoyed the largest naval air fleet in the world. But most of the planes were Curtiss, Nieuport, Farman—and when foreign supply stopped, Russia's naval air activity ceased almost entirely.

Most American seaplanes were used for training, like this five-float Paul-Smith model.

"All clear ahead!" As noted by a Naval historian, a good lookout was really worth his weight in fishnet floats in this N-1 seaplane.

Powerful Burgess seaplane shown at Pensacola, October 28, 1916, was step forward from underpowered Curtiss floatplanes.

Except for few antiquated seaplanes that accompanied Marines to Azores, like this R-9 trainer, Navy used flying boats overseas.

A remarkable photograph of the naval air conflict in WW I; a German Brandenburg W-29 floatplane as it completes a firing pass over a British F-2 flying boat. The German attack has been completely successful, and smoke and flames can be seen rising from the English plane. The crew at this moment are hastily abandoning their machine. U.S. Navy pilots rarely engaged in air fights with the enemy, but when they did so, the battles were brisk, and usually with casualties on both sides. Foreign convoy patrols were also flown with lighter-than-air non-rigids, but the Navy had to rely on foreign equipment. The Navy's first airship, the DN-1, could barely lift from the ground. Five French bases were used for airship patrol, with the non-rigids purchased from that country.

German Fokker D-7 *(above)* excelled in maneuverability, climb, combat worth. Germans originated patterns of air combat in formation tactics, produced the finest, deadliest fighters of the war. The French-built Spad XIII *(below)*, that entered battle late in the war, was best of Allied fighters; it was fast and could outdive all other planes. At beginning of war, U.S. was ranked 14th among world's air powers. Need for planes was so great that from France alone we were forced to purchase a total of 4,784 planes of all types.

THE GLORIOUS TWENTIES

NAVY ENJOYS A GOLDEN AGE: RECORDS FALL, MORALE SOARS

Official policy states "Fleet aviation must be developed to its fullest extent"

Three years after World War I, with the appalling carnage of the great infantry battles still fresh in the minds of the public and its selected diplomats, the Washington Naval Conference (1921–1922) swung a sharp peacetime ax at the navies of the world, and threatened to reduce the military power of our own fleet. The general desire for peace and the United States adherence to armament limitations pacts seriously curbed the Navy's hopes for a powerful new air arm, an outgrowth of lessons gleaned from the experiences of the war just past. The limitations imposed by the Washington Conference were bad enough, but an even more staggering blow was dealt when the Coolidge Administration declared itself irrevocably opposed to military research, development, and construction. For the next three administrations the Navy's air arm labored under strict economy measures. Naval air bases were reduced to only six: Rockaway, Anacostia, Hampton Roads, Key West, Pensacola, and San Diego.

Despite these disastrous restrictions, the fliers of both the Navy and the Army had been fired with the zeal for developing their respective air services; fighting for a share of the paltry military budget for air also meant a grim struggle to acquire national roles and missions. On the Army's side was the burning ambition of General William Mitchell, who proclaimed himself the champion of the Army's cause to advance its role with national airpower. Mitchell used various means to promote his beliefs, and took no pains to temper his dramatic statements to the public and before Congress. Despite his controversial statements, he had a thorough grasp of the potentialities of airpower, and the furor he created served in the long run to advance the status of airpower within both the Army and the Navy.

It was against this generally disheartening atmosphere of crippled economy and political hostility that the Navy blazed some of the brightest trails in its flying history. Both military services regard the years after the war as the Golden Age of Aviation. Navy pilots commanded the respect of the entire world by setting new records for speed, endurance, altitude, and distance. Richard E. Byrd and Floyd Bennett electrified men everywhere with the first flight over the North Pole; other Navy flying teams flew to remote parts of the earth, charting unknown areas for future operations.

Count them—there are nine men in this photograph of USN's NC-1 flying boat, designed by five Navy-civilian pilots and engineers. First flown in October, 1918, a month later it set a world record for carrying fifty-one persons in flight.

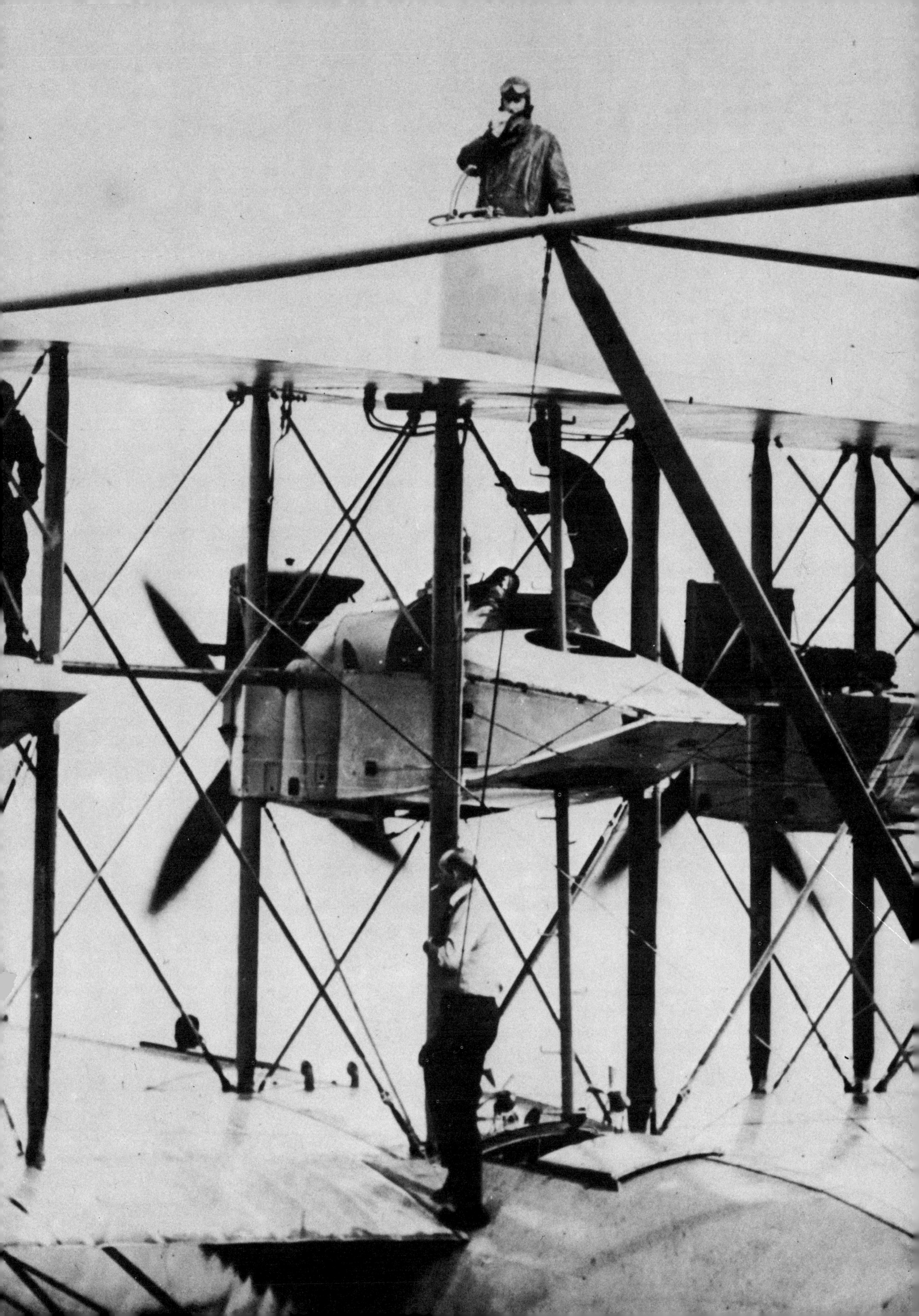

Transocean epic

On May 3, 1919, Seaplane Division One was commissioned, J.H. Towers commanding. Six days later, three great flying boats left Rockaway Beach in an attempt to make the first flight from the U.S. to England. The NC-1, NC-3, and NC-4 ran into severe difficulties; NC-1 sank at sea, NC-3 taxied across the ocean for days at a time, but on May 31, after stops in the Azores, emergency landings in Portugal and Spain, NC-4 arrived in Plymouth, England—23 days after take-off!

After departing Rockaway Beach for Trepassey, Newfoundland, NC-4 experienced engine difficulties, forcing A.C. Read (Naval Aviator No. 24) and Stone (Coast Guard) to land off Cape Cod. They taxied all night to Chatham; for 5 days the airplane was out of the air. Heavy weather, however, grounded her NC-1 and NC-3 sister ships. But from here on, NC-4 flew like a dream. On May 16, 1919, NC-4 took off from Newfoundland, and completed the first transatlantic flight, landing (above) at Horta, Azores.

The NC-3 (above) struggled somewhat hazardously across the Atlantic. After taking off from Newfoundland, Towers was forced down on the open Atlantic, and taxied for two days, arriving at Ponta Delgada, Azores, the day before the NC-4, which was held up by weather after landing at Horta. NC-3 arrived at Ponta Delgada with the wing floats ripped off, and the fabric torn and fluttering in the wind. The NC-3 (left), in somewhat better condition at the start of the flight.

NC-4 taxies triumphantly in Azores *(above)* after completing nonstop flight from Newfoundland; beaching crew takes NC-4 in tow *(below)* in Azores harbor. For this flight started by three planes, Navy positioned 68 destroyers across the Atlantic as "marker buoys" for navigation, and placed five battleships every 400 miles to serve as weather stations. NC-4 required 23 days for trip, although the actual flying time was 54 hours.

Flying (and sailing) o'er the bounding main

On August 31, 1925, Commander John Rodgers, with a crew of four in the PN-9-1 flying boat, and another PN-9 commanded by Lt. A.P. Snody, attempted a nonstop flight from San Francisco to Honolulu. Four hours after take-off, Snody was forced down near one of the "watchdog" destroyers, and taken in tow. Left alone over the Pacific, Rodgers encountered excessive fuel consumption; he passed the destroyer *Reno* 1,200 miles out, and tried to reach the tender *Aroostook* 400 miles ahead. But ship's navigational bearings sent to him by radio were in error. Running out of fuel, he landed under control on the open sea. The radio went out, and search planes, ships, and subs failed to find the flying boat. Rodgers and his crew ripped loose the fabric from the lower wing, fashioned a sail, and set course for Honolulu. Ten days later— only ten miles from Kaui Island—they were spotted by the submarine *R-4*. This flight chalked up an amazing 1,841 miles in the air (a seaplane record); *then* the airmen *sailed* another 450 miles!

Famed PN-9 seaplanes were built at Naval Aircraft Factory, and were first flying boats built with metal hulls. In May, 1925, Lt. C.H. Schildauer flew a PN-9 (*above*) for 28 hours 35 minutes—a new world seaplane record. Despite engine failure and difficulties of attempted San Francisco-Honolulu flight, both PN-9's survived the daring air trek. The PN-9-1, after sailing 450 miles on the open seas for nine days, was repaired and then flew triumphantly (*below*) off Oahu coast.

PN-9-1 in flight, September 19, 1925, over Honolulu after repairs to the lower wing. While the airplane was still missing, and right after the dirigible *Shenandoah* was lost with 14 dead, General William Mitchell assailed the Navy in a 6,000-word statement. He claimed the *Shenandoah* was unsafe and its flight a propaganda stunt, and branded the Rodgers flight a publicity stunt. He accused Navy, War Departments of ''incompetency . . . criminal negligence . . . almost treasonable administration of our nation's defense.'' Three days later, Army ordered Mitchell's court-martial; in 1926 he resigned.

The PN-9-1 flying boat maneuvering into the wind *(left)* prior to take-off for Honolulu. Commander John Rodgers, who led the mission, was Naval Aviator No. 2. Eleven months after the flight was completed, he crashed in the Delaware River, and received injuries from which he died the same day.

The PN-9-1 after entering harbor in the Hawaiian Islands. Note the fabric stripped from the lower wing, which was fashioned into large sails strung between the wing struts. After nine days of sailing on the open seas, the metal-hull seaplane was still in excellent condition, and flew again several days later.

NEW COMBAT PLANES

On May 27, 1920, the U.S. Navy's first Vought VE-7 airplane was ferried from Mitchel Field on Long Island, N. Y., to the Anacostia Naval Air Station just outside Washington, D.C. Not too long before this ferry flight of what was to become one of the Navy's most valuable airplanes, and the beginning of a long line of distinguished combat aircraft, the VE-7 had had its birth in a most incongruous place for a history-making machine—the third floor of the Garside Building in Astoria, New York. Here a business friend launched Chance Milton Vought on his aircraft industrial career. The VE-7 gave the Navy its first airplane with commanding performance and tremendous versatility. It made first flight-deck take-off under its own power from an aircraft carrier, and served as catapult seaplane on warships around the world. High performance in those days: a rugged plane that could do 116 mph.

Vought VE-7 is pulled around in a steep bank by Navy pilot. First production airplane of new Vought firm, VE-7 was the immediate predecessor of history-making airplanes. The VE-9 appeared in 1920, the UO-1 in 1924, and the FU-1 fighter in 1925. Beginning the famous Corsair line, the O2U-1 first flew in 1926, and captured several world's flight records for the Navy. Chance Milton Vought received his flight instruction in 1912 from Wright Brothers, was involved in early aviation pioneering. His UO-1 was the first airplane ever to be delivered in quantity to the fleet, and enabled Navy to experiment with unique combat methods.

Vought VE-7 rolls on her back in Split-S maneuver flown over Pearl Harbor (*above*) in June, 1926. The use of large, land-based bombers like the Marines' Martin MT (*below*) gave the elite flying Corps the chance to branch out in testing new bombing techniques. In addition to working with these planes, Marines perfected art of dive bombing.

Age of flying boats

Immediately after the war, the Navy moved rapidly to integrate performance of its flying boats with the fleet at sea. *Shawmut* and *Aroostook* were converted from mine layers to seaplane tenders; *Wright* was the first designed seaplane tender. New ships gave flying boats floating bases at sea.

Typifying Navy's intensive program to increase combat versatility of its airfleet was this test (*upper left*) of a 37-mm Davis recoilless rifle mounted aboard an HS-16 flying boat. Bow gunner fired first with .30-caliber machine gun to mark his target; he then blasted a few shots with cannon. Weapon was unwieldy, and program was dropped.

Demonstrating new role with the fleet, F5L flying boat on maneuvers sweeps low over the water, curving around warships as it lays a covering smoke screen—note smoke shadow on water. Emphasizing endurance and range of these planes, F5L on April 26, 1919, stayed aloft for 20 hours 19 minutes, covering a distance of 1,250 nautical miles.

In a test of the radio compass as an aid to navigation, on July 6, 1920, an F5L (*above*) left Hampton Roads and flew directly to the USS *Ohio*, 94 miles at sea in a position unknown to the pilot of the flying boat. Without landing, the big plane made a return flight to Hampton Roads, this time navigating by radio signals from Norfolk.

While many Navy planes were gaining in speed, Rear Admiral B.A.Fiske worked hard at developing torpedo strike capability for many aircraft types: began work in 1912 with aerial torpedoes, developed practical torpedo bomber; in 1919 received Gold Medal of Aero Club; made early torpedo tests with flying boats in F5L (*right*).

On July 8, 1927, Lts. B.J. Connell and S.R. Pope flew a PN-10 (above) flying boat with two 600-hp Packard engines to new world duration and distance records, carrying heavy loads (up to 4,400 pounds). With 2,200 lbs. aboard, flew 11 hrs. 7 mins. 18 secs. over nonstop distance of 947.705 miles.

But operations in the old flying boats were not always guaranteed the comfort of world records or, for that matter, even a flight normally completed. Many times this scene (center) was repeated, as one craft went to the aid of another. A Curtiss N-9 trainer tows a powerless H-16 flying boat to shore.

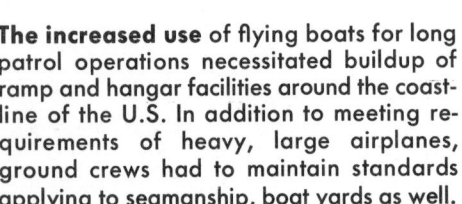

The increased use of flying boats for long patrol operations necessitated buildup of ramp and hangar facilities around the coastline of the U.S. In addition to meeting requirements of heavy, large airplanes, ground crews had to maintain standards applying to seamanship, boat yards as well.

Flying-boat crews developed a lackadaisical attitude toward lumbering through the skies in their great machines, like this crewman of a Naval Aircraft Factory PN-12 patrol bomber. Cruising slowly through the air, the men grasped guy wires and walked along the fuselage or moved out on the wings—"just for the hell of it." Despite this seeming nonchalance, the crews developed operations to high proficiency. With airplane performance increasing steadily, boats assumed more important roles with the fleet.

Even with limited funds available for research and development, Navy made every attempt to produce a new flying boat especially adapted to the needs of the fleet. One of the earliest tries at adapting earlier designs was this flying boat, decked out in a gaudy checkerboard paint design that signifies its experimental status. By 1920, Navy was testing more than 50 new types of instruments to improve flying versatility.

Until catapult floatplanes could be developed in terms of shipboard equipment, and improved performance of the airplanes, the heavy units of the fleet depended more and more on the "eyes" of the flying boats. Separate Scouting Fleet Squadrons, Battle Fleet, were organized, and the boats were integrated into battle maneuvers at sea. (*Left*) An H-type flying boat cruises past the USS *Vermont* as the battleship steams out to sea.

TESTING NEW IDEAS, WEAPONS

Against the political retrenchment that crippled funds for Naval aviation, a bitter fight was won to establish on July 12, 1921, the Naval Bureau of Aeronautics. Despite shortcomings, the bureau was a long step toward keeping the air arm as an integral part of the Navy. Captain W.A. Moffett became adviser to Chief of Naval Operations on "all aeronautic planning, operation, and administration." He overcame limiting organizational barriers, and with unswerving determination raised Navy airpower to new heights, although development control was still not centralized.

Engaged in fleet maneuvers, Marine Martin MT heavy bombers (*above*) lay down a smoke screen to shield the aircraft maneuvers; floatplane torpedo bomber on water prepares to take off before making an attack run from "out of smoke clouds." Floatplane torpedo bomber (*below*) passes over battleship USS *Idaho* as it steams out of Honolulu.

In bomb-development tests of 1919, H-type flying boat (*upper left*) drops a 250-pound missile from rack beneath the right wing. The bomb is in the air, to the right and just below the hull; a second bomb hangs on its rack beneath the left wing. At Hampton Roads, a torpedo bomber-trainer (*left*) of the Atlantic Fleet Torpedo Squadron drops his weapon on signal of the armament officer in foreground. In Hampton Roads tests both dummy and live torpedoes were launched successfully from a modified R-6 by pilot-engineers. These experiments were continued until the new MTB (Martin Torpedo Bomber) became the first plane specifically used for torpedo bombing, and in May, 1920, the first squadron was formed. In 1923, Naval Aircraft Factory bombers were supplied the squadron; a year later these were followed by the Douglas DT. In that same year, the first carrier landing with a torpedo bomber was made.

SEAPLANES BOAST VERSATILITY

On October 26, 1921, the first turntable catapult, Type A Mark I, was tested successfully at the Philadelphia Navy Yard with the successful launch of an N-9 seaplane. The shipboard program called for launching platforms on *Texas* (1919) and *Mississippi*; 30 foreign-made Army planes, including Sopwith fighters on wheels and floats, were turned over to the Navy for catapult tests. "Platforms were built on 5 more battleships," states an official U.S. Navy history, "in contrast to 22 British battleships so equipped. The launchings were successful, but each one was a precarious adventure and landings were unsafe." For a while the seaplanes remained on the sea.

Seaplanes filled many roles with Navy from shore and at sea. Two Voughts (*above*) patrol southward along California coast.

Martin SC-1 (*below*) was heavy, powerful, rugged, one of first planes designed for bombing, torpedo, and scout missions.

Torpedo bomber-trainer makes a practice torpedo run (*left*) at Pensacola Bay, Florida, on May 28, 1920. Dropped slightly off the exact angle needed for clean entry into water, torpedo has porpoised—lunged out of the water. Immediately after, its drive mechanism damaged, torpedo sank to bottom of harbor. Although U.S. Navy torpedo planes became among best in the world (in WW II, second only to Japanese Mitsubishi Type 97 Kate, considered without equal), Navy for years suffered from faulty torpedoes. U.S. "tin fish" were infamous for slow speed, erratic guidance, probable failure.

Douglas DT torpedo bomber (*right*) on April 17, 1923, Lt. R. Irvine flying, and equipped with a new Liberty 420-hp engine, established a world altitude record for Class C airplanes with a useful load of 2,204 pounds. Taking off from Army's McCook Field at Dayton, Ohio, Irvine flew the husky torpedo bomber to altitude of 11,609 feet. DT series were the forerunner of deadly Douglas attack airplanes for Navy; latest propeller and jet bombers are considered world's best. (*Below*) Martin T3M flaring out for water landing, in wheel version was first bomber widely used aboard carriers.

A working Navy

The first of the Navy's Utility Squadrons, VJ-1B, was formed on October 5, 1925, and assigned to Aircraft Squadrons, Battle Fleet. The Navy air arm by now, however, was already well established as a practical, hard-working utility force as well as a combat arm. In June, 1925, Lt. Commander Richard E. Byrd, head of Naval Air Detachment, with the MacMillan Expedition, sailed 3,000 miles to Etah, North Greenland, to begin aerial explorations and mapping. On May 9, 1926, Byrd and Floyd Bennett won applause of the entire world with the first flight over the North Pole. One month later the Navy's Alaskan Aerial Survey Expedition with three Loening amphibians left for an extensive aerial photography survey of Alaska. For their 1926 North Pole flight, both Byrd and Bennett had received the Congressional Medal of Honor; sustaining his exploring drive, on November 29, 1929, Byrd became the first man to fly over the South Pole as well. These events—and many others—stressed the use by the Navy of aircraft, radio, and photography—and gave meaning to the term, the Golden Age of Aviation.

DH-4B ambulance plane (*top*) developed to carry combat wounded out of rear areas. In January, 1928, Lt. C.F. Schilt, USMC, made 10 daring rescues in O2U-1 of wounded in Nicaragua, received Congressional Medal of Honor for flights. Flying boats (*above*) also were used to carry wounded; chicken wire separated patient, whirling propeller!

Floyd Bennett, Naval Aviation Pilot, famed pioneer, for whom Floyd Bennett Naval Air Station is named. Awarded Congressional Medal of Honor for flying Fokker triplane in first flight over North Pole, 1926, with Richard E. Byrd. In November, 1929, Byrd flew over South Pole with 3 other men in plane named for Bennett.

Lt. Apollo Soucek climbing down from seaplane (*above*). Soucek was one of Navy's "great pilots." May 8, 1929—Soucek flew Wright Apache to world's record of 39,140 feet. In June, he set Class C-2 seaplane altitude record of 38,560 feet. One year later, on June 4, he flew Apache to new altitude record: 43,166 feet.

Major T.C. Turner, USMC, arrived in Washington, D.C., leading flight of two DH-4B's (*below*) after a flight of 4,482 miles in round trip to Santo Domingo. For longest unguarded overwater flight to date, the four crewmen were awarded Distinguished Flying Cross.

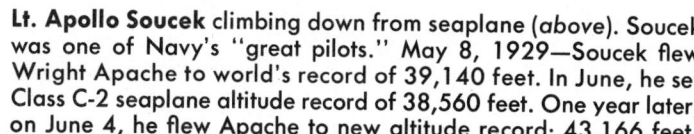

NEW ROLE FOR THE BOMBER

Bombing tests add dimension to airpower

When Brigadier General William Mitchell returned in 1919 from France to the American scene, his arrival seemed certain to focus public attention on the accomplishments of our airpower in the war, and what its future position would be within the Army and Navy. The public was interested; the scandals surrounding the production chaos of World War I were excellent material for large newspaper headlines. Mitchell spared no effort to stress his beliefs. He was honest, eloquent, and he had an almost unerring instinct for drawing attention to his statements.

He was determined that airpower should become a service separate and equal to the Army and the Navy. To prove that airpower had languished as a military stepchild, he stressed what had been done in the war with badly designed airplanes, and claimed that many more lives would have been saved and the war shortened if only aviators had been properly equipped. His charges of incompetence, mismanagement, and a deliberate plan to "keep down the aviators" that he directed at the War Department inflamed Army officials to the point of rage. But when

Mitchell openly attacked the Navy, the General Staff judiciously looked aside. A possible outcome of a Congressional review of Mitchell's charges that the Navy no longer represented the best means of defending the nation, his reiteration before a House Committee that air weapons could be developed ". . . as almost to make navies useless on the surface of the water," delighted Army officials. A possible result of these charges could mean a shift of roles and missions in coastal defense in favor of the Army; the high brass stood back and by willing default gave Mitchell virtually free rein. Mitchell had time and again "destroyed" the Navy in his writings and speeches; from its viewpoint the Navy regarded Mitchell as an inflammatory upstart with no evidence to support his invective. Mitchell clamored for an opportunity to demonstrate in actual tests what his calculations showed: aerial bombing would prove beyond any doubt the total supremacy of the bombing airplane over the warship.

For its part, the Navy was about to conduct its own tests to ascertain the effect of bomb explosions, so that engineers might alter designs of future ships for greater resistance against air attack. The vessels were assembled and ready; Mitchell was reluctantly allowed to participate. He and his men trained eagerly for the tests, agreeing to the rules limiting them to two hits with the heaviest bombs available, and a shipboard inspection after each hit.

The 1921 tests began on June 21. Navy planes attacking with light bombs in 12 minutes sank the German submarine U-117. Eight days later Navy bombers with dummy missiles hit the 11,346-ton *Iowa*. On July 13, new Army Martin bombers engulfed the German destroyer *G-102* with 44 300-lb. bombs, sinking the vessel in 19 minutes. Then on July 18 came attacks against the 5,100-ton German cruiser *Frankfurt*; a combined assault was first with 250-lb. and 300-lb. bombs. The Navy followed with three 520-lb. bombs, and then the Army with a barrage of fourteen 600-lb. bombs that sank the vessel.

"The climax of the first phase of these tests," states a U.S. Navy study, "came with the attack on the *Ostfriesland*, a 27,000-ton German vessel . . . equal to any ship afloat. The tests began by dropping 34 small bombs of

USS Alabama (*opposite*) 11,552 tons, takes hit with 300-lb. bomb. *Ostfriesland* (*above*), hit with 2,000-lb. bomb after two crippling near-misses. Instant of explosion (*below*), two 1,000-lb. bombs on *Alabama*.

which six were hits, then dropping 600-pounders with only two hits. When the ship was inspected after each series of drops, no appreciable below-decks damage was discerned. . . ." Army bombers returned the next morning, scoring hits with four 1,000-lb. bombs. An inspection party showed that "the ship seemed seaworthy and well able to survive more punishment. . . ." That afternoon the bombers returned, each carrying one 2,000-lb. bomb, developed in four months by Army Ordnance at Mitchell's request, for a last do-or-die attack. "The total effect of the third bomb glancing off, the fourth hitting and the fifth and sixth near misses to port and starboard, was sufficient to sink her," reported the Navy.

The tests, it seems, were inconclusive inasmuch as the Navy and Army had never reached agreement on inter-pretation of the test rules and procedures. That battleships were sunk by bombs was obvious, but to what degree would this alter the future role of airpower?

The Army's General Mason Patrick declared in 1921 that Army bombers could perform all the functions of sea search and attack on hostile vessels. Unfortunately for this claim, attacks on anchored vessels proved little when it came to attacks upon ships maneuvering at high speed on the open seas. This the Army Air Forces learned to its dismay at the Battle of Midway in June, 1942, when re-peated attacks by B-17 bombers against Japanese carriers failed to inflict so much as a single hit upon the enemy vessels. Airpower—Navy and Army—was still essentially a fluid weapon, to be equated with the factors of per-formance, opposition, support, and bases.

In 1923, as follow-up to 1921 tests with both Army and Navy bombers, Navy conducted its own bombing experiments. Until these were completed, Navy stated it had not obtained the "required information on bombing effects." The USS *Virginia* (above), 15,000 tons and built in 1926, six seconds after a direct hit with a 1,000-lb. bomb. The *Virgina (below),* shortly before she sank.

A bomb has exploded (*above*) off the stern to port, another (all 1,000-pounders) in a near-miss to starboard, a third bomb explodes in a direct hit on the bow, and a fourth is just exploding in a near-miss off the bow—a tremendous attack by Navy bombers against the USS *Virginia,* September 5, 1923. The ship, a shattered, burning hulk, went down in 27 minutes after 3rd direct hit.

WILD AND WOOLLY AIR RACES

Navy and Army exhibit skill, daring:
Focus world attention on U.S. planes

From 1920 through 1925, air racing in the United States was a pitched battle between the planes and pilots of the United States Navy and Army; there has never again existed such fierce interservice rivalry—or any other occasion when the intense but friendly competition produced so rich a bonanza for the military air services, and American aviation as well. Civilian hopefuls for the coveted Pulitzer Trophy Race and other great air-racing awards could not compete with the prohibitive costs of high-powered aircraft, and left the field virtually to the military. For the five-year period of competition, victory swayed from one service to the other, and men like the Navy's Al Williams, and the Army's Jimmy Doolittle, entered aviation's hall of immortals. The planes they flew represented dedicated engineering and manufacturing; their performance and successes exerted a lasting influence on later United States naval and military designs.

On September 28, 1923, Lt. David Rittenhouse in a Navy Curtiss seaplane won the Schneider Cup Race in England at 177.38 mph; right on his tail in the same model plane was Lt. Rutledge Irvine at 173.46 mph. Navy's high point, however, came on October 6, 1923, when the Navy team in the Pulitzer Trophy Race at St. Louis streaked to a One—Two—Three—Four sweep of the event. *All* planes bettered the time of the previous year's winner, and the first- and second-place planes racked up a new world's record. The winner: Lt. Al Williams in a sleek biplane R2C racer at a blistering 243.68 miles per hour.

Major Marie de Burnside (*right*), entry in 1925 Schneider Cup Race; Army's Jimmy Doolittle won event in R3C2 racer at 232.6 mph. Lt. Al Williams (*below*), one of aviation's all-time greats, taxiing out to take-off position in his Mercury racer. On November 2, 1923, at Mitchel Field, Long Island, Lt. H.J. Brow in Navy Curtiss racer set a new world speed record of 259.47 mph. Two days later, Al Williams, in four flights over a 3-km course, raised record to 266.59 mph.

Navy flight line crew moving an R3C4 racer (*above*) into position to be lowered down ramp into water. Service crews worked day and night to keep planes in best shape. Marine Corps Martin bomber (*below*) takes off to compete in 1923 Merchants Exchange Race. Races and air shows were windows for public to view military aviation in action.

Lt. Al Williams (*above*); as a civilian flying a Grumman biplane fighter Williams thrilled millions with dazzling aerobatics, made his name a household word. Rare photo of Orville Wright (*right*) with Lt. Sanderson, USMC, inspecting the Wright Racer at St. Louis, October, 1923.

Ground crew teams up to turn propeller and start engine of Wright Racer (*below*) winning Navy entry in 1923 Pulitzer Trophy Race. First four places of race went to Navy team, which smashed all previous marks. Lt. Al Williams took first place with a sensational 243.68 mph.

Bluejacket daredevils

Parachute jumping in the Navy wasn't on the same scale as in the Army's paratrooper forces, but a bluejacket who became an airman gained everyone's respect. Navy men who earned the rating of Parachute Rigger leaped or tumbled into space from all types of airplanes under a variety of conditions, to test new parachute designs and to improve upon jumping techniques—information gained the hard way, and that saved many a pilot's life in later years. And while they practiced jumping, they also managed to have some fun at it!

R. E. McLeod (*above*), on wing of F5L trying to open experimental back pack at 1,500 feet; it failed, he used emergency chute.

Lean against the strut (*left*), hang on to a slim cable—nothing to it! Then let go; *that's* the rough part. *This* flier (*right*) isn't going anywhere. Despite what seems to be a casual wave good-by as he stands on wing of N-9, he's just enjoying himself—sans parachute. C.A.M. Scott (*opposite page*)—wearing parachute and sneakers—ready to go.

(*Lower left*) Lt. J.R. Tate, shown in mid-air after pull-off from wing of DT-5 airplane, moments before canopy blossoms out fully. (*Lower right*) Demonstrating jumping technique over Pearl Harbor, October 12, 1925, R.E. McLeod (also in photo at top of page) is holding perfect body position as the opening canopy yanks him clear of DT bomber.

Working aviation

Loening OL-8 amphibian (*above*) was ungainly and slow, but served Navy well as workhorse on exploration flights. Rugged and dependable, Loenings operated with the fleet from carriers, warships, tenders, land bases. A Loening seaplane (*below*) takes off from rough field.

One of the most successful of the earlier planes used by the Navy, the Curtiss N-9 trainer (*above*) performed so well and with such reliability that for many years after entering service, the airplane was still in use with fleet units around the world. In this picture, crewmen aboard the seaplane tender USS *Pelican,* anchored in Port Allen, Hawaii, prime the engine of an N-9 before the seaplane is hoisted over the side and lowered to the water. (*Right*) Pilot of a Loening OL-6 amphibian observation plane prepares to hook on to warship hoist, after returning from patrol mission with Pacific fleet units. In addition to variety of missions with the Navy (and with the Army), the versatile Loening served Rear Admiral H.V. Butler as an early flying command post. It was from a Loening that Admiral Butler first used airborne radio to command fleet's air squadrons.

AGE OF THE CARRIER

Naval aviation gains seven-league boots

The initial phase of United States Naval aviation placed much of its emphasis on developing aircraft that could serve aboard ships of the fleet at sea. This led to the development and use of shipboard catapults and a growing arm of scouts that, combined with the long-range flying boat, afforded the Navy a far-flung aerial reconnaissance and patrol capability. It was readily apparent, however, that if the Navy was to gain from its aircraft their intrinsic worth as weapons, then aircraft carriers—floating islands—must be obtained to exploit fully the combat airplane.

BRITISH SET EXAMPLE

Naval aviators fought hard and consistently within their service for this new weapon, advocating that existing vessels be modified or new ships built for the specific purpose of operating high-performance combat planes. The cause of the aircraft-carrier exponents was furthered by an unexpected source —British foresight and progress in this very same field. In 1914 the tanker *Ark Royal* was converted to a carrier. Then the cruiser *Furious* was converted; from her deck the British staged the first successful carrier attack —a bombing raid against the German Zeppelin base at Tondern. In 1918 the British Navy accepted the *Argus*, the world's first flush-deck carrier.

Encouraged by the British example, the Navy authorized the conversion of the collier *Jupiter* into an experimental carrier; in March, 1922, the vessel was recommissioned USS *Langley*, and from that day on, until sunk by the Japanese shortly after the outbreak of war, served the Navy well. Famous to Naval pilots as "The Covered Wagon," from her silhouette, *Langley* was in business on October 17, 1922, when Lt. Commander V.C. Griffin made the first U.S. carrier take-off. Nine days later Lt. Commander G. deC. Chevalier flew the first plane aboard. Rear Admiral W.A. Moffett, then Chief of the Bureau of Aeronautics, foresaw a powerful carrier fleet and prophetically declared: "The air fleet of an enemy will never get within striking distance of our coast as long as our aircraft carriers are able to carry the preponderance of air power to sea."

STOPGAP CARRIER

Naval aviators realized only too well how much of that statement was foresight and not present-day reality. *Langley* served the Navy admirably as a test vessel, but she was also slow, inadequate in size, and largely barren of proper facilities. It was, however, a worthy beginning, and on her deck the Navy worked out deck tactics, developed equipment, and probed the aerial tactics of warfare at sea.

First U.S. carrier, USS *Langley,* commissioned on March 20, 1922, was of 11,500 tons with a flight deck measuring 64 feet by 534 feet. First U.S. carrier take-off came on October 17, 1922, with VE-7SF; nine days later an Aeromarine eased to the deck for first carrier landing. On November 18, a torpedo bomber was launched from the *Langley's* deck, registering another "first." Many pilots were taught the fundamentals of carrier flying from *Langley* (coming in for a landing, *above;* TS-1 taking off, *left*); developments in handling gear were tested and proved before being used in later, heavier carriers.

LEATHERNECK SAGA

Marines carved own niche in aviation's Hall of Fame

Efficiency was the slogan and *Economy* the watchword of Marine Corps aviation during the years that marked the golden age of military and civilian aviation in the United States. Their initial period of organization and growth demonstrated only too harshly to the flying leathernecks that austerity would shadow every move they made; in characteristic fashion the Marines accepted this burden, and determined to overcome a lack of financial support and equipment with the one item they have never lacked—quality.

The first true USMC expansion in the air came with the outbreak of war in 1917; each service suffered explosive growth marked with chaotic confusion. Less than a month after war was declared the Corps doubled its aviation units by the simple expedient of creating a second organization—the Marine Aeronautic Company, Advance Base Force, at Philadelphia. This, in turn, soon went through the process of subdivision, giving birth to a series of additional units which in turn grabbed eagerly in all directions for men and machines.

We have seen previously the role played by the Marines in submarine patrol during the war from their Azores base, but there are Corps pilots who recall that World War I operations were not nearly as hectic, and often not as hazardous, as stateside

Lt. F.H. Lawson Scribuer, USMC, before his DH-4 bomber, at Managua, Nicaragua. DH-4's were used for strafing, dive-bombing.

Marines flew a variety of old, slow, antiquated airplanes in combat and on garrison duty in assignments around the world. They operated in seaplanes in the Azores during WW I, in Santo Domingo and Haiti, at Guam, and in China. To meet local needs, Marine ground crews often interchanged floats with wheels for ground operations. Even Jenny trainers, equipped both for land and water operations, were flown in combat.

training programs. The group stationed at Hazlehurst, Long Island, for example, on the night of December 27, 1917, had the dubious honor of shivering through a record cold wave of 17 degrees below zero. Then Curtiss Field opened to the Marines in Miami; before the reader envisions luxurious surroundings, first read a memo sent by Lt. H.B. Mims on July 8, 1918, to the USMC commandant, in which Mims describes "lush" Miami:

"Marines are still operating at the temporary field at Miami, living in tents, housing the machines in canvas hangars, which are about to fall down, using a landing field which is made of sand so soft that no grass can be made to grow in it and which is so near sea level that there is a possibility at any moment of having the whole field flooded and making it useless for several days. The surrounding country is almost entirely wild and uncultivated, making it impossible to land machines in only a very few places except right near the present field at Miami."

The Marines, anxious to get into combat, encountered a wall of adamant arguments against any Naval unit flying landplanes; besides this open prejudice, the Army guarded its air control jealously, and the British and French sniffed with disdain at *all* American airmen. A Marine force reached Brest, France, late in July; to Major A.A. Cunningham it was obvious that no one cared one whit about their presence. Cunningham wrote to Mims: "We arrived day before yesterday and found that no one here knew what we were, where we were to go or what we were to do here. . . . The

trouble is that no one in Washington took interest enough in us to cable when we would arrive and what we were for." Undaunted by massive indifference, Cunningham performed some of the best "midnight requisitioning" in Corps history; he commandeered a French-manned train, quickly moved his three squadrons aboard, grabbed all the food in sight and whatever equipment could be dragged away, and chugged off merrily for Calais.

The appalling morass of indifference and confusion that bogged down the Army's aviators also caught the Marines, and they faced the bleak prospect of waiting uselessly on the

ground for delivery of their DH-4 "flaming coffins." During their wait the leathernecks flew with British Squadrons No. 217 and 218; the plan was to blood the Marines with three combat missions each. Sgt. T.L. McCullough became the first Marine to shoot down an enemy plane in combat; on September 9, he flamed a Fokker over Coremarch, Belgium. On September 29, Lt. C.C. Barr became the first Marine aviator to lose his life as a result of enemy action, dying of a leg wound which severed an artery.

For making four passes at tree-top height to drop canned goods and bread to an isolated French regiment, in the face of withering German fire, three

One of the rarer types of planes used by Marines was this Thomas-Morse scout; designed for Army use, it was used as scout seaplane.

Single-engine flying boat (*right*), used by Marines for submarine patrol in Azores during WW I. (*Below*) Typical of operating conditions on Caribbean islands; Navy ground crew lowering a Thomas-Morse scout down a steep mountain trail for delivery to isolated airstrip at Conke Bluff, Cuba. (*Opposite page*) Marines made history with DH-4 biplane bomber. In WW I in Europe they flew bombing missions; in Nicaragua they were used as fighters, strafers, and for dive-bombing. As transport they carried mail, supplies, passengers, and were used to evacuate by air the Marines wounded in battle.

Marine officers (Mulcahy, Lytle, and Nelms) were awarded Distinguished Service Medals; their gunners—Pascal, Wiman, and McCullough—received Navy Crosses.

But the outstanding flying incidents of the war came on two separate occasions, although with the same crew—2d Lt. Ralph Talbot and his gunner, Cpl. R.G. Robinson. For their skill and courage on October 8, flying with the British, and on October 14, flying as part of the first raid in force by the Marines' own Northern Bombing Group, these men were awarded the Congressional Medal of Honor.

On the 8th, with Squadron 218, nine German fighters attacked their DH-4, which was quickly cut off from the British bombers. In a wild, swirling fight they held off the Germans, shot down one of the fighters, and flew home—tattered and happy.

Six days later their DH-4 suffered engine trouble, and dropped from formation. At once twelve German fighters swarmed over their vulnerable, slow bomber. Robinson in the rear seat set one of the enemy aflame; minutes later a bullet ripped through his elbow. Then his machine guns jammed. Talbot broke away from the fighters, giving the wounded Robinson time to clear his guns. That done,

Talbot whipped the DH-4 around and charged the startled Germans. With the nose guns Talbot shot down a second fighter, while Robinson, one hand clenched to his side, continued to spray bullets.

After several more minutes of impossible combat, two bullets hit the gunner in the stomach, and a fourth bullet smashed into his hip. As Robinson, bloody and in terrible pain, tried to keep firing, Talbot dove for the trenches, and zigzagged home at 50 feet, the DH-4 a battered sieve. Ironically, Robinson recovered, but Talbot was killed in a crash on October 25— 11 days later.

In France, three Marine fliers died in combat, a fourth was killed in a crash; three officers and thirteen enlisted men died of influenza. Off the Azores, another pilot was drowned in a crash; four officers and three enlisted men died in crashes in Florida.

Thus ended the first combat action in the air in Corps history; it was, however, only a prelude to years of battle in foreign lands that would lead to World War II, and then to Korea.

On Armistice Day the Corps stood at 282 officers, 2,180 enlisted men, and 175 aviation cadets who had completed training. Less than two years later there were fewer than 1,000

Marines on active aviation duty; this figure was not to rise above 1,500 for another 20 years. It was during this period, when the Marine Corps served around the world and fought in several distant lands, that it truly had to live by its slogan of Efficiency and its watchword of Economy.

It was also a period of two decades in which the fliers of the Corps served the Navy, and their nation, with a performance that can only be described as superb.

THE TURNER DECADE

Although the years following the signing of the Armistice that ended World War I are thought of as a time of peace, the history of the flying Marines was punctuated with successive years of combat. The Marines were sent to Santo Domingo (now the Dominican Republic), to Haiti and to Nicaragua, where they fought little-publicized but bloody "actions" in the revolutions that plagued those small countries. They were balanced on the brink of major fighting in China for many months. And despite the fact that the Marines were all too casually given such missions as flying infantry, these expeditions proved instrumental in shaping the future of Corps aviation. Competition in the Army-Navy air

races, and trail-blazing on long-distance flights helped to distinguish the flying leathernecks as the nation's elite in the air.

During the immediate postwar era, Marine aviation was sustained by little more than the collective fingernails of its surviving pilots. The Marines faced a serious enough problem in allowable manpower—127 pilots in 1919; 67 in 1920; a shaky, all-time low of 43 pilots in 1922—and accidents also took their grim toll. In 1922, 17 new officer pilots joined the Corps; in the same year 9 men, more than half of the new additions, were killed. In the year June, 1923, to June, 1924, 11 pilots donned the flying Marines' uniform; 4 were buried.

Marine aviation in those austere times languished in body, but never flagged in spirit: a fortunate high morale that stemmed in no small degree from the driving power and leadership of a man named Thomas C. Turner. Cunningham had helped to create the embryonic form of Marine aviation; Turner nourished it through its early years. It has never been disputed that Turner was the most ambitious officer in the history of Corps aviation.

A Marine volunteer at nineteen, Turner devoted all his spare time to

Marine's DH-4 bomber carried two nose guns, two guns in rear cockpit.

learning to fly—with Army pilots at a nearby field! Brilliant in the air, he was soon regarded by the Army fliers as "one of our own." Colonel H.H. Arnold did his best to get Turner assigned permanently to the Army; it reached the point where Turner actually became the officer in command of flying at the Army's Ellington Field in Houston. It was the situation every Marine loves to visualize: a single leatherneck surrounded by thousands of Army men, and the Marine unquestionably well in command of the situation.

In 1921 Turner made his first big move to focus the nation's attention on the flying Marines. He led two DH-4 biplanes, survivors of World War I flying, on a Washington-Santo Domingo flight and return—4,842 miles, the longest unguarded overwater flight to date. Turner and each of his men received the Distinguished Flying Cross.

As much as he recognized the need for public support of the Corps' small flying organization, Turner also recognized that most of the strength his Corps needed to sustain itself through the years of little financial support would have to come from the men themselves. To this end Turner brought strict discipline, an unrelenting drive for perfection, his own superb skill in the air, and a leadership that earned for him the highest respect of all his men. The morale of these pilots never wavered; their belief in themselves never faltered.

The struggle for organizational strength of the Corps suffered from the very position of the Marines in the national military structure. Within the Army there raged a heated battle, fired by the proponents for a major airpower organization independent of the restrictions of the General Staff. It was a fight waged with heat and zeal by a growing force of adherents, who used the weapons of oratory, political influence, and industrial friendship with extraordinary skill.

Elements within the Navy fought also for airpower, but here the battle had to be carried forward within the Navy itself. There never existed the belief that the Naval air arm would be divorced from the fleet, nor was this desired; in every imaginable way Naval airpower was an integral part of the fleet's structure, and what still needed to be done to increase airpower strength lay within that same structure. The Army struggle represented an insurgent band striving to be cast free from an over-all framework that smothered aviation. Not so that of the Navy, where the proponents of airpower fought for more planes, more pilots, more carriers; all this to imbue the fleet with truly encompassing military strength—ships on the sea, submarines beneath its surface, planes that could strike anywhere from the fleet as a mobile base, and Marines to move against, and to occupy, positions on the land.

Thus the Marines occupied a position *within* this internal struggle for Naval airpower, and their battle was reduced to the fight to achieve a meaningful status in numbers as a part of the Naval air arm. The Marines recognized the precariousness of their

position. For the primary mission of the Navy was to guard the coastline of the nation, and this important consideration might well bring the Navy to relegate the USMC aviation to a secondary status, doing the menial tasks that Navy airpower did not wish to bother itself with.

The Marines bore—not stoically, perhaps, but certainly without loud verbal protestation—their situation, in regard to flying equipment, as Naval aviation's bastard child. Only after front-line Naval units had used their airplanes for years, were these machines passed on as hand-me-downs to the Marines. On those rare occasions when the flying leathernecks received new equipment, it was only after every last Navy requirement had been met. Like it or not, the Corps was last on line.

SANTO DOMINGO

On February 27, 1919, six Jenny trainers and their crews, under the command of Captain W.E. McCaughtry, arrived at San Pedro de Macoris in Santo Domingo; soon afterward they transferred to Santo Domingo City. For the next four years the 1st Air Squadron, 2nd Marine Brigade, enjoyed the novelty of fighting a hot war against jungle bandits. It was a small but bitter conflict in which the old Jenny performed miracles in the air that its designer would never have believed possible. Fighting the thermals that whipped upward over the hills and jungles the flying leathernecks, in support of Marine ground forces, strafed elusive bandits, flew reconnaissance and, in a DH-4 modified for the purpose, evacuated wounded Marines from the jungle. Even in the roaring, shaking DH-4, a wounded Marine could find relief: the normal trip out of the steaming battle area of three days by mule, ox-cart, and truck was reduced to only two hours.

BANDITS FOR FIFTEEN YEARS

Also in 1919, Captain H.B. Mims with the 4th Squadron—seven old seaplanes and six of the venerable Jennys—arrived in Port-au-Prince, Haiti. Mims' assignment: provide air support for the Marines' attempt to maintain a semblance of order during the island's continuing rebel outbreaks.

Designed as a trainer, Marines used slow Jenny on bombing missions.

For the next 15 years—which is the all-time record for an uninterrupted aerial campaign—the Marines flew in battle. The Corps had available as a *total* fighting force some 80 officers and 1,200 enlisted men, plus the services of 3,000 native troops and police. The object of their attentions: the *caco* rebel leader Charlemagne Peralte and then his successor, Benoit Batraville.

It was a strange war, in which the rebels underwent extended, albeit intermittent, attacks with machine guns and bombs. And if ever there was a war made for a small, understrength flying organization, the Haiti conflict was it. After fighting briskly for weeks, the rebels would vanish. In the respite the Marines patched up their airplanes, accumulated fuel, bullets, and bombs, and waited for the next sudden outbreak. Then came the call for the pilots to locate, attack and, if possible, isolate the various bandit groups weaving through the thick jungles. In addition to their broken schedules for battle, the Marine aviators flew reconnaissance, carried the mail and supplies, and operated a passenger service.

PRELUDE

Revolutions in the rugged country of Nicaragua were almost the norm in the years after the war, but by the mid-twenties the "little war" reached a level of fighting so bloody and violent that the Corps ordered its diminutive air force into the fray. Late in February, 1927, the first detachment, VO-1M, chugged into the town of Managua with six DH-4's on railroad flatcars. Until January, 1933, the flying Marines supported the 2nd Marine Brigade and the Guardia Nacional de Nicaragua against the Moncada and Sandino rebels.

The Marines' first dive-bombing combat operation took place in Nicaragua. Hundreds of bandits attacked a garrison of 37 Marines and 45 Nicaraguan guards at Ocotal; the Marines and natives fought them off in a touch-and-go night battle. At daybreak, when the bandits came back shooting, the outlook was bleak. The nearest reinforcements were a week away.

Two DH-4's strafed the Sandino forces, sending them scurrying back into the jungle. That afternoon Major R.E. Rowell returned at the head of a formation of five DH-4's. As Rowell later reported: "I led off the attack and dived out of column from 1,500 feet, pulling out at about 600. Later we ended up by diving from 1,000 and pulling out at about 300. Since the enemy had not been subjected to any form of bombing attack, other than the

Fueling operations in the old days was a simple procedure; gas was poured by hand.

Courageous flying wins
Marine Medal of Honor

dynamite charges thrown from the Laird-Swallows of the Nicaraguan Air Force, they had no fear of us. They exposed themselves in such a manner that we were able to inflict damage which was out of proportion to what they might have suffered had they taken cover."

In the first organized dive-bombing attack known, and the first time that bombers struck in minimum-altitude attacks in direct support of ground troops, the Marines killed some 70 bandits, and wounded another 175.

Although it was only a series of limited engagements, it was not an "easy" war. Consider the case of a pilot named Wodarcyzk. In the Ocotal battle he made his dive-bombing runs despite a plane crippled by enemy bullets. Several weeks later he flew in three intense battles in a single day, spending seven hours in the air; during the day his gunner was wounded, his plane was hit in the wings and fuselage, and a bullet smacked into his parachute. On this day he flew his twenty-third, twenty-fourth, and twenty-fifth missions, par for the course even in World War II.

Lt. C.F. Schilt, for "almost superhuman skill" in evacuating 18 men in ten flights in a Corsair, was awarded the Congressional Medal of Honor. In the midst of the jungle, Marine troops hacked down brush and leveled part of the town of Quilali to make an impromptu airstrip. Flying this 02U

without brakes—waiting Marines grabbed the wings on landing and dug in their heels—Schilt made his ten landings and take-offs with bullets thudding into the airplane.

Two Marines, early in October, 1927, crashed on Sapotillal Ridge, and the Corps had a foretaste of what would happen when their pilots would one day fall into Japanese hands. Lt. E.A. Thomas and Sgt. F.E. Dowell were tortured, mutilated, and hung by the bandits.

AIR SHOW IN CHINA

For eighteen months in 1927–28 the Marines, to protect American citizens and interests threatened by fighting in China, flew patrols and special reconnaissance flights—a total of 3,818 sorties. They managed to avoid direct fighting with the Chinese, but ground troops fired almost constantly at the American planes—and put bullet holes into seven.

But the outstanding event of the Chinese tour occurred during a stunting exhibition by Captain J.T. Moore before a massed throng in Tientsin. Moore streaked low over the crowd, racked his airplane up in a steep climb, and rolled rapidly as he shot skyward. The pilot was superb, but the airplane was fragile, and both wings ripped off.

Moore dove over the side of the tumbling airplane and parachuted into a moat. The Chinese cheered madly; what a marvelous demonstration!

Vought O2U-1 was the first plane that gave Marines desired performance in the air. In Nicaragua, January 6 to 8, 1928, Lt. C.F. Schilt in 10 daring flights evacuated 18 wounded Marines from airstrip hacked out of jungle village. Despite lack of brakes on the airplane, and constant firing by rebels who surrounded the strip, Schilt made his amazing flights without an accident. For this feat he received the Medal of Honor.

FORGING THE AERIAL

Desp

In November, 1927, the U.S. Navy greeted with understandable enthusiasm the launching of its first great carrier, the 33,000-ton USS *Saratoga*, built on the hull of a battle cruiser, which endeared itself to airmen as one of the toughest, most valiant fighting ships of all time. One month after *Saratoga* was completed, her sister ship, the *Lexington*, moved onto the Navy's warship roster. By January, 1929, both ships joined the fleet and a new era for both the Navy and its air arm was born. Offensive carrier aviation, once little more than a theory, was now reality.

TWO-OCEAN AIR NAVY

The fleet learned how to use carriers for offense and defense; pilots became carrier-trained; personnel became adept in handling carrier-type planes; procurement and maintenance of carrier aircraft developed rapidly, and in every sense of the word the Navy became air-minded. In the 1929 war games, both the Black and Blue fleets used a carrier in attack and defense of the Panama Canal. The 1930 games studied the use of task forces with a unit of a carrier, four cruisers, and two destroyer squadrons. The 1931 games used both carriers as part of a defending force against an attack by surface vessels upon the Canal. By 1932 the value of carriers was so apparent that the current question was whether the fleet needed four or six more large carriers or many more small carriers for efficient operation across the Pacific. Also apparent to Navy strategists was the need for defense of the carriers, and this was reflected in the increased antiaircraft armament of new cruisers, and in the development of antiaircraft cruisers.

Martin T4M-1 torpedo bomber of VT-2B Squadron circling the USS *Saratoga* (March 7, 1932). T4M was one of largest carrier torpedo planes used with Navy, made big *Sara* in the early thirties—along with *Lexington*—world's most powerful warship.

WEAPON

ippled national economy, Navy sets, meets highest standards

Fast, unbelievably nimble in maneuverability, and one of the most rugged airplanes ever built—Boeing F4B-3 fighter of *Saratoga's* "Top Hat" Squadron as it takes off from the carrier deck. Airplanes like these represented a sharp advance over the Navy's former fighters; with the power available that engineers had been clamoring for, they could design new planes able to fight on a par with any in the world. These fighters were so sensitive to any imbalance in flight that the pilot could turn the airplane simply by placing his hand out to his side, in the airstream. The leading fighters of this era were designed and built by Boeing, Curtiss, and later, Grumman. On December 1-9, 1931, the USS *Langley* made the first series of Naval aviation cold-weather tests; the carrier, cruising off the New England coast, used six F3B fighters and six O3U scouts.

USS Saratoga on June 16, 1930; an O2U has just cleared the bow on take-off. Converted from the hulls of incompleted battle cruisers, *Saratoga* and *Lexington* "were to reign as most formidable carriers afloat in any navy." *Saratoga* survived worst of WW II; tired and old, she was sunk in 1946 during Baker underwater atom-bomb test.

T4M torpedo bombers of Squadron VT-10, armed and ready for take-off. In 1929 fleet exercises, Rear Admiral J.M. Reeves provided a dramatic example of *Saratoga's* prowess when carrier was assigned to fleet that would try to "destroy" the Panama Canal. Reeves detached *Saratoga* from the main force of battleships and cruisers, and sent the carrier on a long, fast sweep southward to avoid the defenders. *Saratoga* turned north, launched her aircraft during darkness. Planes swept without warning over Canal locks, and before defense could take any action, "destroyed their objectives."

Martin bomber takes off from *Lexi[n]*
May, 1934. *Langley* experiments deve[l]
deck equipment, handling techniqu[e]
bigger carriers, including flush-deck
pressed air catapults first used in 1[9]

On deck of carrier Lexington (*above*), fighter planes (in foreground) and bombers. (*Below*) Vought fighter landing on *Langley*.
Later the Navy converted the *Langley* to a seaplane tender.

Loening OL-8 (*below*) amphibian drifts in for a landing aboard *Lexington*. Big carriers could handle all types, gave fleet new versatility.

Surveying the Far North

In 1925 Lt. Commander Richard E. Byrd took a Naval detachment to the Arctic as a part of the MacMillan Expedition. With three Loening amphibians, slow but rugged and trustworthy machines, Byrd and his men pioneered in Arctic flying under diverse conditions; they collected scientific data and acquired vital information about the Arctic. Then in 1926, as the Navy continued its major drive to gather data on the Alaskan frontier and in the Aleutians, Lt. Ben Wyatt led three amphibians, with a small tender, on another Alaskan expedition. Other groups made photographic surveys of Central America and the Gulf of Mexico. In 1929 the Navy returned to the Alaskan scene with three OL-8A amphibians, carrying on the trailblazing program.

Alaskan Aerial Survey Detachment (*above*) amphibians at a remote outpost on June 5, 1929.(*Right*) The *Ketchikan*, one of the three Loening OL-8A amphibians, on a photo-mapping flight. The Alaskan aerial survey flights were of vital importance to the United States, because until these Naval expeditions, no reliable information on coastlines, trails, and other vital topographic features existed. Not only the Navy but the Army and many other agencies of the U.S. Government benefited enormously from these military—but peaceful—aerial studies.

Navy Alaskan Survey Loenings en route from Hassleborg Lake to Petersburg, Alaska, August 17, 1929. Following up trail-blazing Navy flights, the Army Air Corps in mid-1934 sent 10 B-10 bombers under Lt. Colonel H.H. Arnold to Alaska to photograph landing sites, mark airways in and out of Russia, and map a 400-mile strip, 50 miles wide.

A new generation of fighters was born to replace the agile F4B series; one of these was the powerful, heavy Curtiss XF11C which featured the recently developed retractable landing gear for military fighters. This type of plane led to early WW II designs.

Today the aerobatic team of the Navy—the Blue Angels—flies supersonic Grumman Tigers, but in the hearts of the old-timers they'll never match the wild, impossible antics of men who flew in teams, like the Sea Hawks, and those that followed. Flying F2B fighters, the pilots of these three airplanes are literally tied together—wing to wing. Almost glued to one another, they took off and climbed in formation, then performed breath-taking aerobatic maneuvers that left crowds gasping with amazement—still tied together! They were Navy's pride and joy.

←

The three Sea Hawks aerobatic team as they posed for camera on August 28, 1928 (left to right): Lt. W.V. Davis, Jr., Lt. W.G. Tomlinson, and Lt. A.P. Storrs, III. The aerobatic team fliers were much more than stunt men, for they came from the ranks of the Navy's carrier pilots, just as the present-day Blue Angels are made up of pilots who volunteer for such duty. Appearing before millions of citizens, they provided a graphic demonstration to the public of Navy flying teamwork and skill, attributes that could—and did—mean everything in air combat.

The Navy accepted delivery of the XOP-1 autogyro (*left*), its first rotary-wing aircraft, at Anacostia on June 1, 1931. The XOP-1, although unsuccessful, provided invaluable experience for rotary-wing operations. Lt. A.M. Pride landed the XOP-1 on the *Langley* in September, 1931, and in June, 1932, the Marines tested the XOP-1 in Nicaragua.

Development of new instruments, techniques gave the Navy the night-flying combat capability it needed to conduct operations anywhere in the world—from carriers and from land installations. These scouts (*right*) based in Hawaii are being run up by ground crew for dawn patrol. They augmented expanding ocean air surveillance.

Typifying the growing strength of Navy in the air, a swarm of F4B fighters thunders over the San Diego Naval Air Station. On June 24, 1926, Congress authorized an aircraft building program for Navy under which the Navy air arm would be increased yearly to reach a total of 1,000 "useful airplanes" in operations at the end of next five years.

WAR WINGS FOR NAVY

The most colorful and popular Navy fighter ever built was undoubtedly the Grumman series F2F and F3F (*above*). The chunky, barrel-shaped biplanes were extraordinarily rugged, and they were famed as a "pilot's airplane." In addition to their role as a fighter, the F2F-F3F airplanes were used by Navy and Marines to bring dive-bombing to a point of "unbelievable accuracy."

U.S. Navy pioneered in meteorological studies around the world, necessary for its ships and planes in operations. Vought SU-1 (*right, above*) was used extensively for aerological research; note aerograph attached to the right strut. (*Right*) Vought O2U laying a smoke screen, August 31, 1933, in tests to develop new equipment. O2U was the Navy "workhorse" in use around the world.

Curtiss FB2C-1's of VB-5B, on maneuvers. FB2C aircraft represented attempt to create an all-purpose "special armament" warplane. Fast enough to be thrown into a fray as fighters, they were equipped to serve as bombers, dive bombers, and could carry enough fuel to operate effectively as scout planes from carriers and land installations.

Lt. Apollo Soucek in his record-breaking Wright Apache, dressed in high-altitude clothes and with sealed oxygen mask. Soucek was world-famous for his altitude flights —he held several world's records, and was known as one of the best test pilots of his day. Soucek's pioneering flights gave the Navy—and the U.S.—much badly needed data about the performance of military pilots and combat planes in substratosphere.

Douglas T2D-1 was a sharp departure from single-engine torpedo bombers; it could fight over longer ranges.

ERA OF THE GREAT GASBAGS

Interior of the 780-foot-long
Akron during construction by G
year Co. It lifted 91-ton l

During World War I, Germany built a total of 88 Zeppelins; by 1918 the great rigid airships used in combat flew at 80 mph, reached as high as 20,000 feet, and carried payloads of 100,000 pounds. (To operate unseen over the clouds, the Zeppelin lowered on a cable a "cloud car," a small gondola that drifted just below the clouds and radioed navigational information back to the airship bridge.) After the war, the seven Zeppelins left intact were parceled out to Great Britain, France, Italy and Japan. The U.S. claimed right of delivery of a new German airship, the LZ-126; this became the U.S. Navy ZR-3. Completed in 1924, she was the strongest airship built to that time. She was flown to the U.S., christened the USS *Los Angeles*, and began a long, successful career. But because of lack of operating funds, the Navy finally had to take the famous airship out of action. After 8 years of service—5,368 hours logged on 331 flights—the *Los Angeles* was decommissioned with honors at Lakehurst.

"The story of the three ships built in this country," states the Chief of the Office of Naval Operations, "is a sad one." And there is no denying this unhappy statement. The ZR-1 was launched in May, 1923, and christened the USS *Shenandoah*. Her performance on fleet maneuvers in 1924 was "not good." On September 2, 1925, Lt. Com-

N2Y-1 (*right, above*), **hooking on** to USS *Akron*. Other countries dropped planes from dirigibles before, but U.S. Navy pioneered in release and hookup as regular operations. First mid-air hookup and pickup was made in 1929 when Lt. A.W. Gorton maneuvered a small UO-1 aboard the USS *Los Angeles*.

Immense size of USS Akron (*below*) is well illustrated in this photo, taken during mooring of the airship at Lakehurst. This is only the ventral fin portion. On November 3, 1931, the giant *Akron* made a 10-hour flight with 207 persons, a world's record.

N2Y-1 (*left*) about to be released from USS *Akron* during 1932 tests of air hookup and release techniques. After *Akron* was lost at sea, Navy re-commissioned German-built *Los Angeles* that had already flown successfully for eight years, and was then retired. After February, 1935, when the *Macon* went down at sea, *Los Angeles* was the only dirigible in the United States, and she turned in five more years of what Navy describes as "sterling service." Proponents of airships are trying today to have an atomic-powered dirigible built, but the expense would be "astronomical."

F9C-2 fighter stowed within capacious hull of *Akron*; sailor can be seen just behind wheels. Five F9C's were carried aboard the giant dirigible. (*Below*) In the hangar at Lakehurst, New Jersey. *Akron* and *Macon* were built at a cost of $6-000,000 each, had a gas capacity of 6,500,000 cubic feet.

mander Z. Landsdowne took *Shenandoah* out of Lakehurst with a full complement of 43 officers and men, en route to Michigan. She never made it. Over Ohio at four A.M., a severe squall hammered at the airship, tore the crew gondola loose, and broke *Shenandoah* in two. Landsdowne and 13 others perished.

In 1931 the USS *Akron*, ZR-4, was commissioned. A giant that was half again as big as *Shenandoah*, *Akron* cruised over a range of 6,500 miles. Eight German Maybach motors, each of 560 hp, drove the great airship (780 feet long) at 80 mph, and *Akron* was designed to carry five F9C fighter planes, each weighing 3,000 pounds. The fighters, which could be launched and recovered in flight, made *Akron* a flying aircraft carrier, and gave her fighter protection no matter where she flew.

For two years *Akron* operated

Rear Admiral W.A. Moffett, with Lt. Commander C. Rosendahl (standing, right) in the *Akron's* control car. *(Right)* In bizarre accident, crewman holds onto lines as *Akron* lifts from ground. This man was pulled aboard and saved; two others fell to their deaths.

successfully with the fleet. On April 4, 1933, she was caught in a severe thunderstorm. Strong gusts snapped the rudder control ropes. *Akron* fell out of control, and smashed tail first into the sea. The airship broke in half and sank, taking with her 18 officers and 55 men. Only three survived. Among the dead: Rear Admiral W.A. Moffett, Chief of the Bureau of Aeronautics. It was a sad and costly blow to the Navy.

Akron's sister ship, USS *Macon* (ZR-5), was commissioned on June 23, 1933, but the airship did not prove valuable to the Navy. Scouting with the fleet, she was invariably "destroyed" by the "enemy." And on February 12, 1935, the *Macon* met real disaster. On maneuvers with the Pacific fleet off Point Sur, California, she suffered a structural failure, settled to the sea, and was abandoned. Of the crew of 80, only two men were lost. The Navy felt that its experience with airships did not justify further expenditures on them—especially at $6,000,000 construction cost for each airship of the *Akron-Macon* class.

The day of the airship was almost over. In 1937 the spectacular disaster of the *Hindenburg*, which burned at Lakehurst and killed many of its passengers, provided the final blow. Despite die-hard adherents, the great rigid airships were through forever.

RECORDS FALL TO NAVY'S FLYING BOATS

Ever since 1927, when a Navy PN-10 flying boat startled the aviation world by setting seven new international records in distance, duration, and altitude at various loadings, American flying boats have been equated with record-breaking performance. As part of the 1926 five-year plan to build the operational flying Navy to 1,000 planes, the Bureau of Aeronautics sponsored the development of several flying boats. Of the three, the Consolidated XPY-1 was by far the most important. It was the first large U.S. monoplane flying boat, its performance was startling, and the basic design was fluid—it was adaptable and could be improved as new design features and more powerful engines became available. One of these follow-up designs of the XPY-1 became one of the most famous airplanes ever built—the PBY Catalina, which served the Navy well before the war, on almost every combat front in U.S. and British colors during World War II, and for many years after the war.

After the XPY, Consolidated engineers burned the midnight oil and came up with another winner, the P2Y, which could fly 3,000 miles nonstop. In September, 1933, Patrol Squadron 5F delivered six P2Y's to Coco Solo in the Panama Canal Zone, flying the 2,059 miles in 25 hours 20 minutes. It was a new world record, and eclipsed the mark of General Italo Bilbo's Italian Squadron, which had flown the South Atlantic from Africa to Brazil—1,864 miles.

Early in January, 1934, Lt. Commander K. McGinnis led the six P2Y's of VP-10 Squadron north to Acapulco (1,667 miles) and then to San Diego (1,616 miles). Here the squadron received assignment to Pearl Harbor. "It was then just a question of whether we would fly over or put the planes on ships," McGinnis recalls. On January 9 the P2Y's flew to San Francisco, and the next day took off for Pearl Harbor —an overwater stretch never before flown by military planes. McGinnis: "They chose the worst month of the year. There were only two or three days in January favorable for a flight of that kind. Now you can go over the weather, but at that time we didn't have the speed or the engines to do it."

The pilots spelled each other at 30-minute intervals across the Pacific. "We flew at 500 feet all night long," McGinnis explained. "We were flying blind by instruments. That was before we had auto-pilots and it was pretty tiring to turn with a turn-and-bank indicator. . . ."

Twenty-four hours and 35 minutes after leaving San Francisco, the six flying boats swept past Pearl

Commander K. McGinniss's P2Y flying boat (*above*) of VP-10 Squadron near Black Point, Oahu, completing his record-breaking flight of 2,408 miles. (*Left*) Improved model of the early P2Y, the P2Y-3.

Harbor. It was another world record chalked up: 2,408 miles nonstop. Later, President Franklin D. Roosevelt declared the flight "the greatest undertaking of its kind in the history of aviation . . . a magnificent achievement."

The P2Y received new engines and other improvements, and became militarily operational with its exceptional range. A new competition to produce an airplane that would fly 3,000 miles at 100 mph, reach a maximum speed of 150 mph, and

weigh 25,000 pounds maximum, was met by Consolidated with the XP3Y-1. Before the new airplane went into production, the designation was changed to indicate that these were patrol planes and bombers—and the historic PBY was born. But before the airplane became known as the PBY, the Navy put the XP3Y-1 into the history books. On October 14–15, 1935, McGinnis and a crew of five flew the airplane from Cristobal Harbor, Canal Zone, nonstop to San Francisco, and marked another new

world distance record for seaplanes of 3,281.402 miles.

It was the PBY that carried the brunt of patrol bomber-flying boat missions in World War II. The more advanced Martin PBM Mariner began replacing the PBY in effective numbers late in the war, and giant PB2Y Coronados, the Catalina's design successor, also began to move into operations. But the line of XPY-1 through the Catalina—and all the records gained in between—typified our flying boats to all the world.

Sikorsky RS-1 transport plane in Hawaiian Islands. Most Navy transports in late twenties and early thirties were flying boats, since landplanes lacked the range for safe, long over-water operations. Both Navy and Marines used transports like the tri-motored Fokker for land operations, but the flying boat was looked upon—both for military and civil aviation—as the only hope for long-range transports. Unfortunately, since there did not exist a strong logistic need for transports, or for fleets of troop carriers, transport development before the war was never seriously pushed, and transport fleet was a hodge-podge gathered from all sources.

Martin P3M-2 patrol bomber (*left*) was of clean, modern design, and paved the way for development of the PBM Mariner used in WW II and Korea. Navy's biggest flying boat was XPB2M-1 Mars, designed to fly 8,000 miles and to carry forty 1,000-lb. bombs; Mars was modified to JRM transport. (*Below*) Coast Guard Fokker, a utility-type amphibian.

THE LAST DAYS OF PEACE

Navy fights for appropriations:
Conflict with Japan threatens

For three consecutive administrations, Naval aviation—despite its memorable accomplishments—suffered chronic budgetary ills. Then came the turn of the decade, a staggering economic depression, and what affected the nation's normal economy was multiplied several times over in respect to military forces. Congressmen concerned with their constituents in breadlines were ill disposed to vote huge sums for military expenditures; the facts of life dictated a crippling austerity for the Navy's air arm. By 1933 there were but thirty students at the once-thriving Pensacola training station; the office of Assistant Secretary of Air was left vacant for budgetary reasons. Of ten recommended aircraft carriers, only one was being built. And the Reserve program, so vital to strength-in-being, found itself deadlocked because of acute financial anemia.

AUSTERITY RULES AIR ARM

President F.D. Roosevelt's first Secretary of War, George H. Dern, peered upon military aviation with unfortunate myopia; openly hostile to military aviation, he denounced air-power concepts as "the fantasy of a dreamer." Unfortunately this perspective was applied in respect to appropriations; the ax was wielded with great enthusiasm, to the detriment of Navy and Army alike. Then new strength seemed to come in through the back door.

Huge sums were appropriated for the new National Recovery and Public Works Administrations, and Naval air enjoyed a sudden, unexpected windfall. Money received from the PWA made it possible to begin construction of two powerful carriers, *Yorktown* and *Enterprise*. Because many air stations lay in areas of unemployment, PWA sums were expended upon these centers of economic neglect. During the next five years Naval air stations prospered in equipment, facilities, and technological improvement; $36,000,000 from PWA sources went into improving runways, lights, hangars, shops, and living quarters at 30 bases.

Our first warship fully designed and built as a carrier, USS *Ranger*, was commissioned in June, 1934. Half the size (14,500 tons) and somewhat slower than big *Sara* and *Lex*, *Ranger*'s usefulness suffered because of her slow speed. But carrier aviation became a true operational reality in the late thirties; *Yorktown* was commissioned in September, 1937, and *Enterprise* in May, 1938. These were sisters of 20,000 tons, but capable of handling as many aircraft

Grumman F3F-3 biplane fighter (*left*) was world's best of its kind matching foreign machines in performance, and boasting unbelievable strength and versatility. Grumman biplane fighters were famous as dive bombers. Unfortunately, replacements for these planes came about slowly, allowing Japan's carrier fighters by 1940 to become world's best. (*Right*) Navy experimented with TBD-1A as a torpedo bomber; abandoned project.

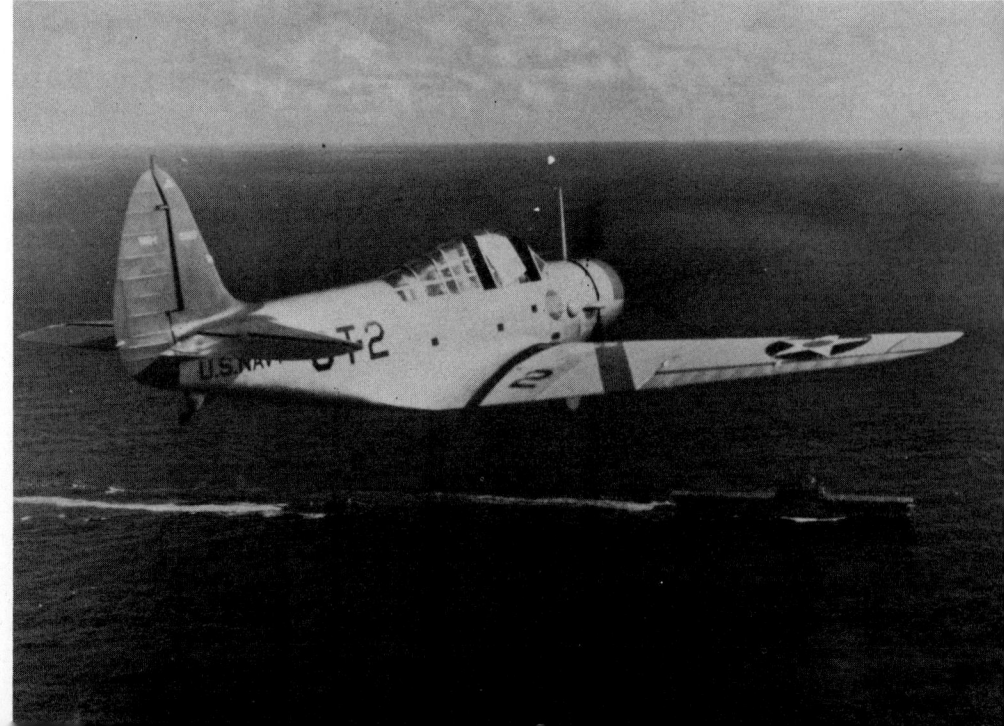

During its operation life, Curtiss SBC scout-dive bomber was second to no other plane in the world. The last of the Navy's biplane bombers, it phased out to SB2U, and then to the rugged, deadly Douglas SBD.

Douglas TBD-1 Devastator flies over USS *Enterprise* (January 14, 1939). The Navy's first production monoplane torpedo bomber, great hopes were held for TBD as powerful carrier weapon. But airplane fell behind rapid technical aviation advances; by time WW II began was underpowered, under-armed, too slow, and naked to enemy fire. Indicative of airpower before WW II: TBD surpassed best British torpedo bomber.

The famed "Razzle Dazzle Formation" of Fighter Squadron VF-2, demonstrated near Molokai, Hawaii. This is not a lucky, accidental shot; the pilots are *holding* this formation! Judicious use of stick, rudder, and power enabled pilots to slip, skid while flying straight ahead. Navy, Marine pilots were world-famous for extraordinary flying skill.

and operating at the same speeds as 33,000-ton *Saratoga* and *Lexington*.

In 1940 *Wasp* was commissioned; and in 1941 *Hornet*, fast and powerful, cut the ocean on her shakedown cruise. Even in 1939, however, as the Navy waited for these two major additions to its air strength, the U.S. carrier Navy was second to none. Not since 1930 had the British completed a new carrier; they had six, none of which was equal to our four operating carriers, and British hopes for naval aviation strength lay in the *Ark Royal* and four other carriers under construction.

SHADOWS OF WAR

It was from the other side of the world that there could be heard ominous rumblings of strength. By the mid-1930's Japan had two large and two small carriers on the high seas, with more in the shipyards. Overnight, it seemed, she had become a force to be reckoned with.

New planes began to appear in the fleet. Scout planes were developed to high efficiency, and served from all types of ships and from land stations. Grumman produced its chunky biplane fighter series (F1F, F2F, F3F) and gave new strength to our fighter force. The SBC biplane dive bomber was as good as any other plane in the world; it was augmented with the SB2U Vindicator, and that airplane was soon to be eclipsed by the sensational Douglas SBD Dauntless. For patrolling, aviation had become so important that in 1938 a $21,000,000 contract was given to Consolidated for its famed PBY Catalina—more than the entire amount expended on Naval aviation some ten years previous.

Unhappily—and unfortunately for the nation—even these measures were not enough. It was true that we progressed; foreign nations had, however, literally thrown away the old rulebook and were racing ahead without the engineering restrictions imposed upon our own firms. The TBD torpedo bomber was a case in point; although of modern monoplane design, it was hopelessly slow, awkward to fly, and a sitting duck. But this would not be demonstrated until appalling battle losses forced the airplane's retirement.

The U.S. public believed that we could be pacifistic, that the Atlantic and Pacific were effective barriers to attack by foreign nations. But this was no longer true—our twenty-year-old battleships and five operational carriers could not control, let alone effectively patrol, the vast expanse of the world's two biggest oceans.

Sturdy, dependable, faithful—the accolade for PBY patrol bomber (*above*) goes on forever. They were slow, vulnerable to fighters, but able to fly tremendous distances. Great endurance gave them ability to shadow enemy ships, maintain constant tracking. Mainstay of Navy prewar patrol aviation, they served in all theaters throughout war. (*Below*) SOC-1 floatplane; catapulted from cruisers, battleships, also was "eye" for fleet.

Grumman J2F (*right*) succeeded old Loening series of amphibians. Designed strictly for utility, the J2F turned out to be one of the world's most useful performers, and served the Navy well almost everywhere in the world. The Grumman plane was used from ships and land bases before the war, all through WW II, and continued as a major operational aircraft for years later. J2F performed in outstanding fashion exploring and opening new trails in remote Arctic areas.

Dispersal of VP-14's PBY Catalina flying boats in the southeast area of Kaneohe Bay, Hawaii, three weeks before attack against Pearl Harbor. In 1940 first additions to flying-boat fleet came with delivery of Martin PBM Mariners to patrol squadrons; in 1941 the first operation squadron with Consolidated PB2Y Coronados, big brother to the PBY, was formed. But "bugs" delayed operations of these planes in large numbers, and PBY remained WW II flying-boat mainstay.

No other airplane is a better example of frustrations in Naval aviation than the Brewster F2A Buffalo. The Navy's first production monoplane fighter, in performance it appeared the equal of any contemporary carrier airplane in the world. Britain's leading Navy fighter, for example, was the biplane Gloster Gladiator. The Japanese were known to be using the Mitsubishi Type 96 (Claude), a monoplane with fixed landing gear and an open cockpit. But the Buffalo's adversary in WW II would be the Zero (entered service in 1940), which was faster, more maneuverable, could climb faster and higher, and carried heavier armament. Planes like the F2A were trumpeted by zealous public-relations men as "world's finest," but when the Japanese Zero fought the overrated Buffalo, the Navy fighter was almost helpless, and our pilots were literally blown out of the skies.

Sikorsky JRS-1 flew Navy transport, cargo missions through Pacific in pre-war days. It was last of big Sikorsky flying boats to serve Navy in quantity.

Chance-Vought SB2U-1 Vindicator scout and dive bombers of VB-3 ''Top Hat'' Squadron, July, 1938. First mass production monoplane dive bomber for Navy, SB2U suffered ill-fated career. After Navy received SBD Dauntless bombers, SB2U's were turned over to Marines. Used at Midway, they were too old, were slaughtered by the Japanese. They were quickly replaced.

The Navy's first airplane to exceed 400 mph in level flight, the Chance-Vought XF4U-1 Corsair was also the first 2,000-hp fighter of the fleet. In early tests the XF4U-1 astounded Naval airpower strategists with its amazing performance. Before entering service it was modified extensively; the synchronized nose guns were removed, and six heavy machine guns placed in the wings, for example. Corsair was the first Navy/ USMC fighter in action to decisively surpass the Japanese Zero in battle performance.

Navy's first twin-engine fighter (*below*) was revolutionary Grumman XF5F-1 Skyrocket, which climbed at 5,000 feet per minute, had heavy firepower, high speed, excellent visibility. Stability problems plagued XF5F-1 (also tested by Army as XP-50), which finally was dropped. Grumman then made twin-engine F7F Tigercat, which saw service in WW II, Korea.

Army and Navy often tested each other's planes for possible use; this is Bell XFL-1 Airabonita, carrier version of well-known P-39 Airacobra. Design was unsuccessful for carriers, was dropped.

FIGHTERS HELD KEY TO FUTURE AIR WAR

The heart of military airpower has always been the fighter airplane, the swift, powerful, heavily armed killer of the skies. Especially with carrier air forces the fighter has played a critical role. A land-based airfield can be bombed, and the damage easily repaired; if the floating island is so badly damaged that it cannot function as an airfield or if it is sunk, then all the naval airpower concerned is lost, the bombers as well as the fighters. The aircraft carrier is a means to an end; the fighter sustains the means, protects it, functions as its rapier so that the bombers—the bludgeon—can destroy the enemy.

Every fighter plane that fought in World War II—except one, the Navy's F6F Hellcat—was designed or flown in the years before the war. Thus the pattern for success or failure in combat was virtually set before the battle. The U.S. Navy almost exclusively pitted its fighter strength in the war against the Japanese; in 1942, F4F Wildcats in Africa fought old American P-36 Hawks and French Dewoitine 520 fighters, but the significant, deciding fighter-vs.-fighter engagements were fought by the Navy across the vast Pacific.

The quality of fighter aircraft of the U.S. before the war suffered an invisible enemy: a combination of ridiculous underestimation of the Japanese as a major airpower and a blind confidence that "if it's built in the old U.S.A., it's got to be the best." Our airpower strategists, Navy and Army alike, blithely ignored all the warnings that Japan was building a superb front-line combat air force, that the Japanese Navy had overnight become second to none with a new fighter known as the Zero. Indeed, the Japanese understood far better than we the vital role of the fighter airplane, for they based their entire pattern of Pacific conquest on the success of the Zero over all aerial opposition. And for an uncomfortable stretch of time that success was overwhelmingly theirs.

They gambled on quality, and until superior U.S. fighters were rushed from production lines to the combat zone, the superior quality of the Zero paid its tremendous dividends.

The three airplanes on this page represent steps in evolution of the U.S. Navy fighter prior to the war. Only one of the three survived the hurdles of severe operational testing—the Chance-Vought F4U Corsair, which blazed a brilliant passage across Pacific skies.

One airplane is not shown—but it fills succeeding pages. This is the Grumman F4F Wildcat, our sole Navy fighter hope in the dark, early days of the war, the Navy's foot-in-the-door fighter that served us so well. Designed originally as a biplane, the Wildcat before the war was converted hurriedly to a monoplane, giving it much superior performance. But perhaps the Wildcat's greatest claim to fame was its successor, the superb Hellcat.

The Douglas SBD Dauntless—greatest killer of Japanese shipping in WW II. No one could have forecast the brilliant role this plane would play, the decisive battles that would be won by its slashing dives. Relatively slow and lightly armed, the Dauntless had amazing stability and control in a dive. It smashed the Japanese across the Pacific, sank more warships than any other American bomber.

Intended before the war as a gradual replacement for the TBD Devastator, the Grumman TBF Avenger program was hastily accelerated when the TBD's were slaughtered by Japanese planes. A big, powerful airplane, the TBF debut took place at the Battle of Midway in June, 1942; overwhelmed by Japanese planes, the TBF force was almost annihilated. But after this unhappy beginning, the TBF turned in an outstanding performance. In WW II they were to fight on almost every Naval combat front, operating as glide and torpedo bombers.

Prior to WW II the Marines developed paramarine tactics to fine art; Douglas R3D-2 transport (the commercial DC-5) was used in tests as drop aircraft. Although Corps suffered badly in aircraft strength—under the government ceilings of 1940 they were allotted 1,167 planes, but had only 204 aircraft on hand by December, 1941—Marine aviators practiced new tactics constantly. In WW II, however, paramarines were not used.

Formations of torpedo and scout bombers, and biplane fighters, pass over battleships of Pacific fleet in 1940 maneuvers. War emergency plans of 1941 dangerously split our carrier force; of three assigned to Pacific fleet, one would protect heavy ships, another would support cruisers for scouting purposes, and third was to be part of a force hitting enemy bases. The early Japanese successes, however, created new task force concept.

JAPANESE SMASH A

BATTLESHIP FLEET MAULED: BUT VITAL
U.S. CARRIERS ESCAPE ENEMY BOMBS

PEARL HARBOR

Japanese photograph, captured on Attu Island in the Aleutians, showing a Zero fighter ready for take-off (foreground) to attack Pearl Harbor; airplanes behind Zero are Mitsubishi Type 97 torpedo bombers. Forty-three Zero fighters went out in first wave, escorting 140 dive, level, torpedo bombers.

Enemy rips Allies across 10,000-mile front

"December 7, 1941 . . . will live as one of the most brilliant military performances of all time. Superbly planned and superbly executed. . . ."

"On December 7, 1941, he [the Japanese] achieved complete surprise. He struck swiftly, boldly, accurately. . . . He made full capital of the paralyzing effect of his initial assault."

". . . From the standpoint of air employment alone, his first stroke was masterful."

These are strong statements. They are frank tributes to the incredible success enjoyed by the Japanese in their assault against Pearl Harbor on the "day of infamy," December 7, 1941. The statements are excerpts from official United States military documents.

The facts of life as they involve the Japanese attack against the Hawaiian Islands are difficult to accept. Much has been said of the sudden raid against Pearl Harbor, but the moral reprehensibility of the enemy blow cannot alter what is fact. The storm warnings were raised many months before. The Japanese were preparing, almost openly, for war. They were insolent, antagonistic in their relations with the United States.

Military orders of the day specified that our forces be on the alert. They were not, and no evasive eloquence can change history.

The Japanese carrier fleet late in 1941 was the most powerful in the world; there were six large and four small carriers. The Zero fighter was unquestionably the world's best, although in the United States the public was showered with glowing stories of our warplanes—"second to none." It was false comfort, propaganda that would cost the lives of our pilots, who believed all too sincerely that nothing the Japanese possessed could possibly match their Buffaloes and Wildcats.

The Japanese prepared the strike at Pearl Harbor to eliminate the U.S. fleet so that it could not interfere with the numerous amphibious operations that were to sweep the Pacific. Japanese moves to picture their own fleet as unwieldy, ill-equipped, and poorly led paid a handsome dividend. Few American officers believed that the Japanese were even remotely capable of more than one major naval or amphibious operation at one time.

On November 5, 1941, the Commander-in-Chief, Imperial Navy of Japan—Admiral Isoroku Yamamoto—issued Combined Fleet Secret Operations Order No. 1; it was a grandiose command to "drive Britain and America from Greater East Asia."

The Pearl Harbor Striking Force under Vice-Admiral Chuichi Nagumo consisted of the modern carriers *Zuikaku* and *Shokaku* (30,000 tons), *Akagi* and *Kaga* (27,000 tons), and the modern light carriers *Soryu* and *Hiryu* (10,000 tons). There were also two battleships, three cruisers, nine destroyers, and three supply vessels.

On the afternoon of November 28, 1941, military and Naval commanders in Hawaii received from the War Department in Washington a

Mitsubishi Type 97 Kate torpedo bomber on take-off roll. Forty Kates carried torpedoes, 49 Kates were loaded for high-level bombing; plus 51 Aichi 99 Val dive bombers. First bomb dropped by a Val struck at 7:55 A.M. on Ford Island; first torpedo exploded at 7:56 A.M. in *West Virginia*, just before bombs and torpedoes hit other ships.

Flak bursts and thick smoke over Pearl Harbor; second wave is just attacking.

message containing this statement: "Japanese future action unpredictable, but hostile action possible at any moment."

On the morning of December 2, steaming toward Pearl Harbor, Nagumo received his final secret orders. The signal was: "*Niitaka Yama Nobore.*" (Climb Mount Niitaka.)

Millions of words of testimony have attempted to affix the blame on those responsible for the Pearl Harbor debacle. Unfortunately, political considerations have transcended the straightforward recital of military events, and the endless accusations and countercharges have only confused the matter hopelessly. Consider, however, these highlights leading up to the attack.

We ignored the sighting—at 3:42 A.M., several hours before the attack—

Zero fighter taking off for Pearl Harbor. Eighty-three Zeros engaged in attack, operated perfectly as escort screen and strafers. They shot down planes from *Enterprise*, as well as fighters taking off from Pearl.

Warship's fuel tanks explode in a tremendous blast of flame; burning battleship is shown at right. First wave of planes attacked for 30 minutes, destroyed or crippled 70 per cent of all targets.

of a Japanese midget submarine by USS *Condor*, only two miles outside Pearl Harbor. At 6:45 A.M. the destroyer USS *Ward* noted smoke marker bombs dropped by a PBY near the submarine, and opened fire with her deck guns, then dropped depth charges. At 6:53 A.M.—one hour and two minutes before the first bomb fell—*Ward* radioed Pearl Harbor: "We have attacked, fired upon, and dropped depth charges on sub operating in defensive area." No action was taken.

The carrier *Enterprise* was steaming toward Pearl Harbor. Two hundred miles from the Naval base, at 6:15 A.M., the carrier launched several planes which were to fly to Ford Island. At exactly forty-five minutes past six, in the *Enterprise* radio room, the scream of an American pilot burst over the radio. It was the voice of Ensign Manuel Gonzalez of Scouting Squadron 6. Gonzalez had flown within sight of the Japanese bombers and their escort; the Zeros were swift and sure. One hour and ten minutes before the first bomb fell on Ford Island, Gonzalez' scream of *"Don't shoot! This is an American plane!"* was heard aboard *Enterprise*. No action was taken.

One hour and ten minutes before the first attack, an Army radar station picked up a *blip* on its screen; it was a single airplane, unidentified, bearing at high speed toward Oahu. The radar operator who tracked the "unknown" for 15 minutes was told to disregard the sighting; and so the Zero floatplane fighter, catapulted off the cruiser *Chikuma* to reconnoiter Pearl Harbor, went unmolested.

A second radar warning was provided. At exactly seventeen minutes past seven, the Army radar station reported "many" planes approaching Pearl Harbor. The first indication on the scope showed the Japanese force 132 miles from Oahu, bearing in from 3 degrees east of north at 150 mph. Because a flight of B-17's was expected from California, the radar report was ignored.

At thirty minutes past seven, Boatswain's Mate Milligan was on the deck of the destroyer *Allen*. Looking up, he noticed 20 to 25 planes orbiting slowly in formation at about 5,000 feet. It was a beautiful sight, with the sun glinting off the wings of the planes. By one of those calamitous quirks of

Fifty-one of these Aichi 99 Val dive bombers struck Pearl Harbor in first attacking wave. Second wave, bombing at 8:40 A.M., included an additional 80 Vals. The dive bombers were extremely effective. At Kaneohe, the bombers destroyed 27 of 33 PBY Catalinas, damaged the other 6. With their Zero escorts strafing, Vals destroyed 47 out of 48 Marine planes in Hawaiian Islands.

While smoke pours from warships and shore installations, Naval personnel begin task of mopping up aircraft hangar area on Ford Island. In the first few minutes of the attack, Val dive bombers destroyed half of all Navy planes on Ford Island, and succeeding attacks wrecked many others. Four Navy planes from USS *Enterprise*, low on fuel and trying to land, were shot down by our own flak.

fate, Milligan did not have binoculars with which to study the planes. If he had, he could have seen that the aircraft circling Pearl Harbor—*for 25 minutes*—bore on their wings the red ball of Japan. The planes were Aichi 99 dive bombers that reached Pearl Harbor before the arrival of the slower torpedo bombers; they circled unmolested for nearly a half hour, then dove.

At fifty-five minutes past seven on the morning of December 7, 1941, the first bomb fell on Ford Island.

THE LOSSES

In the devastating air attack with 353 carrier-based warplanes, Japan's pilots either sank or rendered useless for a long time to come the battleships *Arizona*, *California*, *Oklahoma*, *Nevada* and *West Virginia*; three destroyers; the target ship *Utah*; the minelayer *Oglala*; and a large floating drydock. Heavily damaged: battleships *Maryland*, *Pennsylvania* and *Tennessee*; light cruisers *Helena*, *Raleigh*, and *Honolulu*; seaplane tender *Curtiss*; repair ship *Vestal*.

Japanese pilots either crippled or destroyed more than 150 Navy airplanes; they shot eleven Navy bombers out of the sky without loss—fully armed planes that never fired a shot in their own defense.

They ripped Army ground and air installations into a bloody shambles. They destroyed 141 Army fighters and bombers, and damaged dozens more. They set aflame and demolished hangars, storage shops and warehouses, barracks, piers, cranes, munitions dumps, and other vital installations.

They killed 2,844 men from the military forces on Oahu, and wounded another 1,178 Americans. In the two hours of the attack, our Navy lost about three times as many men as it lost by enemy action in its two previous wars—Spanish and World War I.

To accomplish all this, to deliver what the Navy lists as a "complete victory" and a "crippling blow" to the "U.S. Pacific Fleet," the Japanese lost but 29 airplanes and 55 men.

STRIKING BACK

Although the Japanese broke the back of our battleship fleet in the Pacific, they failed to inflict damage upon the core of the Navy's offensive striking force—the three carriers of the Pacific fleet. *Saratoga*, just out of overhaul, was moored at San Diego. *Lexington* was at sea about 425 miles southeast of Midway, where she was to deliver Marine bombers. *Enterprise* was steaming toward Pearl Harbor.

During what may accurately be described as the most crucial period of the war—from Pearl Harbor through the Battle of Midway in June, 1942—the three Pacific fleet carriers, plus the *Hornet* and *Yorktown*, rushed from the Atlantic (*Wasp* remained in those waters until June 10), steamed more than 180,000 miles, carried out numerous raids, and fought two decisive battles that turned the course of the war.

The first mission of the Navy was, as it always has been, the defense of U.S. territory; and because this included the military installations in Hawaii, one carrier at least was retained in the Central Pacific area. During the

Navy line crews and other personnel immediately after attack attempt to salvage planes at Kaneohe base and Naval Air Station.

Carriers make first strikes at Japanese

early months of hostilities, *Enterprise* performed this mission. This did not preclude striking at Japanese bases to the westward, so that *Enterprise* together with *Yorktown* attacked installations in the Gilbert and Marshall Islands in the first U.S. carrier action of the war on February 1, 1942. *Enterprise* alone carried out raids on Wake, February 24; Marcus, March 4; and provided air cover for *Hornet's* attack against Japanese homeland April 18, 1942 (see pages 110–111).

These raids were planned to relieve pressure elsewhere, particularly far to the south where Japanese forces threatened to cut the line of communication between the U.S. and Australia. In early 1942, when Japanese naval forces outnumbered those of the Allies, the objective, and it was necessarily a limited one, was the lifeline to Australia, where General MacArthur was assembling ground, sea, and air power for a counteroffensive. *Lexington* had gone southwest from Pearl Harbor in early February. It had an initial brush with the enemy on the 20th of that month when detected while steaming in for a surprise attack on the Japanese base at Rabaul in the Admiralty Islands. The engagement (the attack was cancelled when Japanese planes sighted *Lexington* 350 miles out) showed that the guns and planes of a carrier group could furnish an effective defense against land-based air so long as odds were about equal.

Shortly after the raid on the Marshalls and Gilberts, *Yorktown* joined *Lexington* and together they struck enemy installations at Lae and Salamaua on the north coast of New Guinea on March 10. This action, even though it checked the Japanese advance only slightly, was important tactically because the two air groups operated as a unit under a single command in the air, an advance over earlier operations when the aircraft from two carriers had attacked different targets in the same general area simultaneously.

We had begun to strike back, but we were still in serious difficulty. *Langley* (converted to a seaplane tender) went down under a massive air attack near Java; *Saratoga* took a submarine torpedo and was in Bremerton for repairs.

Japanese photo taken during first minutes of attack against Ford Island. Dive and torpedo bombers have just completed first target runs.

A graphic portrayal of the accuracy and effectiveness of the Japanese bombing. In the background is the wrecked battleship USS *Pennsylvania*; in the foreground, smashed and gutted, lie the USS *Cassin* and USS *Downes*. At a cost of only 55 men and 29 planes, the Japanese carrier force crippled our battleship fleet, wrecked half the Pearl Harbor cruiser force, ripped destroyers and other warships, and left the shore installations a shambles.

NATION CHEERS DARING RAID

"Their flight was one of the most courageous deeds in all military history"
Vice-Admiral William F. Halsey

In the first brief months of war the American public suffered a tremendous shock—a nation that we had scorned as a military power, derided as a land of bamboo and bifocals, was teaching us the finer points of war. American morale plunged as the Japanese stormed over a 10,000-mile front; we were guilty in our headlines of sinking nonexistent ships and shooting down imaginary planes. The nation needed an honest bracer, a heady boost for its sagging morale.

The answer was a tightly knit cooperative project between the Navy and the Army; *Hornet*, escorted by *Enterprise*, would carry 16 AAF B-25 bombers to attack the Japanese homeland. It was a move in which the Navy faced tremendous peril, for the nation could ill afford to lose these two precious carriers. Credit for the overwhelming success of the attack is shared by all, from James H. Doolittle, who led the air mission and earned the Congressional Medal of Honor, to the Navy crewman whose arm was sliced off by a B-25 propeller.

Hornet rendezvoused on April 13 in mid-ocean with *Enterprise*; on April 17 the two carriers and four escorting cruisers refueled 1,000 miles from Tokyo, left the destroyers and tankers behind, and raced for Japan. Japanese Intelligence had alerted patrol bombers and picket ships; the latter sighted the task force. Still 650 miles from Japan, the 16 bombers were launched.

The B-25's, each carrying one ton of bombs, struck at Tokyo, Kanagawa, Yokohama, Yokosuka, Kobe, Osaka, and Nagoya. The damage was slight, but Americans everywhere walked a little straighter.

The pictures on these two pages show different scenes of the Army B-25 bombers taking off from *Hornet*. Planes raced down deck that pitched dangerously from heavy swells. All 16 bombers made take-off without accidents, although several dropped dangerously near the water after clearing deck. The Mitchells flew to Japan at 15- to 20-foot height, hit the home islands with complete surprise; Japanese called the tactics "brilliant." To evade fighters that scrambled into air, one B-25 streaked over Japan at minimum height, flying beneath electric power lines to shake off pursuers. After launching B-25's, U.S. carriers fled—and eluded heavy Japanese bomber force seeking them out.

FLASH: "SCRATCH

For first time in war Navy—in the air—stops the Japanese

Shoho takes a devastating attack by 93 Navy planes. As bombers attacked, our fighters flamed seven defending Nakajimas, opened way for bombers. In 15 minutes *Shoho* took the terrific beating of 13 bomb hits and 7 torpedo strikes, blew apart and sank. Lt. Commander Bob Dixon radioed: "*Scratch one flattop!*" We had finally struck back—hard.

ONE FLATTOP!"

The first carrier offensive of the war, carried out against Roi, Kwajalein, Maloelap, Wotje, Jaluit, Makin and Mili, was an attack unpretentious in scale but important in effect. The raids against these bases in the Marshall and Gilbert Islands did little real damage to the Japanese, but they boosted Naval aviation morale; much more important, they discovered the weaknesses of the enemy, and provided the hard core of experience needed by commanders who would soon take on the responsibility of new fleets. They were experiments in carrier warfare, conceived and born of the necessity to defend a shattered fleet, and of learning the methods to be employed by the fast carrier task force of the future.

The first aerial fight between opposing carrier planes occurred during the abortive raid of February 20 by *Lexington* against Rabaul. Three hundred fifty miles from her target, *Lexington* was attacked by 18 enemy planes. Lt. Edward "Butch" O'Hare gained national fame, the Congressional Medal of Honor, and ace status by shooting down five torpedo bombers in a single engagement, likely saving his carrier from destruction.

When *Enterprise* on March 4, as part of Task Force 16 under Vice-Admiral W.F. Halsey, struck at Marcus Island, the Japanese were forced to sit up and take notice —an American carrier was only 1,000 miles from the homeland, carrying out offensive action less than 90 days after the start of war. Then came the strikes at Lae and Salamaua on March 10, followed by the Doolittle attack on April 18. Events now led the American and Japanese carrier forces into their first direct, violent engagement.

Intelligence reported that troop transports escorted by the light carrier *Shoho* and two large carriers would enter the Coral Sea by the end of April; the evaluation of the Japanese move pointed to an invasion of vital Port Moresby in New Guinea, and a flanking move to bring Australia under direct Japanese attack. *Lexington* and *Yorktown* were ordered to rendezvous near the New Hebrides, and to "operate in the Coral Sea commencing 1 May."

The issue was to be joined on May 7, but *Yorktown*, which had completed refueling at sea first, received word of an invasion force landing on Tulagi in the southern Solomons. On May 4, *Yorktown* planes sank a destroyer, several small boats, and destroyed a seaplane base at the cost of three aircraft. Early on the 5th the carriers again rendezvoused, refueled from the tanker *Neosho*, and kept up a far-reaching reconnaissance patrol.

Now the Japanese carriers *Shokaku* and *Zuikaku* rushed into the picture. On May 7, 61 Japanese planes caught the *Neosho* and the destroyer *Sims*, turning the tanker into a mass of flames and sending *Sims* to the bottom (*Neosho*, gutted, was sunk deliberately on May 11). The same morning, Admiral Fletcher of *Yorktown* ordered 93 planes out to hunt for the enemy.

Douglas SBD Dauntless bombers (*above*) of *Yorktown* swing over Tulagi Harbor after raid that sank one destroyer, four barges. (*Right*) SBD scout leaves carrier for patrol mission, hunting out Japanese force. (*Opposite page*) The 30,000-ton *Shokaku* turning hard and fast to avoid bombs and torpedoes; a heavy bomb has just struck the water off the bow. Three SBD's finally caught *Shokaku* and each sent a 1,000-pound bomb crashing into the ship. Badly damaged, she transferred her planes to *Zuikaku* and limped back to Japan. Both carriers were knocked out of action for at least two months, and were unable to participate in Battle of Midway as planned—a dividend of the Battle of the Coral Sea that may well have affected the course of the entire war.

114

Emerging from thick storm clouds, the heavy American force had the great fortune to sight *Shoho* and her covering cruisers and destroyers. It was a moment dreamed of by our carrier pilots, and the sky seemed to fall down on *Shoho* as all 93 planes swarmed down for the kill. Thirty-six minutes after the first sighting, *Shoho* was a riddled, blasted, flaming hulk, and sank quickly. At a cost of three bombers, we had sunk the first carrier to be lost by either side.

The battle was still to be joined in full fury. Admiral Takagi launched 27 planes from his two big carriers to attack our ships; in the storm-filled skies these were torn apart by Wildcats, which shot down 9 planes. Confused enemy pilots tried to land in the dark on the American carriers. Withering point-blank gunfire drove them off, and 11 more bombers went down. Only 7 out of 27 returned.

The second day's battle began at 1057 hours; *Yorktown* planes hurled two bombs into *Shokaku*. But it was a costly morning. Japanese bombers raced in low and from both sides of the carrier released eleven torpedoes at *Lexington*; two crashed into the port side. Shortly afterward, two heavy bombs smashed into her deck. *Yorktown*, after dodging eight torpedoes, took one large bomb. A few minutes later word was received that bombers from *Lexington* had again scored hits on the enemy.

By noon, the Japanese had lost 43 planes, the Navy 33. *Shokaku* transferred her planes to *Zuikaku* and limped away to the north. *Zuikaku* did not press battle any longer, and it was just as well. *Yorktown*, burning fiercely, brought her own fires under control, and resumed flight operations. But *Lexington*, holed by bombs and torpedoes, was doomed.

Tactically, the Battle of the Coral Sea was a draw. Strategically, however, it represented significant victory. The enemy expedition had turned back, and Moresby for the moment was spared. By the time the Japanese returned, hoping to take the vital base, we had accumulated sufficient strength to inflict a decisive defeat—a long-term payoff of the Coral Sea.

FIRST SEA BATTLE IN WHICH WARSHIPS NEVER ENGAGED IN FIRE

BITTER COST OF BATTLE

Fire, explosions rip <u>LEXINGTON</u>

The *Lady Lex*, as she was known to her crew, was a gallant, powerful, fighting ship, and one of the greatest carriers in the world. But in the Coral Sea, despite the damage inflicted on the Japanese carriers *Shokaku* and *Zuikaku*, and despite the frantic efforts of Wildcat pilots, and even SBD dive-bomber pilots acting as a fighter screen, the Japanese got through. Admiral F.C. Sherman, on *Lexington's* bridge, reported the enemy attack as "beautifully co-ordinated." Five bombs and two torpedoes ripped the *Lex*; heroic efforts saved the ship. Then gasoline vapor ignited between decks, dooming the great carrier. Destroyers saved 2,735 men; 216 were lost. The survivors wept as *Lady Lex* went down.

Wildcats (*above*) flew escort for bombers attacking enemy carriers, provided defensive screen for *Lexington*. (*Opposite page, top*) SBD bombers, with 4 machine guns, were used as fighters to defend the USS *Lexington*.

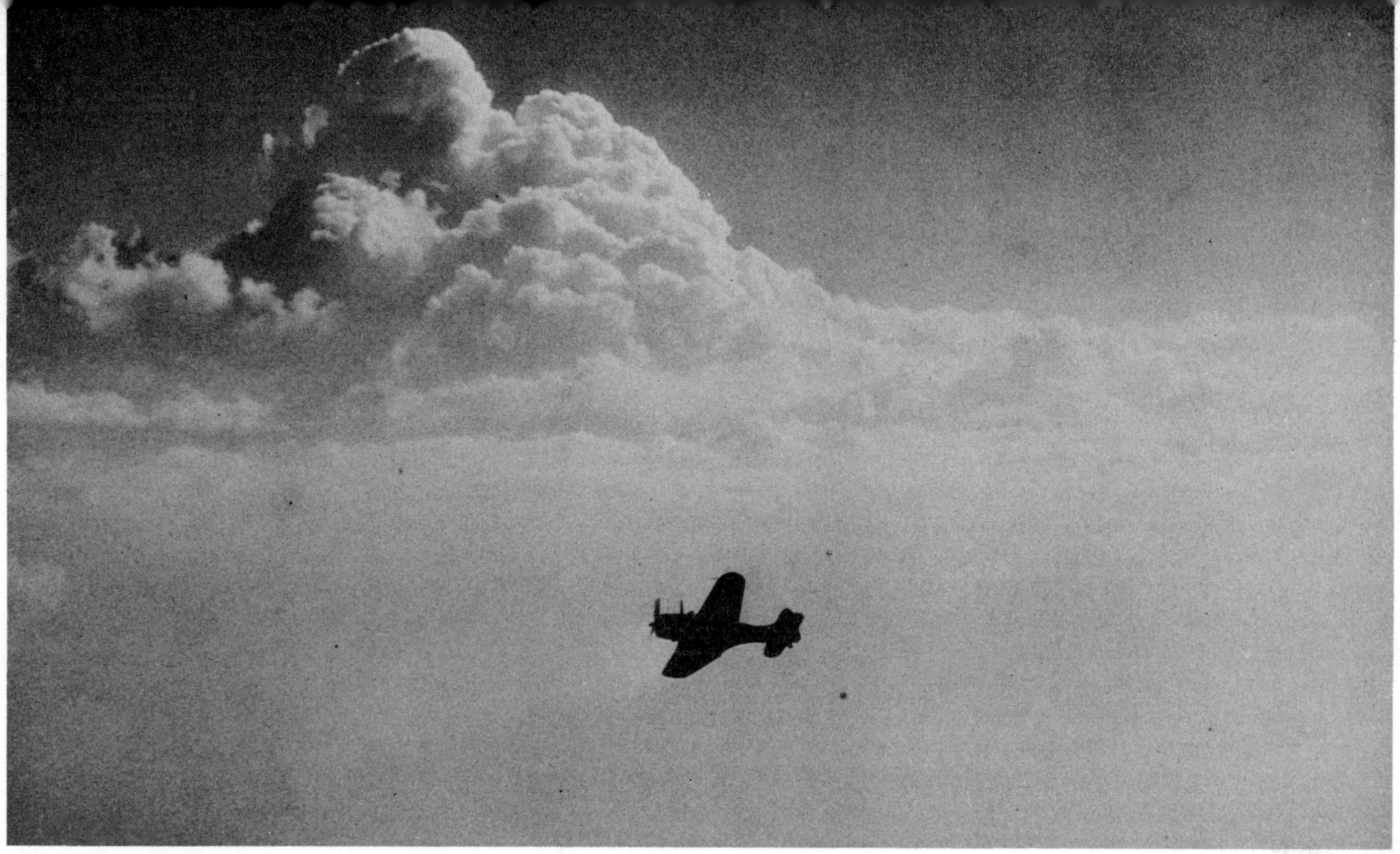

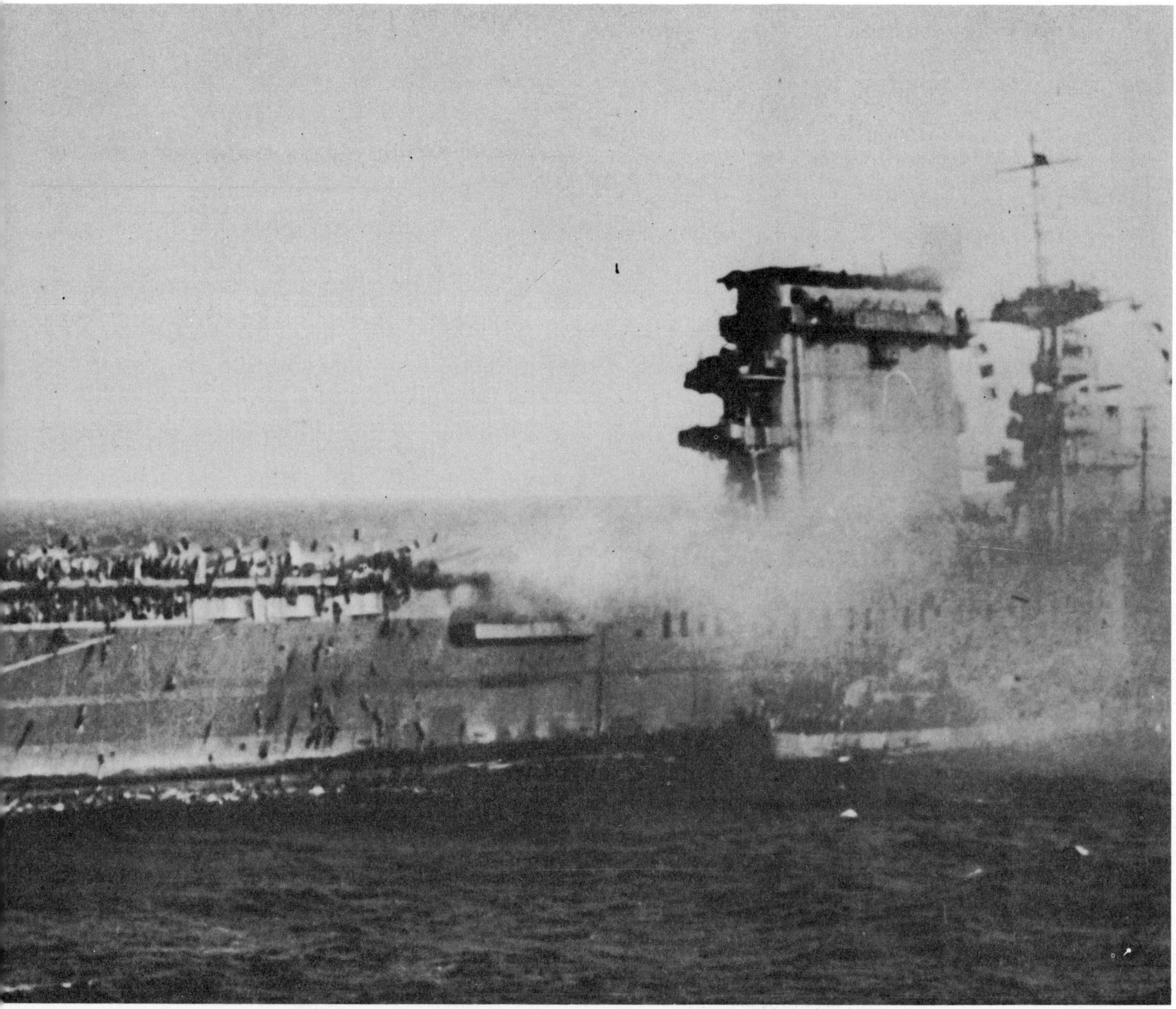

MIDWAY . . .
TURNING POINT OF THE PACIFIC

Japanese strategic offensive broken:
Enemy fleet is shattered

Admiral Isoroku Yamamoto—remembered in Washington long before the war as one of the toughest poker players ever to serve as a naval attaché in the capital—was one of the few Japanese who held a keen evaluation of American strength and resources. Early Japanese gains, no matter how overwhelming, did not blind Yamamoto to the fact that unless he could annihilate the U.S. fleet in 1942, he must—by his own interpretation of the future—lose the war.

To draw the fleet into battle, he planned a force to attack and occupy Midway Island. The U.S. Navy must defend Midway because of its proximity to Hawaii and the U.S. mainland: this was Yamamoto's bait. To close the trap the wily admiral assembled a tremendous force. Nagyma had the 4 remaining carriers from the Pearl Harbor strike, 2 battleships, 3 cruisers, and 12 destroyers.

The killer of Midway (*left*)—Douglas SBD Dauntlesses sank four large carriers and the heavy cruiser (13,000 tons) *Mikuma* (*below*). The cruiser *Mogami* rammed the *Mikuma*, then both ships were heavily bombed. Note wreckage of Marine SBD on gun turret.

Four enemy carriers sunk

Admiral Kondo would protect 12 transports with 2 battleships, 10 cruisers, the carrier *Zuiho*, and 20 destroyers. Yamamoto personally led the "Main Body"—another force of 3 super battleships, 4 other battleships, the carrier *Hosho*, 3 cruisers and 13 destroyers.

Our own Navy was ill equipped to combat this overwhelming enemy fleet, although maximum use was made of secret Intelligence reports that accurately outlined Japanese plans, composition, routes, and timetables. We still faced what amounted to an alarm-

ing situation. *Yorktown* limped into port on May 27, and was drydocked; in a superb effort, shipyard workmen labored 48 straight hours and, incredibly, refloated her on the 29th. *Saratoga* was in San Diego; she could not leave until June 1. *Wasp* was in the Atlantic. *Hornet's* air group lacked battle experience, but at least *Enterprise* was primed and ready.

In short, Admiral Nimitz had 3 carriers against 6 of the Japanese. Against Yamamoto's 3 fast super battleships (68,000 tons) and 8 other battleships, he had none. (Without sufficient air cover, Nimitz wisely kept our slow battleships in San Francisco; our fast dreadnaughts were in the Atlantic.) Against 16 enemy cruisers, he had 9; against 45 destroyers he had only 15. Helping Nimitz somewhat were the Navy, Marine, and Army fighters and bombers on Midway Island.

On June 3 a PBY sighted the Japanese force 700 miles from Midway, almost at the exact spot pinpointed by Intelligence. That afternoon 9 B-17's bombed the carriers, didn't score a hit, but came home with reports of "terrific damage to the enemy." At midnight 3 black PBY-5A's found the Japanese by radar,

lumbered in at minimum altitude, and hit a tanker with a torpedo.

At 5:34 A.M., on the 4th, a PBY sounded the long-awaited warning of "Many enemy planes heading Midway." In this first phase of the battle the Japanese Zeros literally slaughtered Marine pilots in Wildcats and old Buffaloes, and the bombers damaged heavily the Midway installations. Of 24 Marine fighters, 14 went down.

From Midway, 4 Army B-26's went out to hit the Japanese fleet; Zeros cut down 2. Six Navy TBF's tried; 5 fell burning into the sea. A force of 28 Marine SBD and SB2U dive bombers then tried. Results: 12 planes shot down, 5 heavily damaged. Fourteen B-17's tried again from 23,000 feet; all returned. Results: Not a single hit on the Japanese fleet; we had already lost 33 planes and their crews.

Hornet and *Enterprise* launched strikes at 0700, followed by *Yorktown* at 0840. *Hornet's* Torpedo Squadron 8— every man begged to make the strike although the 15 old TBD bombers lacked the gas to return to the carrier —attacked the main enemy force. *Every* plane went into the sea. Score: No hits. Soon the other torpedo planes reached the enemy, but of the total of

TBD Devastator (*above*) with torpedo en route to attack Japanese carriers.
TBD squadron (*below*) is in position on carrier deck for immediate take-off.

Part of the second attacking dive-bomber wave, two SBD Dauntless dive bombers (*above*) positioning to dive against carriers.

But Zero fighters
slaughter Navy planes

Brewster F2A Buffalo fighters (*above*), used by Marines to defend Midway Island, were slaughtered by superior Japanese Zero fighters. After the battle, embittered Marine survivors condemned their airplanes as "death traps," perhaps useful only as trainers.

Two Navy torpedo-bomber types that fought at Battle of Midway were Grumman TBF Avenger (*above*) and Douglas TBD Devastator (*left, returning to carrier*). This was combat debut for TBF; of the six airplanes that went out from Midway, Japanese fighters and flak blew five bombers out of the air. It was a tragic beginning for the airplane that became the Navy's standard torpedo bomber for the rest of the war, and that turned in spectacular achievements. The TBD, an offshoot of prewar service, just did not have the performance or stamina to withstand modern combat, and the planes were slaughtered without ever hitting a Japanese vessel. Had the TBD's, however, been armed with reliable, fast torpedoes, they might have enjoyed some success. But our torpedoes were so slow that Japanese carriers simply turned and outdistanced the missiles.

121

YORKTOWN takes torpedo, bomb hits: Sub attack dooms carrier

41 bombers, the Japanese shot down 35. And not one American plane scored a single hit!

The time was exactly 10:24 A.M., the fateful moment for the Battle of Midway. Zero fighters were right on the water, cutting to pieces our torpedo bombers. Flak guns were at maximum deflection, blasting away at the TBD's. At this moment the SBD Dauntless dive bombers of *Enterprise* and *Yorktown* appeared overhead—and history was made.

In perfect visibility three of the four Japanese carriers lay below. The pilots pushed over and screamed down, engines roaring, at terrific speed in almost vertical dives. The flak shifted suddenly and the Zeros swerved, but nothing could stop the plunging bombers. They started at 17,000 feet, streaked down to 2,500 to release their heavy bombs. Almost at once the entire battle was decided.

Soryu took direct hits with three 1,000-pound bombs, *Akagi* took two bombs, and *Kaga* reeled under four hits. They never took on any of their airborne planes, never launched any more. In minutes all three carriers were sheets of flame. That afternoon *Kaga* exploded and sank. U.S. submarine *Nautilus* caught the blazing *Soryu* and laced three tin fish into her side. *Akagi* burned all night and went down the next morning. All three carriers took their planes with them and most of their pilots, the hard core of skilled, experienced Japanese naval airmen; for this the Japanese suffered for the rest of the war.

Hiryu escaped undamaged, and we paid dearly for that. Surrounded by a powerful surface fleet, *Hiryu* sent her planes out in strikes; they hit heavily. *Yorktown* took three heavy bombs and two torpedoes. Burning, her engines dead, listing badly, she was abandoned. In an effort to save her the destroyer *Hammann* moved alongside;

on June 6 the Japanese submarine I-168 loosed an accurate torpedo salvo. Both *Hammann* and *Yorktown* went down.

The battle continued. . . . *Enterprise* SBD's caught *Hiryu*, smashed her with eight direct hits and left the fourth Japanese carrier a holocaust of flames before she went down. Other dive bombers sank the cruiser *Mikuma*, and heavily damaged the cruiser *Mogami* and two destroyers.

At battle's end we had lost *Yorktown*, *Hammann*, 132 planes, 307 officers and men. Japan suffered the staggering loss of 4 large carriers, 1 cruiser, 234 planes and 2,500 officers and men.

A handful of aviators in dive bombers had gained mastery of the air, and with it mastery of the sea as well. Midway was the most decisive battle of the Pacific war. Although bitter fighting lay ahead, the Japanese offensive had been fought to a standstill, and the tide of war had turned.

Crippled by bombs, *Yorktown* (*left*) limps along at highest possible speed when bombers race in; water geyser is from aerial torpedo strike. (*Above*) Fire detail fights flames. First abandoned, then reboarded, ship was taken in tow. Submarine attack doomed carrier.

COLD, WET FORGOTTEN WAR

Weather worse foe than enemy

The Japanese grand strategy to secure the Pacific and Asia, and to destroy the American fleet, had specific objectives related to a rigid timetable. If Japanese forces could move quickly and entrench themselves on islands the Americans needed for land-based airpower, and could destroy our carrier fleet—then the United States must fight a long, bloody, and terribly costly war. For the Japanese, who had pioneered in the use of the fast carrier task force, realized only too well that in the vast domain of the Pacific, land-based airpower could only be effective in conjunction with (1) a powerful military fleet to fight, and reduce the strength of, enemy forces, and (2) a logistic capability that itself could exist only on the basis of success of the first premise. Without the American Navy as a swiftly moving power, American land-based airpower would wither on the vine of its own logistics weaknesses, and the short range of its tactical aircraft.

Thus from the Japanese point of view, the thrust into New Guinea and the Solomons was but the first phase in their strategic offensive. Then would

Caught by fast-moving fog, PBY-5A Catalina amphibian, with depth charges still under its wings, makes an emergency landing.

Navigator aboard PBY *(left)* in Aleutians prepares to catch an anchor buoy on return from patrol flight. *(Right)* After blinding snowstorm and high winds had stopped all operations for two days, PBY-5A amphibian at Cold Bay, Alaska, is loaded with heavy bombs for long, dreary patrol mission. The ability of the Catalina to operate from land or water areas, and to fly long hours over 2,000 miles and more, made the PBY an airplane exceptionally well suited to the Aleutians struggle. The rugged structure and reliability of the machine saved many crews.

Lockheed PV-1 land-based patrol bomber of Squadron VB-136, flying off coast of Adak Islands. Navy brought PV-1's to area because of greater speed, heavier armament.

come the capture of Midway, destruction of the Navy in accomplishing this; and, as a side maneuver, the occupation of the Western Aleutians. These bases would establish the solid perimeter defense for the new empire, and simultaneously pose a serious threat both to Oahu and Australia.

While Nimitz wrestled with the problems facing him with the impending Battle of Midway, Intelligence informed him of the scheduled Japanese thrust into Alaskan waters. Naval forces in that theater were pitifully weak; 3 air stations, a few small surface vessels, and 10 PBY patrol bombers. The Army had fields at Kodiak, Cold Bay, and Umnak, and 50 bombers at Kodiak. To bolster this meager force, Nimitz assigned for Alaskan defense 5 cruisers, 14 destroyers, and 10 more PBY's—all that could be spared.

ALEUTIANS BECAME POWER VACUUM

The Aleutians have what can only be described as miserable, stinking weather—rain, snow, mist, or a low overcast, can be expected 365 days a year. The PBY's and Army bombers faced insurmountable problems in the bleak and hazardous weather, and sea patrol was an unrewarding hit-or-miss proposition. Consequently, the Japanese force of two light carriers, *Junyo* and *Ryujo*, slipped by our search planes, eluded the picket boats, and

launched their planes. They struck hard at Dutch Harbor, losing only 8 planes to Army fighters in two days.

Screened by this initial success, Japanese forces landed simultaneously on June 7 at Attu and Kiska. Both were undefended. This was the beginning of the Japanese occupation of the Aleutians: a nine-month phase of bitter, dreary, wet and cold war. The Japanese slowly and tenaciously tried to build up airfields and keep what they had; the Americans, with the faithful old PBY's and Army bombers and fighters, just as slowly and tenaciously tried to blast them out.

It was a miserable war in which the Japanese were far down on the list of enemies, after ice, cold, snow, rain, mud, and all the other niceties of the Aleutian chain. We lost comparatively

few planes in combat, but suffered badly from the weather. An airfield that was in plain sight to bombers and fighters approaching from a distance, would be blotted out from sight in sixty seconds flat, remaining that way for hours while the planes gradually exhausted their fuel. Steel matting runways became inundated with mud and water, and the planes that took off from these strips later found vital equipment inoperative because of the frozen slush.

Those men assigned to this bleak and forsaken part of the world knew a war of boredom, misery and frustration, punctuated infrequently by the sporadic Japanese attacks. But no matter how rare these strikes, a man was just as dead if he stood in the way of a bomb.

Naval air crews, like those of the Army fliers with whom they flew and fought, were largely forgotten by the public in their Aleutian outposts. The island chain held vital strategic importance, but neither the Japanese nor Americans could overcome weather problems to carry out full-scale campaigns.

126

Planes were kept in constant readiness (*above*). Upon return from long patrol mission, this PBY crew at Attu refuels their bomber.

Heavily clothed for protection (*below*) from wind, snow, and cold, crewmen check PBY's tied down in 80-mph gale at Adak.

SUB KILLERS—THEN
INVASION OF NORTH

H.M. Honsaker, PBY turret gunner on patrol in Biscay Bay. PBY war was usually quiet, monotonous, but not for one Catalina of Squadron VP-84. In 1943, when the PBY was escorting a British convoy off the coast of Africa, a four-engine FW-200K bomber began a bomb run against the ships. Badly outmatched in speed, armament, and maneuverability, the PBY pilot ran for the German plane on a collision course, with every gun blazing. Three times the Focke-Wulf started its attack; three times the PBY charged; three times the German broke off. Wounded and burning, the attacking bomber turned tail, and fled.

AFRICA

Silent, deadly war

While the Navy in the Pacific stopped the Japanese and began a limited offensive, our Atlantic Naval forces fought a bitter, losing war with Hitler's submarines. In 1942 the Germans were sinking merchant ships at the rate of nearly 3 a day; during this period 8,000,000 tons of Allied shipping plunged to the bottom, while only 17 sub kills were made by U.S. forces. Of these, 9 were made by Navy planes. Fearing air patrols, German subs dove at the sight of aircraft, and the wolf packs avoided like the plague areas of air coverage. Subs moved into U.S. coastal waters early in 1942, but when air patrols and a coastal convoy system made things too hot for them, they turned south and made the Caribbean a shipping graveyard. Eight air wings of four patrol squadrons each were used by the Navy in this monotonous war, where results were measured only in shipping statistics. Although kills were few, the number of merchant ships sunk in the Eastern Sea Frontier diminished from a high of 23 in April, 1942, to zero in August. Much of the credit for this positive change in statistics went to fliers based from Argentia in Newfoundland, to Jacksonville, Florida. The Navy hastened the conversion of escort carriers to cover convoys in mid-ocean, but, paradoxically, these were to prove themselves first in the invasion of North Africa, when ship-based air support for U.S. landing forces was a primary requirement. After this operation in November, 1942, the escort carriers were "turned loose" against the subs, and hunter-killer operations were developed, and practiced in earnest. But sub-hunting was a job for all types of planes, from the single-engine OS2U Kingfishers, to the four-engine PB4Y Privateers that operated in the Bay of Biscay in defiance of German fighter patrols.

Hookmen rush (*above*) to retrieve bridle of TBF Avenger which has just been catapulted from deck of USS *Santee*, operating in the North Atlantic on antisub patrol. All pictures on this page were taken aboard *Santee*.

Maintenance crewman (*left*) works on TBF torpedo bomber. As sub killers, TBF's carried depth charges instead of torpedoes; great load-carrying ability of the big Grumman plus good endurance made it deadly for submarines.

Preparing F4F Wildcat fighters (*above*) for take-off from *Santee* in invasion of North Africa, November, 1942. *Santee* became famous for Atlantic duties; provided air support in North Africa, destroyed German blockade runners, and rang up steady victories against German subs in Atlantic.

TBF Avenger being raised to *Santee* flight deck on forward elevator (*below*). Much of the escort carrier's success was due to close teamwork between F4F fighters and TBF bombers. *Santee* planes were among first equipped with *Fido* torpedoes, which homed on German subs despite evasive actions.

Deck spotter (*above*) on *Santee* in November, 1943, as the carrier prepared to launch convoy patrol TBF's. Escort carriers operated with convoys and hunted submarines in killer task forces.

131

Baby carriers bring war to enemy

The first escort carrier to engage in antisubmarine warfare in the North Atlantic was the *Bogue*, which began operations in March, 1943. Escort carriers operated as the center of a small independent task group; this type of force was extremely effective in breaking up U-boat wolf pack attacks. In all, the escort-carrier groups sank 36 German submarines; techniques developed in the Atlantic formed the basis of all future antisubmarine warfare.

F4F Wildcat fighter (*above*) takes off into dusk for early evening patrol. (*Below*) F4F with depth charges poised for morning take-off.

Her fighters and bombers (*left*) out on patrol, escort carrier waits for their return.

Carrier, shore-based planes and blimps turn sea into sub grave

Antisubmarine operations called for every weapon available to break the crippling German U-boat offensive, which reached its peak with a force of 300 subs in commission, many of them operating in the dreaded wolf packs. The Navy for its antisub campaign used everything from single-engine observation planes and fighters to its four-engine bombers, and worked closely with the Army Air Forces in the campaign to push the subs back from the approaches to the eastern United States, and from the Gulf of Mexico. As blimps developed in performance, they played an increasingly important role in long endurance flights over convoys—and no convoy protected for its full voyage by Navy blimps ever lost a ship to a submarine. Along the eastern U.S. coast, so intensive was the search for subs that even tiny private airplanes went out on patrol, armed with small bombs.

Late afternoon patrol (*above*) is ended by TBF coming in for landing on USS *Santee* in the North Atlantic. (*Below*) Ground crewmen help steady an OS2U Kingfisher, loaded with two depth charges, as it taxies in high wind at east-coast base. Kingfishers flew sub patrols in the worst winter weather.

Navy blimp, armed with depth charges (*above*), cruises over convoy in North Atlantic. (*Below*) The payoff. German U-boat caught in the surface is attacked with depth charges and heavy strafing by patrol bomber. On second run the submarine went down.

Flying boats, heavy bombers
flew long, weary sub missions

One of the Navy's greatest squadrons, which kept open the vital sea lanes at the peak of the German submarine campaign, was VP-84, flying the faithful, slow, cumbersome, and vulnerable PBY Catalina. But with this airplane VP-84 chalked up an astonishing record of achievement. Operating in conjunction with two Royal Air Force squadrons of Hudsons and Liberators, VP-84 served under operational control of RAF Coastal Command. When the U.S. squadron was relieved, one of the RAF pilots who had flown from the same base wrote: "No. 84 has co-operated with us from Reykjavik for 11 months, in which time it made 31 attacks and killed 5

[later assessments made it 6] U-boats, a really magnificent record for one squadron in Iceland. We see them and their old PBY's going with real regret." VP-84 served for 45 consecutive months. It patrolled the North and Middle Atlantic, served in the Caribbean, covered the approaches to the Panama Canal. The squadron flew in the far reaches of the Pacific from the Galápagos Islands to Northern California. VP-84 was cited "for extraordinary heroism in action against enemy forces in Atlantic waters." VP-84 was an outstanding squadron, but it was only representative of the patrol bombers that did such tremendous work during the war.

Maintenance crews (*left*) working on Martin PBM Mariner flying boats at Naval Air Station, Banana River, Florida, ready the planes for next day's sub missions. (*Right*) Consolidated PB4Y Privateer gave Navy a long-range, fast, heavily armed bomber for escort. PB4Y's carried 3 tons of explosives.

After patrol mission (*left*) at minimum altitude because of heavy storm clouds, PB4Y returns to England from Bay of Biscay flight. Operating from British Isles, American patrol bombers worked with RAF Coastal Command, co-ordinated closely all U-boat patrol missions.

Radar-equipped PBM's (*below*) gave the antisub flying-boat fleet a tremendous gain in seeking out German U-boats. After being pushed back from U.S. east coast, subs concentrated on Caribbean shipping. This PBM is in hangar at flying-boat base at San Juan.

F4F Wildcat (*right*) receives take-off signal from carrier off North African coast, November 8, 1942. Wildcats fought Curtiss P-36 Hawk fighters, much more maneuverable than the Grummans, and the French pilots—members of the famed Lafayette Escadrille—gave the inexperienced Navy fliers a hard time of it. Wildcat pilots tried to battle in individual dogfights, French remained in pairs and broke up the Grummans. Strafing runs by the F4F's were particularly devastating; one attack by 6 Wildcats set aflame 8 Douglas bombers and 3 Curtiss fighters. On first day we lost six pilots; one man was killed on strafing run when he dove into the ground.

Army P-40F Warhawk (*left*) fighters being delivered by USS *Ranger* to North Africa, January, 1943. Planes took off from *Ranger*, landed at Army fields. During invasion on November 8, 1942, auxiliary carrier *Chenango* carried 76 P-40's to operate from Port Lyautey airfield as soon as base was secured by troops. (*Below, left*) SOC catapult planes from U.S. warships flew gunnery direction missions, also strafed French troops, dropped depth charges on tanks and bombs on gun batteries. (*Below, right*) SBD dive bombers attacked French warships, gun emplacements, and fought off almost constant attacks by German subs.

TORCH—850 SHIPS INVADE NORTH AFRICA

Fleet is greatest armada in military history

Naval aviation fulfilled two major roles in 1942 in the Mediterranean-North Africa theater. In April, 1942, the beleaguered British island of Malta was in dire straits. Carrier *Wasp* went to the aid of the British Admiralty by making two "Missions to Malta"; on April 20 *Wasp* launched 47 Spitfires within flying distance of Malta, repeated the maneuver again on May 9. The reinforcements enabled the RAF to hold its own until the Allies won through in Africa.

The event that shook the world, however, was Operation Torch, a combined British-American assault on North Africa in November, 1942. This was the largest amphibious operation in history, carried out by a tremendous fleet involving some 850 vessels. The attack forces struck at Oran, Algiers, and Casablanca.

Available to the American operation was only one carrier, the faithful old *Ranger*, supplemented by four small auxiliary carriers converted from tankers. These were rushed to completion for the African landings, and actually sailed from Hampton Roads with the yard workmen still aboard!

The French struck at our F4F Wildcats and SBD dive bombers, plus some TBF's, with a numerically equal force of Dewoitine and P-36 fighters, plus DB-7 (A-20) attack bombers. One pilot of the "Red Ripper Squadron," "Windy" Shields, shot down two fighters and a bomber before four P-36's cut up his Wildcat. It was a wild battle on the first day; on the second the F4F pilots flew in pairs against the more experienced French fliers. "Chuck" August shot down three P-36 fighters in a mad scramble. But in three days it was over, and the French, who fought briefly but valiantly, capitulated.

NAVAL, MARINE AVIATION EXPLODES IN SIZE: TRAINING PROGRAM IS HARD-PRESSED T

High requirements for carrier pilots maintained

Pearl Harbor found the Navy with only 4,000 qualified combat pilots out of 6,000 fliers on hand. Immediately there existed a need for 30,000 pilots—per year—and the Naval aviator training program went into high gear. The cadet was wrung out in 26 weeks of pre-flight, then went into primary training and the famous N3N "Yellow Peril" biplanes. For 11 weeks, and later 15, he struggled through six stages of primary flying. If he managed to bridge the gap he moved to intermediate training; carrier pilots went into the SNJ Texan (SNJ student practices carrier landings, photo opposite), and multi-engine students into the Beech SNB. In these planes the student pilots had a taste of everything except advanced combat tactics. After 22 weeks of intermediate, the pilot was commissioned a reserve officer, and moved to operational training. Here he became accustomed to service planes, and learned to fly as a member of a combat team. He gained proficiency in carrier landings. And after assignment to a squadron, the pilot received still further training to prepare him for the life-or-death tactics of combat. By war's end Naval aviation had grown to a powerful force of 60,747 pilots (there were 10,049 Marine pilots) and 41,000 planes of all types. The 1940 force of 7,772 enlisted technicians mushroomed to 32,827 ground officers and 343,950 enlisted ratings. For sheer combat power, Naval aviation was second to none.

EET PILOT DEMAND

End of a long, hard day (*below*) of training; SNC-1 trainers parked for the night at Corpus Christi, Texas. Combat records sustained the Navy's basic philosophy that pilots should be competent officers as well as skilled pilots, that quality should come first, and that Navy teamwork was essential. Many times during the war the Navy was faced with the temptation to cut requirements to meet the critical quotas for pilots; this was never done, however, and with results that paid off. By the end of the war, the ratio of Japanese plane losses to our Naval planes was six to one, with campaign scores running as high as 1,796 enemy planes compared to 120 of all types of Navy's.

North American SNJ-4 Texan (*above*) on student solo flight. SNJ's were used for gunnery, bombing, rocket attack training.

Pilot-instructor at Kingsville Field, Naval Air Training Center, Corpus Christi, Texas, demonstrates to cadets in his charge the proper method of approaching an aerial target for gunnery training. All Naval and Marine pilots received gunnery, bombing training.

The two pictures on these pages represent the new trend in the Pacific air war that began 1942 . . . men on our carriers keeping the decks cleared for fast-moving action and (*right*) a swarm of torpedo-carrying Avengers on a grim hunt for the enemy fleet. The Battle of Midway unquestionably restored the balance of power in the Pacific that the Japanese had smashed from our grasp; now a new struggle—the invasion of Guadalcanal and a series of bloody engagements fought in the waters of the Solomons—placed that balance in serious jeopardy. For the six months from August, 1942, on, the U.S. and Japanese navies hammered at one another in wild and fearful fighting. We did not win all those battles, and although headlines back home did not reflect that thinking, we came to respect the Japanese ability to fight hard, swiftly, with skill, and with courage almost beyond belief. The Japanese Navy, for propaganda reasons derided in stateside newspapers, demanded our very best in combat, and the fact that we sustained our forces, and from that savage six months began to forge ahead, is only more to the credit of our seamen, Marines and soldiers, and our airmen. From August 23 to 25 we fought the Battle of the Eastern Solomons, indecisive in its conclusion but intense in terms of struggle. The enemy carrier *Ryujo* went down, but the *Enterprise* was critically damaged by three hits, one of seven occasions when the *Big E* was to be battered by the Japanese. Our position grew more precarious when a submarine on September 15 sent three torpedoes crashing into *Wasp*, and that valiant carrier burned, exploded, and sank. On October 26, in the Battle of Santa Cruz, our carrier planes mauled *Shokaku* and *Zuiho*, but *Hornet* was engulfed by a swarm of bombers and ripped to a hulk that finally went down. The war was not yet a year old, and we had now lost four great carriers—*Lexington*, *Yorktown*, *Wasp*, and *Hornet*, a calamitous blow to our rising hopes to strike back with increasing fury at the enemy. Through the Guadalcanal campaign we lost more ships than the Japanese and paid dearly in men's lives for what we gained. Both sides were so badly hurt that for a while operations actually decreased. But when new, fresh strength was gathered, it was clearly the U.S. Navy that went eagerly out to hunt.

THE HARD ROAD BACK

Offensive-defensive begins
Both sides suffer losses
"Hunting season" opens

A PLACE CALLED GUADALCANAL

The first strategic offensive of the United States in World War II was actually the *offensive-defensive* assault in the southern Solomons, known as Operation Watchtower. Its goal: to seize and occupy the islands of Tulagi and Guadalcanal. On August 7, 1942, the 1st Marine Division went ashore on Guadalcanal, seizing an airfield the Japanese were building in the strategic jungle island. Three heavy carriers maintained an umbrella of planes over the invasion, and despite superior Japanese naval forces in the area, remained to block efforts to throw us back into the sea. By nightfall of August 8 we were securely on Guadalcanal and Tulagi, but holding our positions became an extended, furious, and costly battle. Twelve days after the Marines were ashore, the first Marine planes landed on the airfield which was to become famous as Henderson Field; Army fighters and Navy bombers followed to give the Marines air cover.

In the second day of the invasion, however, we took it on the chin with our Naval forces. A Japanese cruiser force brazenly moved to point-blank range and sent four cruisers—three American and one Australian—to the bottom. After this, warships came down at night through the "Slot" and blasted our forces on Guadalcanal while the Tokyo Express—destroyers acting as troop transports—delivered Japanese reinforcements.

We had much to learn in those days. The Japanese had superior patrol bombers and torpedo bombers, and they were far more skillful in fighting at night. Until 40-mm guns were installed on our ships late in 1942, we were desperately in need of medium-range flak weapons to counter the Japanese pilots who streaked into point-blank range to deliver bombs and torpedoes. This was proven at Santa Cruz in October; guns such as these might have saved *Hornet*, which took a terrible beating from hits with three torpedoes, six bombs, and two suicide crashes on her deck. The new battleship *South Dakota* in the same battle, armed with these weapons, braved the worst of Japanese air attacks and blew 26 bombers out of the air.

The climax of the drawn-out, crippling campaign came on November 13–15, when the Japanese made their supreme effort to retake Guadalcanal. In the jungles the Marines and Army troops fought a savage hand-to-hand battle. At sea we reeled from the loss of two cruisers and seven destroyers; the Japanese staggered from the sinking of two battleships, one cruiser, three destroyers.

Eleven troop transports bound for Guadalcanal were caught by Marine, Navy, and Army planes, and in unremitting attacks our pilots sank or burned all eleven, inflicting terrible casualties on the Japanese. That closed the book on Guadalcanal. Six months to the day after our landing in the Solomons, the beaten, exhausted Japanese evacuated Guadalcanal.

Wildcat fighters (*left*) on Henderson Field, Guadalcanal. Marine and Navy pilots in Solomons campaign fought some of the outstanding pilots of Japanese Navy, including top-ranking aces Sakai, Nishizawa, Ota, and others, who flew Zeros to Guadalcanal from fighter bases at Lae.

Ace Joe Foss: 26 kills.

Wildcat fighters (*above*) at Guadalcanal bore brunt of air-to-air combat against Japanese, fighting Zeros, dive, torpedo, and level bombers. Chunky Grummans operated under primitive conditions, bore up with outstanding performance. Outclassed in maneuverability, speed, and climb by the Zeros, their superior construction paid off time and time again by bringing pilots home in airplanes shot to pieces. On January 15, 1943, Marine ace Joe Foss got 3 planes and ran his score up to 26. Three months later, Lt. J.E. Swett in an F4F in 15 minutes shot down 7 bombers, earning the 22-year-old pilot the Congressional Medal of Honor. (*Right*) Number 1 ship-killer of Solomons campaign was faithful SBD; crew discusses results of raid. (*Below*) Betty pilots attacking U.S. troop transports.

SBD Dauntless prepares to swing into dive-bombing attack against Japanese installations on Wake Island during raid of October 5, 1943. SBD's after occupation of Guadalcanal carried load of Navy bomb strikes in New Georgia, New Guinea, Russell Islands, Bougainville, and other Solomons islands. Now attacks on Rabaul began in earnest.

F6F Hellcat (*above*) coming in for landing aboard USS *Yorktown*. (*Right*) *Enterprise* throws up a wall of flak in Battle of Santa Cruz, October 26, 1942. *Big E* took three hits, but survived to fight again.

ANGRY, BLACK SKIES

After Guadalcanal, we concentrated on the rest of the Solomons, fighting our way onto the Russell Islands, New Georgia, and Bougainville. Two battles fought in the Kula Gulf in February, 1943, closed the Japanese route to the South Pacific.

We had begun the long road back. In the Pacific—with new *Essex*-class carriers of 33,000 tons and smaller *Independence*-class carriers of 10,000 tons, with fast new battleships, cruisers, destroyers, and a vast flotilla of amphibious craft—the Navy began to drive up from the south to the heart of the enemy. Our strategy presupposed that if superior force could be brought to bear upon the Japanese from the sea, any point could be taken and held. If the aircraft within range of that same point were once destroyed,

then land-based planes could keep all enemy bases within range neutralized. Then, if the U.S. fleet maintained itself in the forward area, the enemy could neither relieve nor recover his garrisons except by fleet action—and exposure to our expanding Naval air force, now equipped with superb new airplanes, Grumman F6F Hellcats and Vought F4U Corsairs among them. Carriers in 1943 operated in task groups of three or four, and they formed the spearhead of the tortuous route to Tokyo.

There were many setbacks, and an appalling loss of life and matériel. But the significant fact is that, backed by the greatest sea-air power in history, the plan succeeded. The first battle of this new offensive was the assault upon the Gilbert Islands on

November 20, 1943. Fighters and bombers from eleven fast carriers softened up the atoll of Betio. Then eight escort carriers gave the amphibious forces a constant air support. Losses in men were formidable, but the atoll was taken, and in the following months bloody fighting wrested from the Japanese, Kwajalein, Majuro and Eniwetok. Three fast carrier groups plunged through the Central Pacific, virtually neutralized the "impregnable fortress" of Truk, and destroyed hundreds of Japanese planes. And no one would ever forget Tarawa in the Gilberts, where the Marines crammed into 70 hours an entire war. And at Makin, the Navy sadly reported the loss in battle of Butch O'Hare, who once single-handedly saved the old aircraft carrier *Lexington*.

DYING MEN, DYING SHIPS

The blazing aircraft carrier in the above picture is the *Wasp*, famed for her delivery of 94 Spitfires to the island of Malta in the Mediterranean in 1942 which helped save the British fortress. *Wasp's* Pacific career was short; on September 15, 1942, in the Solomons, a Japanese submarine put three torpedoes into her side. Internal fires raged out of control, and *Wasp* was through. All of the four large carriers lost by the Navy—*Lexington, Yorktown, Wasp,* and *Hornet*—went down in 1942, before new task group tactics were devised. During the war, out of 110 U.S. carriers of all types, only 11 were lost; in addition to the four named, the 10,000-ton *Princeton* sank during the Battle for Leyte Gulf. Our escort carriers carried no armor; one was torpedoed in the Atlantic, suicide planes sank three, naval gunfire one, and a submarine broke the *Liscombe Bay* in half during the Gilberts campaign. It was the worst carrier loss ever suffered by the Navy—700 men went down with the ship.

Crewmen of USS Saratoga (*above*) lift gunner Kenneth Bratton out of TBF turret; Bratton was wounded in strike against Rabaul on November 5, 1943. (*Below*) Another TBF lands aboard USS *York-town* (CV-10; second carrier to carry the name) after strike. Rabaul was hit again on November 11 for second attack in a week. In this raid, pilots from *Bunker Hill* introduced new SB2C Helldiver.

HUNTING SEASON OPENS

We were now ready to begin the kill . . . and this deck signal officer was a perfect representation to all pilots: "*Go!* The hunting season is open. . . ." New fighters and bombers, new carriers, vastly improved antiaircraft, combat operation, fire-fighting techniques and procedures gave the Navy its eagerly sought vital qualitative edge in carrier warfare over the Japanese. Battle-wise, seeking retribution, the carrier task forces began a Pacific blood-bath.

On June 16, 1943, one of the war's most furious air battles was fought over Guadalcanal. In an attempt to smash our airpower and local sea forces, the Japanese attacked Guadalcanal with an armada of more than 60 bombers and 76 escorting Zero fighters. Every available Navy, Marine and Army fighter—about 100 planes in all—met the Japanese, and at a cost of 6 fighters lost, "went wild" in air combat. That day alone the Japanese lost 107 of their warplanes!

Fast action on carrier decks called for a lot of co-ordinated muscle power—as this photo shows. There are more than 90 men respotting this single F6F Hellcat fighter! Pilot (center foreground) walks away from his plane, tired from a mission in which Japanese hit his fighter several times with machine-gun bullets. On board USS *Yorktown,* December, 1943. (*Right*) Refueling superb F6F Hellcats aboard USS *Nassau* somewhere in the vast Pacific.

Nemesis of Japanese fighters (*left*), the Grumman F6F Hellcat was fast (390 mph), heavily armed (6.50-caliber guns, large ammunition load), and the most maneuverable American fighter built; Japanese aces said it was only U.S. fighter that could turn with the nimble Zero. (*Above*) SBD dive-bomber pilot gives last-minute instructions to his plane captain before taking off from *Yorktown* for attack against enemy islands. (*Below*) TBF from *Yorktown* circles *Marcus*, burning fiercely, after slashing carrier raids in September.

F4U Corsair snagged to a halt (*above*) by arresting cable aboard USS *Charger*. Corsairs first saw action on February 13, 1943, in land-based raid against Bougainville. Most Japanese considered Corsair most effective of all American fighters. F4U had six guns, outclimbed Zero, and exceeded 400 mph. (*Below*) F6F Hellcat takes off past native children.

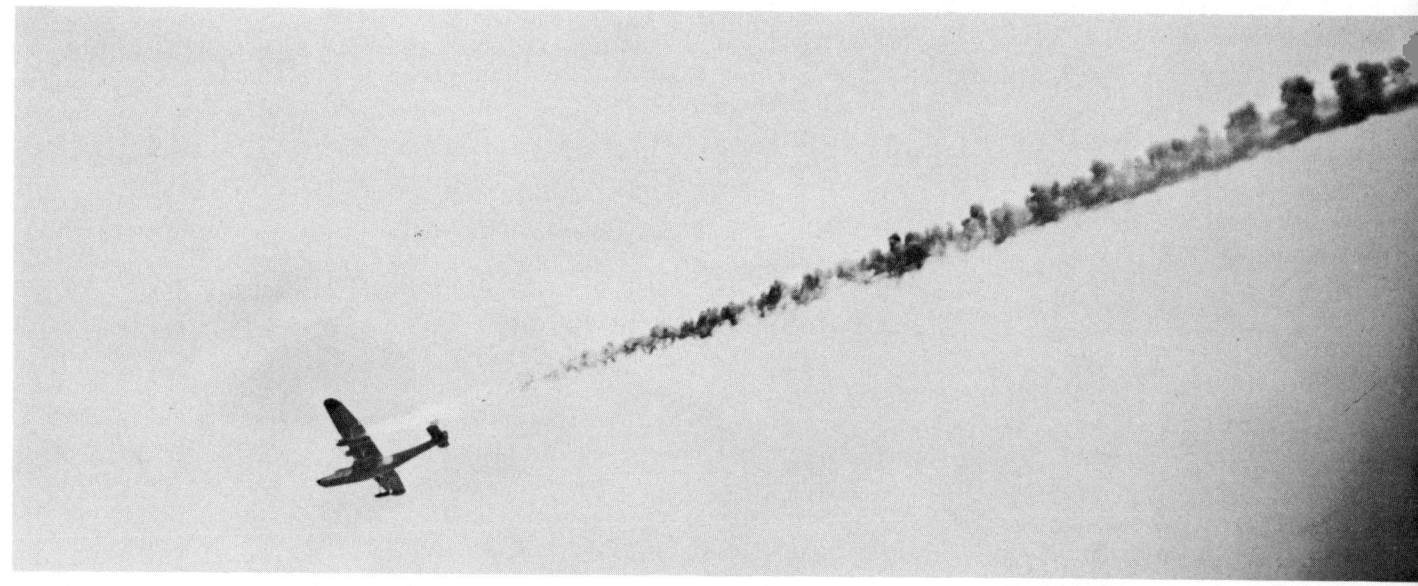

Even the heavy patrol bombers got into the act. In August, 1943, a Consolidated PB2Y-3 Coronado flying boat, flown by Lt. C.J. Alley of Squadron VB-104, encountered a Japanese Mavis four-engine flying boat in South Pacific. Despite heavy Mavis armament of guns and cannon, PB2Y-3 closed in to point-blank range, set aflame Mavis wing tanks.

These eleven Hellcat pilots have good reason to shout and cheer. Their jubilation is result of furious air battle in which they intercepted 20 Zero fighters heading for Tarawa (November, 1943). In the wild melee that followed diving attack by the Hellcats, the eleven pilots scattered the Japanese formation. Lt. Eugene R. Hawks alone flamed five Zero fighters in less than five minutes to become an ace, while the rest of his teammates shot another twelve Zeros out of the sky. Seventeen out of twenty—without losing a single Hellcat fighter; no wonder the "Pistol Packin' Airedales" pictured here were happy!

MURDERERS' ROW

Carriers smash inner shell:
Bring war to Japan's doorstep

It was in the Marshalls that the Navy demonstrated most dramatically its new mastery of combining air, surface, submarine, and ground forces to project massive fighting power across the seas. The invasion of the Marshalls—Kwajalein, the Majuro atolls, and Eniwetok—was similar to the Gilberts operation, but was executed with greater precision and effectiveness. Six large, fast carriers and 6 light carriers of the *Independence* class were organized into four groups and given the name of Task Force 58; accompanying them were 8 fast battleships, 6 cruisers and 36 destroyers. On the evening of January 29, 1944, this powerful fleet started to blast the Marshalls; two days later, when the troops stormed ashore, there was not a single Japanese aircraft operational in the Marshalls. The fleet poured 15,000 tons of bombs and shells into the enemy defenses, and the saturation was so effective that the invasion became a model amphibious operation that achieved outstanding results at a low cost.

The final blow of the Marshalls campaign was executed by Task Force 58 in the Carolines on February 16 and 17, and later against Saipan in the Marianas. Truk was blasted into smoking ruins; Task Force 58, reorganized into two groups to smash at Guam, Saipan, Rota, and Tinian, demonstrated its defensive prowess when for thirteen consecutive hours the carriers fought off a determined enemy attack—and emerged untouched.

From here the carriers rampaged through the Pacific. A blow at the Palaus in March, 1944, cost the Japanese 28 cargo vessels sunk and another 18 damaged. Then came the Marianas, the acid test for the elaborate forces created for the Central Pacific campaign. These were large volcanic islands

Symbol of Navy's great striking power (*below*); USS *Ticonderoga* at anchor in Ulithi Harbor. (*Right*) In a dramatic photo, a Japanese cruiser maneuvers frantically in Manila Bay to escape a Helldiver attack. Hit minutes later, the warship exploded and sank quickly.

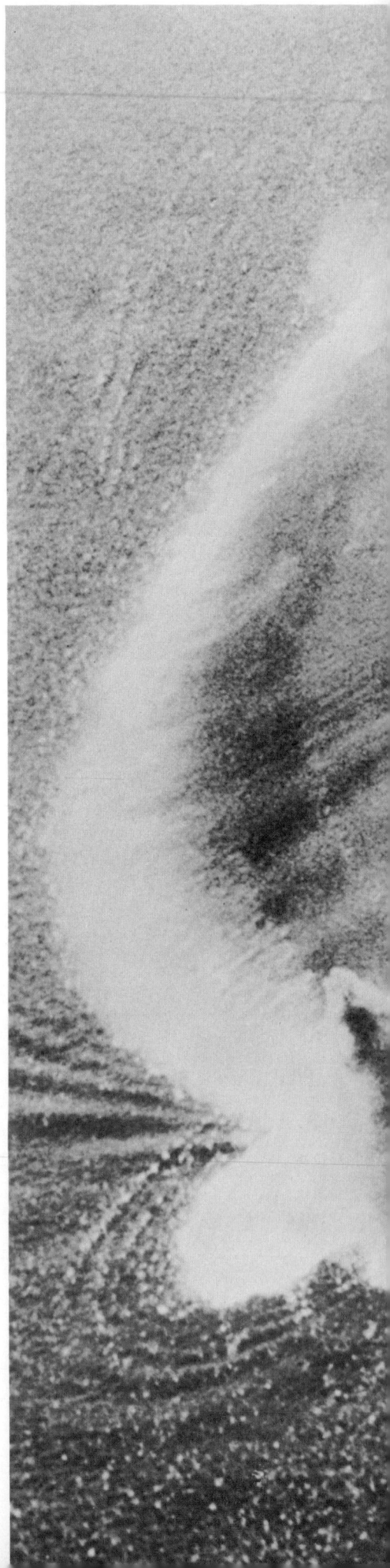

Hellcat fighters aboard the USS *Essex* (*above*) having their motors revved up for early morning take-off. F6F's virtually wiped out opposing Japanese fighter forces in Philippines, gave our bombers run of the skies.

Preparing for massive air strikes against Luzon in the Philippines; aviation ordnancemen load .50-caliber belts into wing of F6F Hellcat fighter (*above*) aboard USS *Lexington*. Enjoying a brief interlude between swift attacks against Japanese islands, deck crewmen (*below*) nap or just relax aboard *Hornet*, bound for Marianas.

Ordnance man dollies heavy depth charge down hangar deck of *Yorktown* (*above*) for loading into TBF Avenger. Avengers flew constant sub patrol around our carriers because of increased enemy underseas activity. *Liscombe Bay, Saratoga, Wasp* were among carriers hit. Later in war, TBF's carried antisub rockets.

158

Hellcat pilots rush to their planes aboard *Hornet* (*above*). Between September 9 and 24, 1944, Mitscher's carrier forces raged through Luzon and central part of Philippines. 800 Japanese planes were destroyed in the air and on the ground; 241 vessels were sunk. We lost 54 planes, but Task Force 58 was not damaged.

Deck crewmen aboard *Essex* stand by SB2C Helldivers (*above*) waiting for take-off orders. Powerful dive bombers carried 4 20-mm cannon and 2 .50-caliber machine guns in addition to bombs, became most feared of all Navy carrier bombers. F6F Hellcat fighter circles *Essex*-class carrier (*below*) before coming in to land, December, 1944.

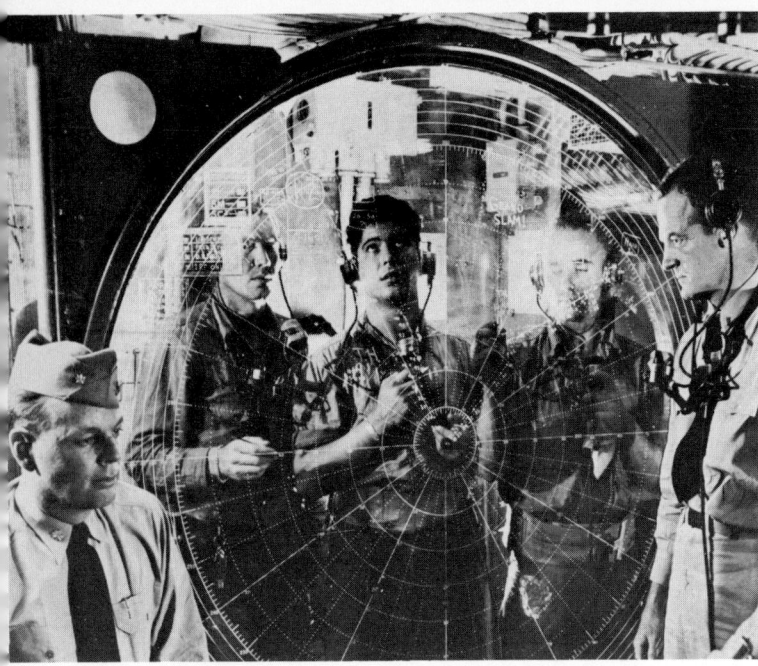

PACIFIC BECOMES NAVY LAKE

Plotting movement of friendly and Japanese aircraft, in Combat Intelligence Center of *Wasp* (CV-18). Accurate, rapid control of aircraft was vital to success of vast offensive missions. For the Philippines invasion, 800 vessels and 1,600 U.S. aircraft were used!

capable of sustaining prolonged enemy resistance. On June 11, 1944, Task Force 58 began to work over the Marianas, and also sent two task groups to neutralize the Bonin and Volcano Islands closer to Japan. The amphibious forces hit Saipan on June 15; four days later the Japanese made their supreme bid to smash our carriers. The tales of that day have become legendary, and Hellcat fighters raked Japanese airpower to a shambles. In what became famous as the "Marianas Turkey Shoot," 366 Japanese planes were shot out of the sky. The next night—to recover planes coming in low on gas, and in darkness—Admiral Marc Mitscher, in a display unprecedented for wartime, ordered every vessel of Task Force 58 to turn on all running lights, searchlights, and to fire star shells to guide the planes home. Many landed in glides, without a drop of fuel.

By June 20, enemy airpower was broken. The total effect of the carrier raids cost the Imperial fleet 1,500 skilled pilots, the pick of their naval aviation. They had tried desperately but without success to stop our fleet, and now Japan faced the prospect of having its cities gutted by a storm of B-29's. Their inner defenses were split open; a vital southward communications link was crushed.

In the late summer of 1944 the forces of Nimitz and MacArthur converged upon the Philippines. The Palaus and Morotai, in the Halmaheras, became stepping stones to the islands from which we had once been thrown out. In October, Task Force 38 bombed, strafed, rocketed Japanese positions in a severe battering. Sixteen escort carriers gave the Naval air force battle air superiority, and troops stormed ashore at Leyte. Six days later, contact was made with the Japanese fleet, and precipitated the massive sea fight, the Battle for Leyte Gulf. In the end, the Japanese were dealt a crippling defeat. The road northward now lay wide open.

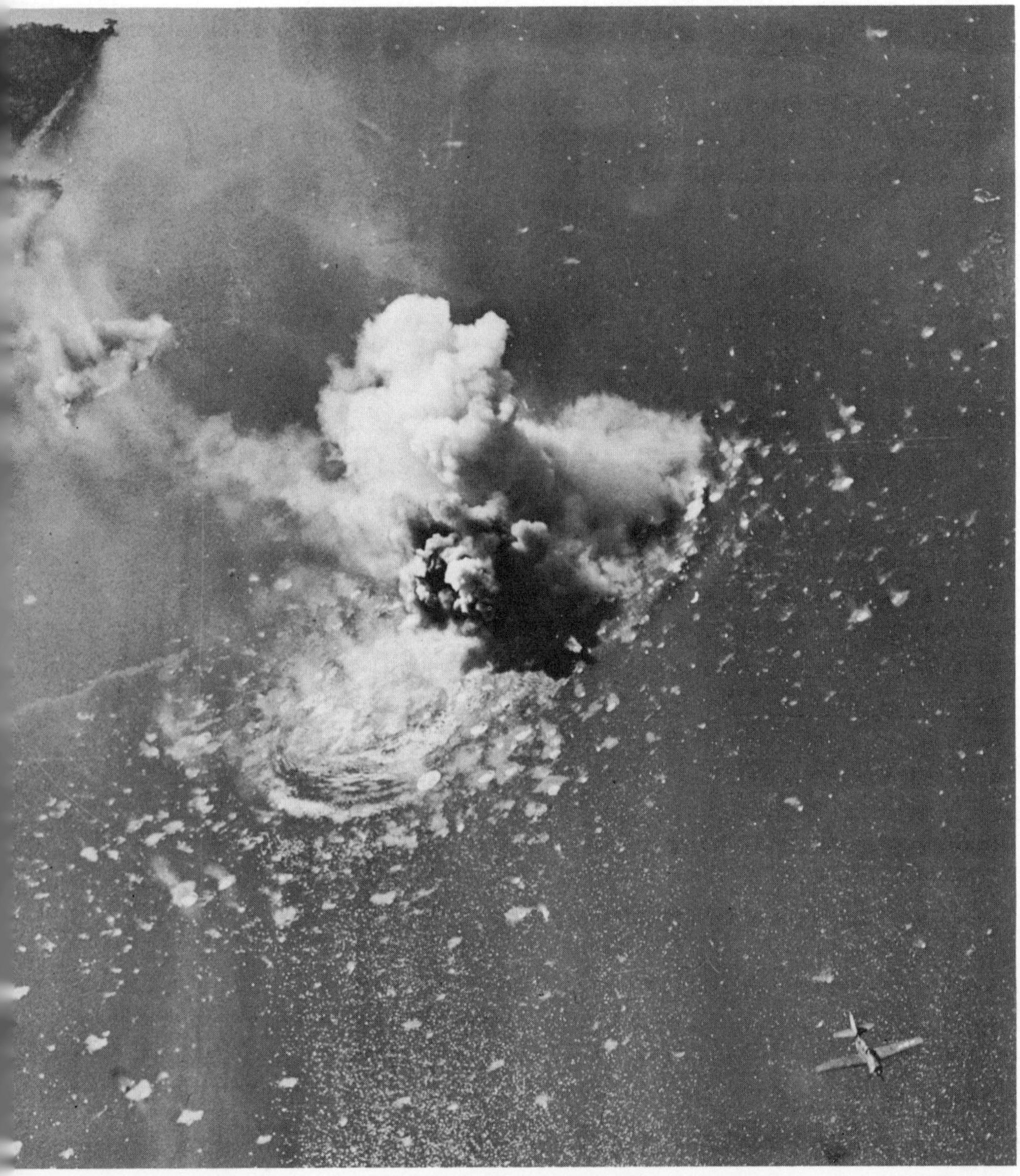

Smashing Japanese attempts to reinforce their troops in Philippines, Helldiver (*left*) explodes Japanese transport off coast of Marinduque Island, south of Luzon. Bow of broken transport protrudes from smoke cloud; at the far left, another transport has just taken a direct hit from another SB2C.

Helldiver finishes antisubmarine patrol, swings in for landing aboard *Intrepid* (*above*). Helldivers stormed against Japanese shipping, and in Philippines, were responsible for greatest damage and number of ships sunk. Its heavy bomb load and high speed made the SB2 Helldiver deadly.

Heavy F4U Corsair fighter whistles in for landing aboard USS *Essex* (*right*) after strike on Luzon. Between October 12 and 16, 1944, when Navy attacked Formosa in support of Luzon operation, more than 1,000 planes engaged in fierce air fighting, 400 of them in vicinity of U.S. carriers. Corsairs were effective against new Japanese fighters.

161

Plane spotter in action aboard *Yorktown*, off Saipan (*above*). SB2C pilot in damaged airplane smashed into carrier bow (*right*) on landing. Plane disintegrated, pilot escaped unhurt. Action was the same in Europe (*below*); on deck of *Tulagi*, off southern France.

Deck crews needed fleet feet

When the carriers moved their warplanes, loaded with potential hell in the form of high-octane fuel, bombs, ammunition, rockets, whirling propellers, it behooved the deck crews to be alert, to move *fast* if necessary. LSO's, deck spotters, plane handlers, ordnancemen and others received little publicity, but their skill and devotion to duty provided the backbone for carrier operations.

Arresting gear failed to snag hook of F4F Wildcat; fighter careened down deck, smashed into parked aircraft. Deck crewmen are tossed like tenpins (*above*) as F4F whips around on one wheel and plunges out of control into parked planes.

Ensign P.L. Ferber piloting Vought OS2U Kingfisher (*above*) over invasion force moving toward island of Anguar, five miles southwest of Peleliu, September 17, 1944. Kingfishers and other catapult planes remained over invasion areas to direct ship's gunfire.

Douglas R5D Skymaster of Naval Air Transport Service (*below*) over Golden Gate Bridge, bound for Pacific Islands. Four-engine transports carried vital priority cargo to battle areas, flew thousands of badly wounded troops and seamen back to the States.

Black sheep and a new rulebook

WW II began for the Marines' air arm in devastating fashion; Ewa air station, 10 miles west of Pearl Harbor, was torn to pieces on December 7, 1941. Of 48 Marine planes in the Hawaiian Islands, 47 were destroyed, but the leathernecks made a comeback that was unparalleled in the history of the war. On August 8, 1944, the last Marine kill of the war brought their score to 2,355 planes shot down. The list of Marine aces was impressive—121 pilots had shot down five or more Japanese planes apiece.

2nd Marine Air Wing Corsair (*above*), taking off from airfield only 1,500 yards from bitterly contested Five Sisters Peak on Peleliu, still has wheels down as napalm drops on dug-in troops.

In one of war's strangest incidents, POW Lt. Minoru Wada voluntarily led Marine force of PBJ Mitchells and F4U Corsairs (*above*) to 100th Japanese Division Headquarters, where Marine force almost wiped out target with fragmentation bombs, napalm, rockets, and heavy strafing. Marine Sgt. C.T. Imai acted as interpreter for Major M.H. Jordan, who led the attack. (*Right*) Marine PBJ bombers being serviced just off airstrip at Espiritu Santo. Combat debut for PBJ (AAF B-25) was March 15, 1944, when USMC Squadron VMB-413 attacked Rabaul. PBJ was used by Marines against Japanese ground positions, as well as their shipping.

In the F4U Corsair (Squadron VF-17 F4U lands at Bougainville; *above*) the Marines found just what they had been looking for— a fighter faster than anything the Japanese had, that could climb 3,000 feet per minute, had twice the range of the older F4F Wild-cat, and that was superbly rugged. It was the fighter with which the Marines wrote history after its combat debut on February 13, 1943. In the air war over the Solomons and Rabaul, Marine fliers in aerial combat shot down 1,520 of the 2,500 planes Japan lost.

Corsair taxiing out to active runway at Bougainville (*left*); crewman on wing guides pilot along taxiway. In Pacific war, from land bases and carriers, Corsairs shot down 2,-140 Japanese planes, flew a total of 64,051 combat sorties. Most unusual kill with a Corsair went without question to Lt. R.R. Klingman. Over Okinawa he was one of four F4U pilots who chased a Japanese photographic plane to 38,000 feet. Closing to within 50 feet of the Nick, Klingman discovered his guns were frozen. The Marine pilot closed to ramming distance, sawed with his propeller through rudder and into rear gunner's cockpit. Klingman made three "propeller passes," sawed off the right stabilizer and rudder, watched the Japanese plane spin in.

"Scratch another meatball"—Saipan, June 18, 1944.

DEFENDING THE CARRIERS

The Battle for Leyte Gulf, which raged October 23–26, 1944, was the greatest naval engagement of all time. It was actually a series of three separate spectacular engagements: Surigao Strait, Samar, and Cape Engaño, all taking place at the same time. In operations that included every type of ship from PT boats to giant battleships (the Japanese lost the 68,000-ton battleship *Musashi* to intense attack by Helldivers and Avengers), Naval aviation harassed the approaching enemy and disposed of his carrier force while it was moving from the Empire to do battle in the Philippines.

One clear pattern emerged from these great conflicts—our carriers were the enemy's primary target, and the Navy went to every effort to assure that these vital ships were protected. Yet the swarms of Japanese planes meant that some would always get through, and there was always the threat of submarines, and elements of the powerful surface fleet breaking free. On October 24, a bomb hit the light carrier *Princeton*, started intense flames among parked aircraft and then set off ammunition stores; the blazing wreck was sunk by one of our destroyers. Japanese heavy warships in Leyte Gulf smashed and sank the escort carrier *Gambier Bay*, badly damaged the *Kalinin Bay* (15 hits) and *Fanshaw Bay* (4 hits).

Then came a dreaded addition to the Pacific war—deliberate crashes into our ships. The kamikaze—crude but lethal. In November, 1944, five of our carriers in the Manila area were struck. On January 4, 1945, *Ommaney Bay* suffered a kamikaze hit, burned and exploded, and went down.

Riddled by antiaircraft fire, enemy bomber whirls crazily (*above*) over USS *Yorktown* during attack against Truk in 1944. Left gear leg has dropped free, right wing and fuselage are blazing. This was second Jill bomber shot down in seconds. (*Below*) Crewmen on a carrier raiding Saipan and Tinian, February, 1944, cheer happily as Japanese bomber making attack on their ship goes down, crashing into sea only yards away.

Burning from direct hits, Japanese dive bomber (*above*) roars in against USS *Essex* in Philippines area, November 25, 1944. Seconds later, as photographed from USS *Ticonderoga*, the bomber crashes on the *Essex* flight deck, forward of number 2 elevator (*below*); 15 men were killed and 44 wounded; despite damage, *Essex* continued operations.

Flying through "impenetrable wall" of flak, Kate torpedo bomber (*above*) races for the USS *Yorktown.* Bomber burned, crashed into sea without hitting carrier. (*Below*)Tail of twin-engine Betty bomber juts from sea as airplane's fuel tanks spill flaming gas on water. Japanese pilots often attacked U.S. carriers, while flying only a few feet above water.

CARRIER PLANES RAMPAGE ACROSS PACIFIC, SMASH AT JAPAN

Navy is master of Pacific but kamikazes take fearful toll of U.S. ships

In the Battle for Leyte Gulf, the Japanese lost 4 carriers, 3 battleships, 8 cruisers, and 9 destroyers. In subsequent battles, what remained of the Japanese fleet was hunted down, smashed with bombs and torpedoes, and sent to the bottom. With Naval responsibility in the Philippines out of the way, support was given to the invasion of Iwo Jima. On February 10, 1945, the single most powerful force of the war assembled and moved toward Tokyo. Eleven large and 5 light carriers, with 1,200 aircraft aboard, 8 battleships, 17 cruisers, and 81 destroyers rampaged off the main island of Honshu, smashing airfields and factories. The Navy then concentrated on Okinawa and Kyushu, and the Japanese faced a fleet almost beyond comprehension in size. More than 1,200 ships of all types were involved. In addition to Task Force 58, which operated between Okinawa and Kyushu, more powerful than the Japanese Navy at its peak, there were 12 to 17 escort carriers to the southeast, and a fast and powerful British force of 4 fleet carriers, 1 battleship, 6 cruisers, and 18 destroyers, positioned to cut off attacks from Formosa. Against so overwhelming an aerial and surface armada, not even the hordes of suicide planes could avail Japan. Right to her doorstep, the Pacific had become a Navy lake.

Helldiver pilot on *Lexington* (*left*) gets take-off signal. Bombers and fighters teamed up from carriers to wreck Japanese airpower; in last 3 months of 1944 Navy destroyed 3,-800 enemy planes in air and on ground.

On April 6, 1945, in a desperate attempt to smash the U.S. invasion fleet off Okinawa, the 68,000-ton battleship *Yamato* (sister ship to the *Musashi*) sortied from the Inland Sea, accompanied by a cruiser and eight destroyers. A submarine shadowed the world's greatest battleship, radioing position reports to our carriers. The following morning a swarm of Helldivers and Avengers engulfed the *Yamato* in a wave of fire. Eight heavy bombs crashed into her decks and burst within her hull; eight torpedoes blew open her sides. The *Yamato* exploded violently (*above*) and went down. But the carrier planes drew more blood. The cruiser and four destroyers also went to the bottom of the sea.

171

Corsair returns to USS *Franklin;* deckman directs pilot up flight deck as he folds wings (*above*). The Corsair flew sustained attack missions to support troops on Okinawa, firing bullets and rockets, dropping napalm and bombs to dig die-hard Japanese from caves.

Murderers' Row—powerful carriers of U.S. Pacific fleet in Ulithi Atoll before leaving for Japanese waters. Pictured below are the *Wasp* (CVA-18), *Yorktown* (CVA-10), *Hornet* (CVA-12), *Hancock* (CVA-19) *Ticonderoga* (CVA-14), and *Lexington* (CVA-16), far left.

In January, 1945, Task Force 38 made a fast run through Luzon Strait to burst out in South China Sea, an area rimmed with bases containing 1,000 Japanese warplanes. On January 12, Helldivers (*above*) and other bombers with fighter escorts covered 450 miles of the Indochina coast, raiding shipping, airfields.

Helldiver of Task Force 38 leaves behind two Japanese tankers burning from group attack. In all-day strikes, Navy sank 40 warships, tankers, merchant ships.

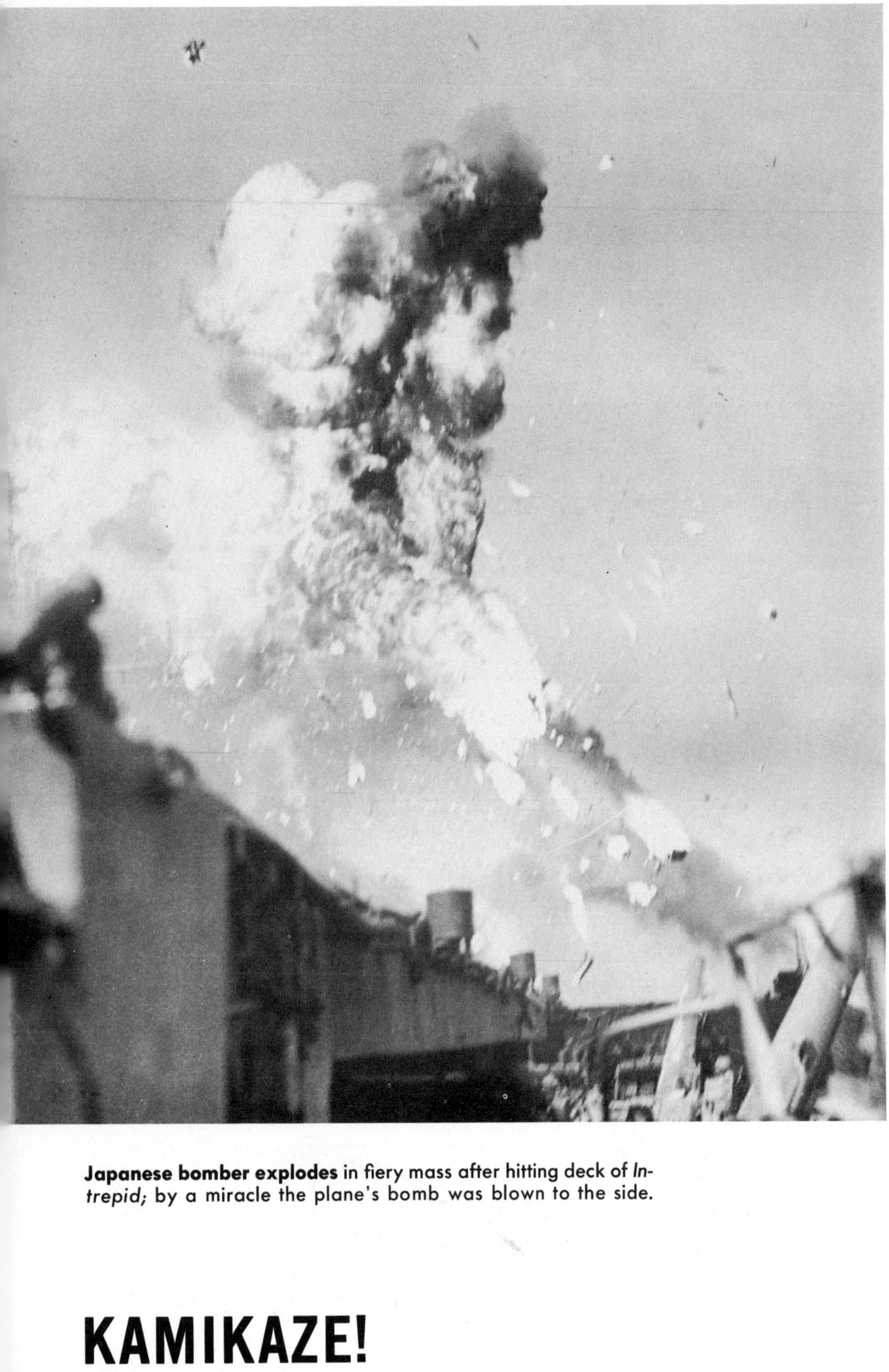

The only enemy aerial reaction of consequence to the Iwo Jima invasion came on February 21, when a dusk raid from Japan reached the support carrier force. Within three minutes, *Saratoga* was burning from four kamikazes and three bombs, but withdrew under her own power. Two suicide planes smashed into the escort carrier *Bismarck Sea*; she sank quickly. On March 19, the Japanese sharpened their aim. Off the coast of Kyushu, two heavy bombs exploded with devastating effect on *Franklin*, setting ablaze planes on the deck; only heroic efforts saved the carrier. The new *Wasp* took a severe hit, and withdrew from battle. In our surface defense against the swarming, determined Japanese planes, our own ships hit *Enterprise* so badly she had to return to Ulithi.

But it was Task Force 58, in Okinawan waters on April 6 that really brought the enemy out in full suicide strength. Led by skilled veterans in 420-mph fighters, hundreds of planes —everything from rocket-powered winged bombs to trainers—descended on our fleet. Hundreds were shot down, but they were so numerous that many got through to their targets. When the Okinawa campaign ended on June 21, 36 of our ships had been sunk by air attack, and we had lost 763 planes in the battle. Another 368 vessels were damaged, and personnel losses aboard ship were staggering— 4,907 killed, 4,824 wounded. It was the worst three-month period in the Navy's history.

Japanese bomber explodes in fiery mass after hitting deck of *Intrepid;* by a miracle the plane's bomb was blown to the side.

KAMIKAZE!
Suicide planes wreak bloody havoc

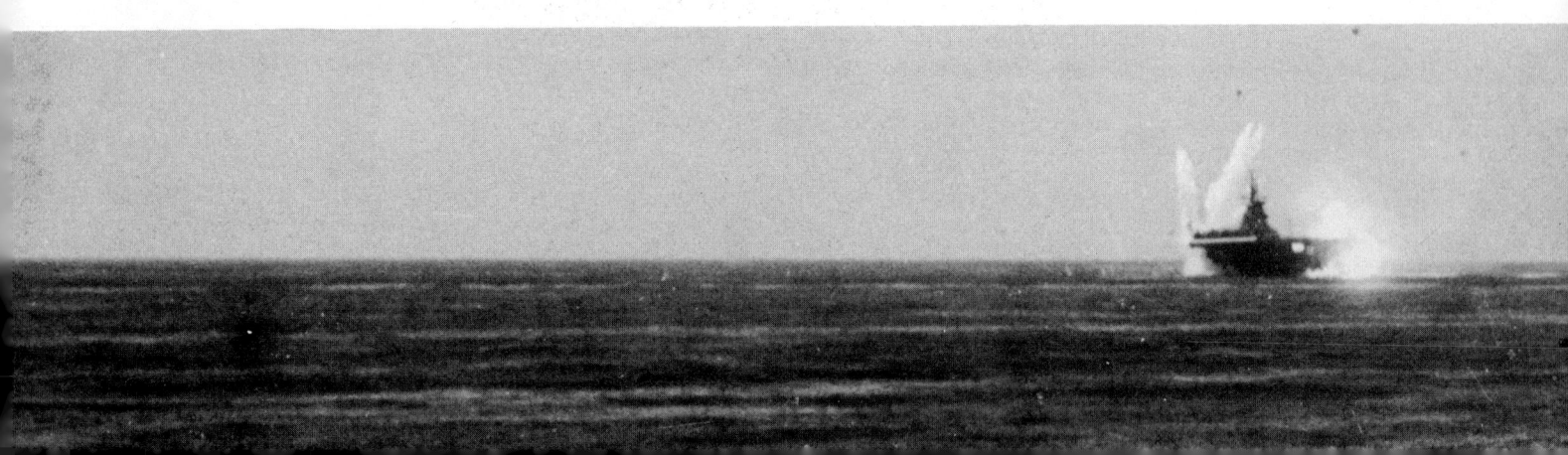

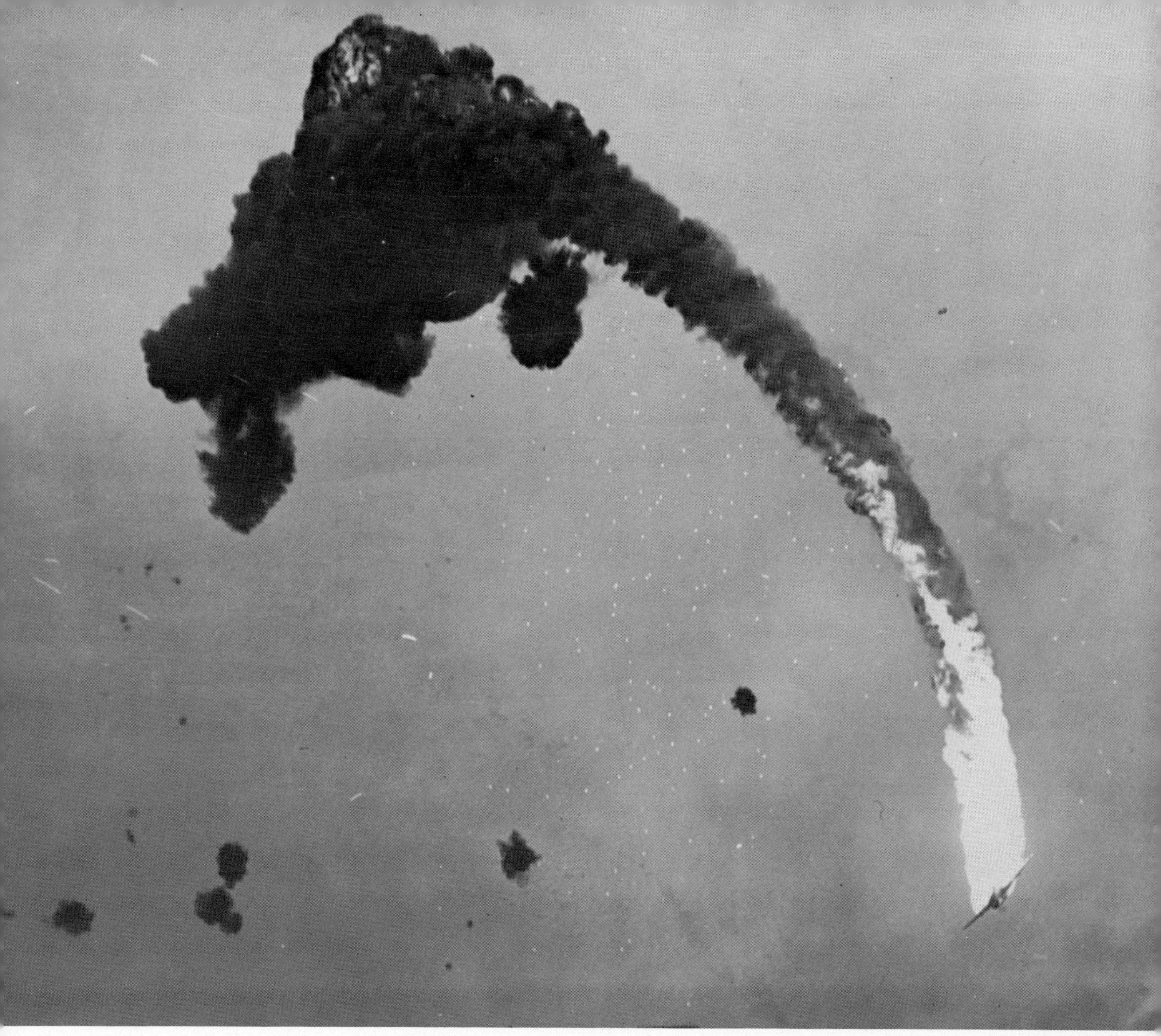

Judy bomber blazes fiercely (*above*) after being shot down by antiaircraft fire from the *Wasp*, March 18, 1945, off the Ryukyus. This was one of dozens of planes shot down in mass attack. (*Below*) Twin-engine Frances passes over carrier, then explodes.

As seen from the *Yorktown* (*left*) one suicide plane crashes aboard the deck of *Intrepid* while its bomb explodes beside the carrier; the second plane barely misses the *Intrepid* and crashes near the high water geyser from the bomb. Battered four times by suicide planes and air strikes, each time the big *Essex*-class carrier returned to fight again.

Crewmen run for their lives (*above*) on deck of carrier USS *Franklin* as blazing wreckage streams across the deck and over the island, after an explosion of Japanese dive bomber in island superstructure. Ball of fire and explosion show clearly by radar; metal cascades down on deck.

The USS Bunker Hill takes two kamikazes in 30 seconds—May 11, 1945. While operating with a fast carrier task force in the "Slot" between Okinawa and Kyushu, the two suicide hits, acting as fuses to the gasoline-filled and bomb-laden planes, started off one of the most heroic battles of the Pacific. Fighting suffocating flame and exploding rockets and bombs (*left*), the gallant crew, her heroes unnumbered, sacrificed 392 dead and 264 wounded to save their ship. The saga of the *Bunker Hill* was similar to that of USS *Franklin*, hit on March 19 by two 500-lb. bombs. Gutted by flame, listing badly and suffering 832 killed and 270 wounded, she limped thousands of miles back to New York. *Saratoga* off Iwo Jima took four kamikazes into her flight deck, a fifth into her hull; with 110 killed and 180 wounded, the "Fighting Lady" made it back to the U.S.

Hellcat fighter defending fleet off Japanese coast was hit in flight by enemy suicide plane; wounded, the F6F blazing, the pilot brought his crippled fighter back to the carrier, landed, and escaped with his life.

Massive pincers close on Japan

In the defense of Okinawa the Japanese lost more than 4,000 aircraft in combat; of this number at least 2,000 fell to the guns of Task Force 58's planes, while other carrier aircraft accounted for an additional 500—the remainder being destroyed by land-based airpower. With this force out of the way, the Navy unleashed a thunderbolt at Japan, and the greatest sea armadas in history roamed at will up and down the Japanese coast-lines. Carrier planes blackened the skies, while battleships and cruisers moved to point-blank range to blast industrial targets with their heavy guns. The air over Japan was crowded in these final days of conflict, for the B-29's stormed in from the Marianas, and P-47 and P-51 fighters flew from Iwo Jima to add to the carnage. United States and British Navy planes hit targets day after day, and hundreds of Air Force and Marine tactical aircraft poured into Japan from Okinawa. Unable to resist, the Japanese watched helplessly as the planes raced over the country at tree-top level, exhausting all possible targets.

With the Japanese fleet beaten from the seas, the bombers from the U.S. carriers ripping Japanese home-

By late spring of 1945 the Japanese naval air force was through; too many planes had met the fate of this bomber (*above*).

Operating from airfields in the Marianas won by carrier airpower, and supported by the Navy's extensive Pacific supply system—bombs, fuel, spare parts, food, tools, medical supplies, etc.—Army Air Force B-29's burned Japan's cities to the ground. It was the final closing of the massive pincers, the total destruction of the enemy's home industry.

Carrier planes smash the *Haruna*—Kure area, July 28, 1945.

land targets hunted out the remnants of the Imperial Navy. In the Kure anchorage they found a bonanza—the flight-deck battleships *Ise* and *Hayuga*; the battleship *Haruna*; the carriers *Amagi, Kaiyo, Katsuragi,* and *Ryuho*; and the cruisers *Tone, Aoba, Oyodo, Iwate,* and *Izuma.* On July 24 the Navy delivered a final knockout blow to these already-damaged survivors of the enemy fleet. *Ise* was almost blown out of the water with ten direct hits and

many near-misses; *Hyuga* also took ten direct hits. With the exception of the carrier *Ryuho,* previously damaged and cleverly hidden by the Japanese, every warship either settled to the bottom, or capsized and then sank. Not satisfied with this, the planes came back four days later and pounded the warships into scrap. "By sunset that evening," wrote Admiral W.F. Halsey, "the Japanese Navy had ceased to exist."

VICTORY IS OVERWHELMING

The two atomic bombs, over Hiroshima and Nagasaki, were the psychological climax to a defeat that had already been inflicted upon the Japanese. In between the two bombs, on August 8, Russia entered the conflict, a vulture coming to feast upon the near-corpse of Japan. The signs of victory were clear—the great carrier air fleets operating with impunity (*above*) over the homeland itself, and the cities that had become terrifying wastelands of ash.

The Navy's carriers could now accurately assess their role in the greatest war ever fought. Some 6,484 Japanese planes were shot out of the air against carrier losses of only 451; another 5,854 were destroyed on the ground, 48 per cent of all the planes lost by Japan. Carrier aircraft sank 711,156 tons of war vessels, more than any other agent; they sent 1,390,959 tons of merchant shipping to the bottom, second only to kills scored by the submarines. The record was full—the carriers had held the line; turned the tide. Then they led the tidal wave of power back across the Pacific, to inflict a defeat that was absolutely unquestioned in the minds of the Japanese.

Ace of aces

The Navy's "Ace of Aces"—Commander David McCampbell, who shot down 36 enemy planes in aerial combat; set an all-time American fighter pilot record by shooting down nine enemy planes in a single engagement. Awarded the Congressional Medal of Honor. As Air Group Commander of the USS *Essex*, McCampbell led a division of seven F6F Hellcat fighters against a Japanese force of sixty bombers, diving into the enemy formation. In the wild battle that followed, McCampbell shot nine bombers out of the sky, while his wingman shot down six, and the remaining five pilots scored a total of nine kills—twenty-four without the loss of a man. No bomber reached McCampbell's carrier.

THE U.S. MARINE—
HE DID IT THE HARD WAY

NAVY GAINS GRAVE RESPONSIBILITIES

USN becomes nuclear-armed, jet-equipped global airpower

With the greatest war of history now the province of the historians, Naval aviation plunged into the heady new world of nuclear weapons (Bikini *Able* test shot, 1946, *above*), jet fighters and supersonic speeds, and the explosive miracle of modern electronics. The war had a sustaining drama of life-and-death, but the postwar era was just as dramatic in its intensity of purpose and its promise of accomplishment. Beyond the problems of adapting jet fighters to carriers—on July 21, 1946, the FD-1 Phantom made the first jet fighter trials aboard a carrier—the Navy worked to create an entire new line of carriers, and the "angled deck" was born. Special research aircraft with jets and rockets smashed its way to new speed and altitude records, continuing a time-honored tradition. The entire planet had become the Navy's sphere of operation, and it probed not only the upper atmosphere, but with great rockets reached out at hypersonic speeds into the forbidding airlessness of space. It was an overwhelming new world of jets, rockets and missiles, nuclear weapons and electronics . . . all demanding Naval aviation's best.

185

AD-3 approaching USS *Boxer*.

Reach into the stratosphere

As pioneers in blazing new trails for aviation, Navy and Marine pilots co-ordinated their efforts with scientists of the National Advisory Committee for Aeronautics, and focused world attention on startling new records in flight. On August 15, 1949, Douglas test pilot William Bridgeman flew the D-558-II Skyrocket to a new altitude record of 79,494 feet. Among the pilots who pushed the rocket-powered sweptwing D-558-II to world altitude and speed records was Lt. Colonel Marion Carl, USMC (*above*), who in the predecessor Skystreak airplane had already grasped speed records for the Navy. To accomplish these goals, aviation medicine took a giant stride forward with the development of new high-altitude suits and pressurization equipment. Record-breaking became a habit with the new jet/rocket Naval air arm.

Sleek and fast, pioneering Douglas D-558-I Skystreak (*above*) jet research aircraft takes off from Muroc, California, on August 25, 1947. With Major Marion Carl, USMC, at the controls, Skystreak raced a 3-km course to set new world record of 650.6 mph.

Aboard the USS Norton Sound at sea (*below*) in scientific program of exploring atmosphere. As part of "Operation Skyhook," small balloons carried instruments aloft to measure temperature, density, pressure of the atmosphere at different world locations.

Flying high-performance fighter planes in carrier deck operations has always demanded the highest pilot skill; normal problems, however, were enormously complicated by jet fighters with higher stalling speeds, additional danger of heavy jet engine behind pilot. Grumman F9F-5, flown by Commander G.C. Duncan, hit edge of USS *Midway*, broke in half, exploded (*above*). Duncan escaped!

Wake of carriers and battleships turns the ocean into strange, beautiful design (*left*) as McDonnel F2H Banshees fly formation over their ship. High-performance Banshee gave the Navy its first mass-production jet fighter that flew brilliantly from ocean level to more than 50,000 feet. Cannon-armed F2H fighters also carried bombs, napalm, rockets, served with the fleet in every part of the world, and in Korea; it is still operational.

Demonstrating new Naval air capabilities, a heavy P2V hurls back thick clouds of smoke from rocket bottles as it races down deck of USS *Coral Sea* (*right*) on March 7, 1949. Six months later, P2V-3 took off from USS *Midway* at sea off Norfolk, flew across the Caribbean to Panama Canal, then to Corpus Christi, Texas, and on to San Diego, California, for its first landing! Total elapsed flight time: 25 hours 40 minutes. Total distance flown: an astounding 4,880 miles.

Banshee jets on flight deck of USS *Coral Sea* (*above*) during maneuvers in Mediterranean. (*Below*) Fueling wingtip tanks of F2H-2.

New missions, new planes

In the amazing Douglas AD Skyraider (*above*) the Navy gained one of the most versatile war machines ever created. Strikingly rugged, powerful AD's carried greater bomb load than WW II B-17 heavy bombers, and were in use as dive bombers, torpedo bombers, and even fighters. Considered one of the most "perfect" airplanes ever built, Skyraider integrated requirements for scout, dive, torpedo, and patrol bombers.

Giant Martin JRM-2 Mars flying-boat transport (*above*) was part of small JRM fleet that began operations in 1944. The JRM-2, named Caroline Mars, on March 4, 1949, set a record by carrying 269 passengers on a Pacific flight. The next year the Caroline Mars flew from Honolulu to San Diego with 144 persons aboard.

The postwar aviation era brought with it the need to throw away operations maps in use for years. New Russian bombers that could reach out for thousands of miles with atomic bombs created an overnight, urgent requirement for effective air patrol. Navy helped to meet new mission with radar-packed Lockheed PO-1W (*below*).

KOREA: ON THE BRINK OF TOTAL ATOMIC WAR

Lt. Commander Harry M. Dater, former Head, Naval Aviation History and Research Section, USN: "As the shadows fell across Tokyo Bay [September, 1945], men hoped once again that the killing had stopped at least for their lifetime, if not for good. Seldom has this ageless dream been so quickly shattered. Almost on the morrow of victory, the shadow of international communism fell across large areas. For the professional military man, who must prepare in peace for a possible war, the outlook was grim but far from hopeless. On the debit side he could see the vast hordes disciplined to the communist will, but he knew that the United States had in its designers and engineers, its production experts and skilled workers, a precious technological asset that could, if properly developed, offset the enemy's advantage in manpower."

No one ever said it better.

AD-3 Skyraider laden with rockets, napalm (*opposite page*), ready for launching from USS *Princeton* for Korean strike. (*Above*) Corsairs on USS *Philippine Sea* before take-off to Korea.

Ordnancemen and flight-deck crews bring
1,000-lb. bombs to *Philippine Sea* deck
(above) for shackling to AD Skyraiders.

Ordnancemen load rockets (*above*) on AD Skyraiders aboard
Boxer. AD's made first strike, July 3, 1950, from *Valley Forge.*

B.N. Washam, prone on deck of USS *Antietam* (*below*) isn't lying
down on the job; he's waiting for signal to pull F4U wheel chocks.

Crewman stands on wing ladder (*above*), fuels Grumman F9F Panther aboard USS *Boxer*. On July 3, F9F's flew first mission, shot down 2 YAK-9's over Pyongyang.

Aboard Philippine Sea off North Korea in snowstorm, deck crewmen (*above*) check sway braces of napalm bomb on F4U Corsair.

Men make the carriers

Ordnanceman wheels bombs along deck of USS *Antietam* (*below*) for Corsair fighters. Strike was made February 25, 1953.

F9F Panther, one of the fastest Navy fighters of Korean War (*above*), but much slower than Russian MiG-15, filled variety of missions in Korea, including strafing, napalm and bombing runs, rocket firing for flak suppression. F9F and F2H jets also flew as escort fighters for B-29's bombing rail yards.

Skyraider taking off from *Bon Homme Richard* (*left*) was Korean War's most versatile warplane. They were used for attacking every type of target, as night and all-weather bombers, as radar-equipped anti-sub patrols, and with countermeasure equipment, to confuse enemy's radar sites.

Crewmen respot Corsairs, Skyraiders on USS *Princeton* (*below*) after Korean strike. In first 10 months of fighting, Corsairs flew 82 per cent of all Navy, Marine ground support missions. F4U-5 used in Korea could hit 450 mph, carry staggering weight of bombs, napalm, guns, and cannon for low-level raids.

Grumman F9F streaks down deck of *Antietam* (*above*) as catapult officer and deck "talker" crouch to escape jet blast. Aboard *Princeton* a crewman (*left*) stays low as F9F wing streaks over his head. Navy used both F9F and F2H jets from carriers; Marines used F9F from shore fields. "Jet take-off characteristics and their high consumption of fuel proved less than ideal for the carriers we operated during the Korean War," states Navy. Their unusual speed, however, made the jets excellent flak-suppression planes.

F9F being spotted on *Philippine Sea* flight deck (*right*) for launching. By July, 1953, a total of 16 aircraft carriers had seen operations in Korean waters; 13 of these were U.S. warships, 2 were British, and 1 was Australian. Every third or fourth day the U.S. carriers retired from the battle scene to replenish fuel drained by the jet fighters. During the entire active Korean War, Navy and Marine units lost 537 aircraft to enemy flak, 4 planes in aerial combat. Combined air strikes and Naval gunfire (4 battleships, 8 cruisers, 80 destroyers) killed estimated 35,000 troops, sank 1,400 large and small vessels, destroyed 4,500 large buildings, plus thousands of trucks, tanks, cars and trains.

Banshee fighter, having dropped its bombs, starts dive for strafing run against truck concentration in village near Name Chon River (*above*) in North Korea; pilot is Commander James B. Kain. (*Left*) Lt. Robert Pitner in F4U from USS *Boxer* circles over Wonsan to observe effects of bombs he has just dropped on bridge. (*Below*) Two F2H-2's from carrier *Kearsarge* trouble-hunting over Wonsan Harbor, looking for supply-carrying junks.

Busting up bridges, dams

Names like Heartbreak Ridge, Little Gibraltar, and Punch Bowl were written in blood into the history of Korea as the most bitterly contested mountain posts of 1951. Between July 3, 1950—the first attack—and July, 1951, when the initial truce talks began, carrier aircraft exacted a fearful toll of the enemy. In the newspaper accounts back home the Fifth Air Force, which did a magnificent job in Korea, overshadowed the results of carrier aircraft—and this is surprising, for those results were tremendous. In those 12 months planes from the Navy's carriers destroyed 83 Communist planes, ripped 313 bridges, destroyed 12,789 small and large military buildings, 262 hostile junks and river craft, 220 locomotives, 1,421 railroad cars, 163 tanks, and almost 3,000 support vehicles as a result of interdiction and close support missions. In the first and only use of aerial torpedoes in Korean combat, 8 Skyraiders and 12 Corsairs from USS *Princeton* attacked the Hwachon Dam. Conventional bombing attacks had failed, but the torpedoes dropped by the Skyraiders (see below) ripped the dam and wrecked the floodgates; water from the reservoir poured into the Pukhan River and effectively slowed a Communist army advance. Korea gave Navy the opportunity to test bomb-laden drones in battle. On August 31, 1952, two Skyraiders from USS *Boxer* remote-controlled an F6F-5K drone into a bridge at Hungnam, North Korea.

Two Skyraiders from *Bon Homme Richard* rolling into vertical dives (*above*) to begin bombing runs against supply center at Tanchon, North Korea, on November 14, 1952. (*Below*) Direct hit by Skyraider's aerial torpedo smashes the floodgates of Hwachon Dam.

It was in Korea that the helicopter—used by the Navy, Marines, and Air Force—truly ''came of age.'' The ungainly choppers performed miracles in evacuating wounded, for artillery spotting, emergency supply flights, and for direct combat duties. Maneuverable and adaptable to the rugged terrain of Korea, the helicopter—like the Bell evacuation model in the above picture—could land on mountain ridges and along, or immediately behind, the firing line. Marine Squadron VMO-6 helicopters set a new record when in a single day they evacuated 77 litter cases from the mountain ridges east of Hwachon reservoir. Circuiting helicopters, moreover, rescued aircraft crews downed behind enemy lines. And they were great morale boosters for pilots of fighters and bombers operating from the carriers, as they constantly stood by to rescue any man who went into the sea.

"Hit and Git" tactics devised by rocket-firing Marine teams with helicopters gave them powerful weapon. 11th Regiment Sikorsky helicopters airlifted teams to firing sites, where Marines set up, blasted away with withering salvos from rocket launchers. Waiting helicopters snatched up launchers, took on crews, rushed away (*above*) before Chinese were able to pinpoint the launching site.

AD Skyraider is directed to loading site on Briscoe Field, on Yo Do Island (*below*) in Wonsan Harbor, Korea. Skyraider is from USS *Valley Forge*, with other fighters and bombers operated from front-line airfields to increase carrying capacity and fuel load for missions. Of all the planes used by Navy, Marines and Air Force in the Korean War, the Skyraider was considered the most effective.

Seriously damaged by Communist antiaircraft fire over its Korean target, a crippled AD Skyraider attempting to land crashes aboard *Philippine Sea* (*above*). Airplane broke in two, wings tore free, and fuel tanks exploded. (*Below*) Ensign F.D. Jackson, his face riddled with glass shards, flew into cable stretched across Han River. Badly wounded, he made safe landing on *Philippine Sea*.

Small war but death is the same

It was a "small war"—but demanding of an enormous expenditure of matériel. The 1st Marine Wing *alone*, not including any Air Force, Navy, or other Marine organizations, flew 118,000 sorties, dropped 91,000 tons of bombs, fired 192,000 aircraft rockets, and shot 34,000,000 rounds of ammunition. (In the massive B-29 attacks against Japan in World War II, a total of 96,000 tons of bombs was dropped—only 5,000 tons more than the Marines in tactical aircraft dropped in Korea!) At times missions in Korea matched almost anything of World War II. In a two-day strike at the huge hydro-electric power plants near and along the Yalu, 223 carrier and 77 Marine AD's, F4U's, and F9F's hit the target while 100 Air Force F-86's flew top cover. When these 400 planes left, another 100 F-86's cruised over the Suiho plant, while waves of fighters and bombers from three carriers smashed the power stations. Then 120 F-84 fighter-bombers took over. After this, another wave came in—323 carrier planes and 60 Marine aircraft. That was enough—more than 1,000 planes had wiped out the ground objectives.

High landing speeds, explosive fuel loads of jet fighters made combat carrier operations extremely hazardous for deck crews. On USS *Essex,* September 16, 1951, an F2H-2 Banshee returning from Korean strike landed successfully, then "ran away" on the deck. Fighter crashed into parked planes, exploded in giant ball of flame (*right*) that engulfed deck crewmen, burning them terribly. Aftermath (*below*) shows smashed jets.

An epic is ended

Because the Communists had no true naval forces to face the U.S. Navy, and because their rare attempts to send planes over our carriers met with immediate defeat, control of the seas around Korea was never disputed, and the carriers' principal mission to support the land campaign and to participate in the air offensive was carried out with extraordinary efficiency. It was a war that taught the Navy much, and assured its full maturity in the age of jets and atom bombs. It was a war that also proved the astounding strength of Navy jets (*above:* its nose torn away by flak, F9F returns to *Philippine Sea*), and its ending is symbolized in the return of an F4U-5N Corsair night fighter (*below*) to the *Leyte,* and in a deck crewman at day's end lashing an F2H Banshee (*left*) to deck of the *Essex.*

NEW AGE DAWNS

Control of the sea is a term that has acquired a drastic new perspective, for it encompasses the three dimensions of military activity—on the surface of the earth, down into the ocean depths, and far up into the very airlessness of space. This is the current domain of sea-power, a fusing of responsibilities into a single immense force. The policies of seapower do not emerge from dusty tomes; rather, they are shaped by atomic realism. And because control of the sea cannot hope to be realized, or sustained, without control of the air overhead—the New Age has dawned around a hard core of qualitative air-power, and a Navy designed to function on the basis of its ability to deliver slashing air attack anywhere on the globe at any time. In a very real sense military power is indivisible; there is little purpose in air or sea power unless there is a means of exploiting properly that power. Success in this exploitation is the sustaining element of freedom in a troubled world—the U.S. Navy fully meets this responsibility.

The four catapults of the great carrier USS *Forrestal* enable the warship to operate at a pace many times that possible of our carriers that fought in WW II or Korea, and also to accomplish this goal with larger, heavier, and higher-performing aircraft. Utilizing the *Forrestal's* angled deck catapult, a heavy, supersonic Vought F8U Crusader is hurled into the air (*above*). Indicative of the amazing performance of the Navy's modern warplanes, the powerful Crusader was world's first operational fighter to exceed 1,000 mph in level flight. (*Right*) The new *Saratoga*, equipped with jet fighters and heavy twin-jet bombers, on the high seas.

Bombers perform tactical, strategic air missions

In 1944, Britain's Admiral of the Fleet Lord Keyes made an analysis of United States Naval successes, in which he said in part: "The success of the battle for the Philippines was only made possible because the United States Navy has been free to develop its own naval aviation. It has been done with amazing skill and enterprise and on a gigantic scale. Furthermore, it has shown that in the complex business of waging war on the seas, it cannot be set down as a maxim that any one factor can be exclusively decisive." This basic premise of sea/airpower has not changed. Certainly contemporary technological gains have modified naval air techniques, but in the main these have served only to enhance the tremendous striking power of the modern navy. With airplanes that fly at better than twice the speed of sound, that reach to 100,000 feet above the earth, that can fly at supersonic speed for thousands of miles while carrying bombs measured in their destructive power at millions of tons of high explosives, our Navy contains awesome strategic might. It is hard to accept, however real it may be, that in a single launching of its aircraft one modern carrier can send out many times more destructive power than was carried by all bombers of all combatants in every war since the airplane first flew.

USS Ranger on Pacific maneuvers.

Largest bomber now in carrier service is Douglas A3D (*above: launching from USS Forrestal*) Skywarrior. With a range exceeding 3,-000 miles with a full combat load, A3D outreaches WW II B-29's. (*Below*) Douglas AD-6, late model Skyraider, is still tops for ground support.

Modern aerial refueling techniques give new jet fighters and bombers unlimited range; "probe and drogue" technique is demonstrated (*left*) by AJ bomber-tanker refueling F9F Cougar photographic-reconnaissance fighter. In 1954 three Cougars spanned the U.S. in record 3 hrs. 45 mins.

Smallest high-performance bomber in the world, Douglas A4D Skyhawk (*below*) is one of the most spectacular combat machines in the world. Holder of several world records for speed, Skyhawk became operational in 1956. It performs all types of attack missions, is superb for "toss bombing" strikes.

A3D Skywarriors on long-distance combat maneuvers

In simulated combat run, swift A3D (*above*) took off from USS *Shangri-la* at sea, raced to inland target at average speed of 606 mph 1,543 miles away, had enough fuel to return to its carrier. (*Below*) A3D being moved to carrier hangar is towed from deck elevator.

Returning home after extensive service in the 1957 NATO exercises, USS *Forrestal* has its heavy A3D jet bombers lashed to the flight deck (*above*) as it moves into storm.

Deck crewmen aboard USS *Intrepid* (*left*) preparing to launch squadron of A4D Skyhawks in late afternoon. Carrier was at sea for day-and-night tests with new planes.

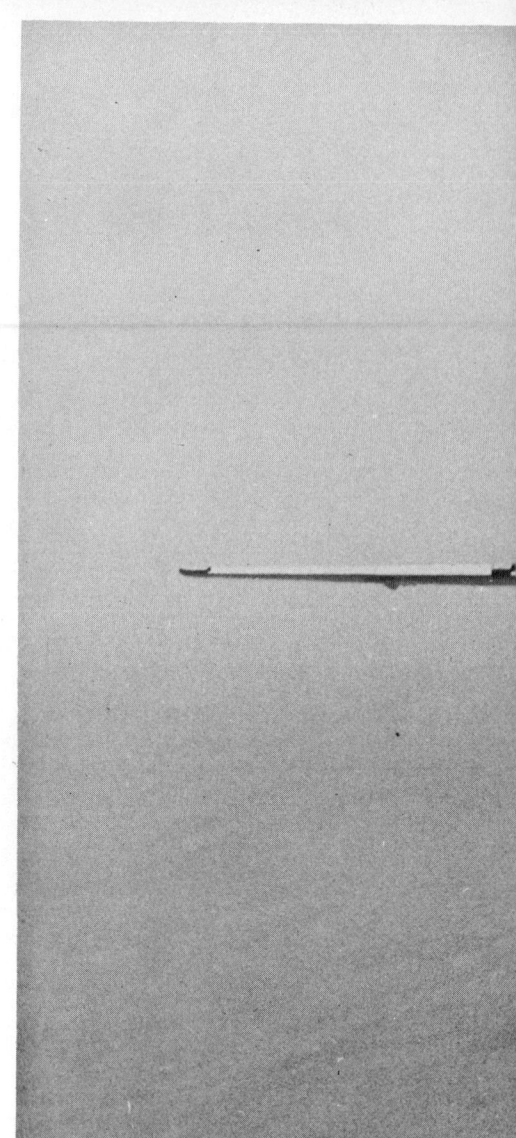

A NEW BOMBE

The tactical guided missile has been an integral part of the Navy's air-weapons systems for years, including a wide variety of air-to-air, and air-to-ground homing and guided missiles. In this dramatic photo (above) Douglas F4D Skyray has seconds before launched an infrared-seeking Sidewinder missile, which exploded against evading jet drone.

No airplane has ever excited Naval air planners so much as the new North American A3J Vigilante (above), a rakish, powerful twin-jet bomber that pushed Naval aviation into the Mach 2. category. Able to fight from treetop level at high supersonic speed and to race for thousands of miles at more than twice sonic speed at 60,000 to 70,000 feet, the Vigilante is the equal of any combat plane ever flown in the U.S. or the Soviet Union; indeed, in this country, only the great Convair B-58 Hustler can match it. What best illustrates the tremendous versatility of this most powerful of all Naval air weapons is that the Vigilante can operate from the modern aircraft carrier. With this combination, every world target is within Navy's supersonic reach with thermonuclear bombs.

UTFLIES THE FIGHTERS

North American FJ-2 Fury just prior to touch-down on flight deck of USS *Coral Sea* (*below*). Assigned largely to Marine fighter squadrons, Fury has been replaced with newer fighters like F4D Skyrays. As in World War II and Korea, Marines stress tactical ground support, paralleling jet-fighter and bomber developments with troop helicopters.

Heavy attack carriers operational with the fleet have four large deck-edge elevators to move plane (F8U; *above*) up to flight deck.

Jet-age Navy hasn't changed in one major respect; carrier efficiency still needs skill, and agility of fast-moving deck crews (*above*).

More than 1,000 feet in length and fitted with four catapults, modern carrier decks swarm with activity (*below:* AD's and F9F's).

Afterburner of F4D deltawing fighter hurls back stream of fire aboard USS *Lexington* operating in Formosan waters. With two catapults, carrier can launch supersonic jet fighters at intervals of 20 seconds; aircraft are recovered at 26-second intervals. When no scheduled aircraft are being readied to depart, interceptors like F4D's are kept spotted on the catapults and others behind them to augment the existing Combat Air Patrol that is active in air whenever carrier operates away from U.S.

Grumman S2F Tracker (*above*) can operate from smallest carrier in Navy, is considered the most efficient antisub plane ever built.

Vought F7U-3M Cutlass, giant missile-firing twin-jet fighter (*below*), moves into position on flight deck for catapult launching.

Supersonic McDonnell F3H Demon leaves deck of mighty new *Saratoga,* largest carrier operational in the world. More than 70,000 tons fully loaded, *Saratoga* is 1,040 feet in length, and 252 across at the extreme width. Each of the four deck-edge elevators will take a 75,000-lb. bomber, and four steam catapults allow maximum launch and recovery operations. More than 4,000 men are needed to operate the giant, but the Navy's newest seagoing island—the great, atomic-powered USS *Enterprise*—requires even more. The new *Big E* displaces nearly 90,000 tons, accommodates 70 jet fighters and bombers of Vigilante size. Eight nuclear reactors, four propellers give it a speed of 35 knots.

DAZZLING WORLD OF CARRIER AVIATION

While their squadron mates in a dawn launch leave contrails in the sky, three Crusaders from Squadron VF-32 prepare to launch from *Saratoga's* angled deck catapult.

Banshee wings point starkly against the horizon on deck of *Hornet*.

Taking a breather, mechanic rests in tail section of Panther jet.

Downwash from Marine Sikorsky HR2S-1 helicopter creates a dramatic water pattern (*left*) as the "chopper," largest in the world in production, hovers at low altitude. Giant craft carries tremendous loads, including mechanized vehicles, operates as major element of carrier-based troop assault force.

On October 31, 1956, seven Navy men in a Douglas R4D Skytrain landed on the ice at the South Pole—the first to stand at that spot since Captain R.F. Scott of the Royal Navy reached it in January, 1912. Scientific exploration has since its inception been a major activity of Naval aviation, and Antarctica in recent years has received world attention. A P2V lands on McMurdo Sound ice runway (*above*) on skis. (*Below*) Douglas R5D at McMurdo prepares for a rocket-boosted take-off in a dramatic 60-knot snowstorm.

AMAZING WORLD OF THE AIR

The world of Naval aeronautics knows no rest; qualitative superiority in the skies demands a ceaseless search on the ground and on the Navy's testing fields. Every manner of aerodynamic principle is dissected; wherever possible it is flown, tested, and, if it passes the hurdle of engineering scrutiny, it may survive to become operational.

A3J Vigilante taxies (*left*) to runway in desert for flight test. (*Above*) Navy conducts extensive research in VTOL fighter designs.

As part of vertical take-off and landing platform, Navy is testing one-man Hiller flying platform (*below*) for use by combat Marines.

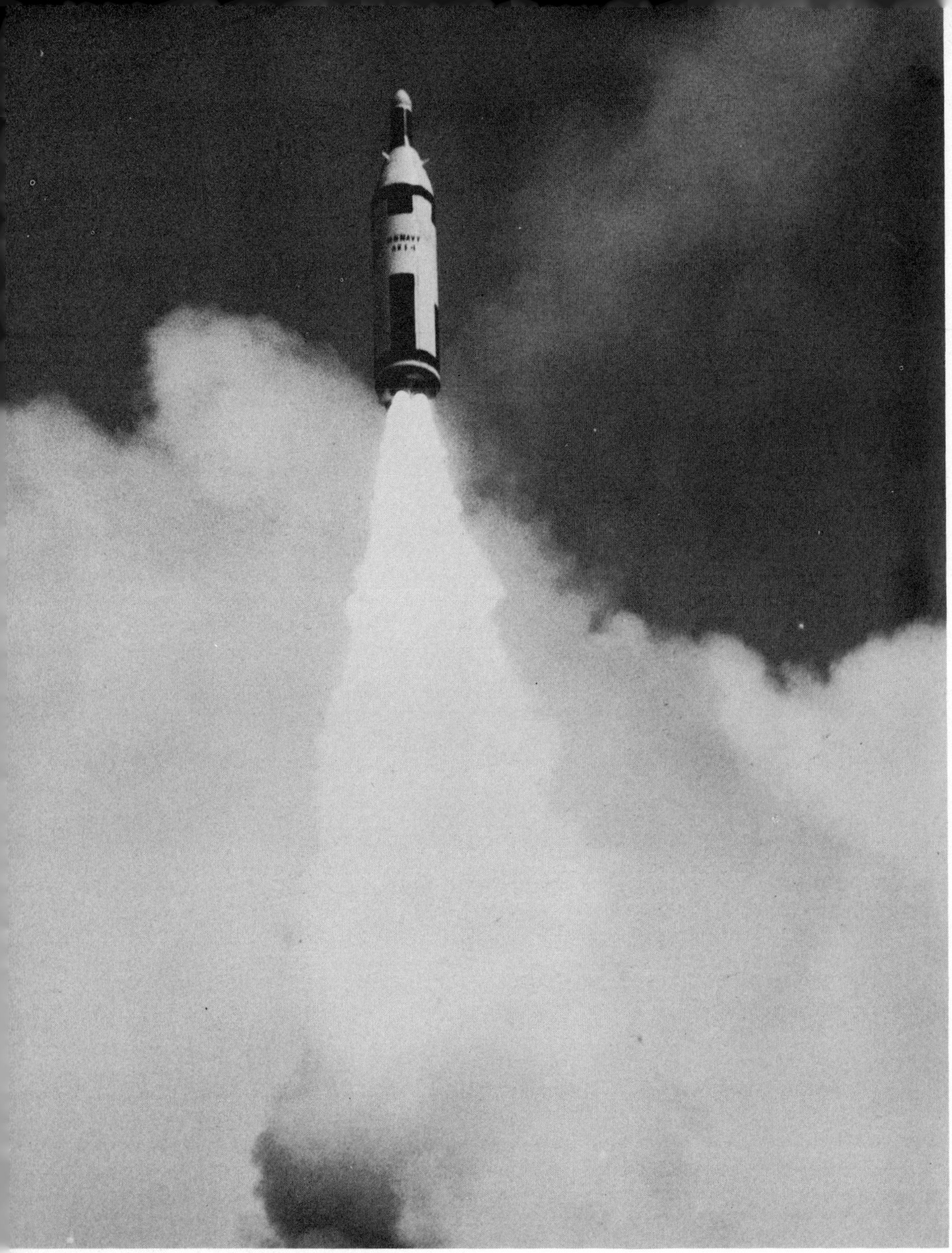

The "Fleet Ballistic Missile"—Polaris—is a weapon that was created under all the pressures that would exist during an actual war; top priority was given this critical missile as soon as its potentialities were recognized. Much more than simply developing a weapon, the Navy—and its brilliant team of industrial contractors—has had to accomplish break-throughs in hundreds of technical fields. The result—in the form of the operational Polaris missile (*left:* a test at Cape Canaveral) as it will be mated with the *George Washington* class of nuclear subs (*below:* world's fastest, USS *Skipjack*)—gives the U.S. a mobile-based ballistic weapon.

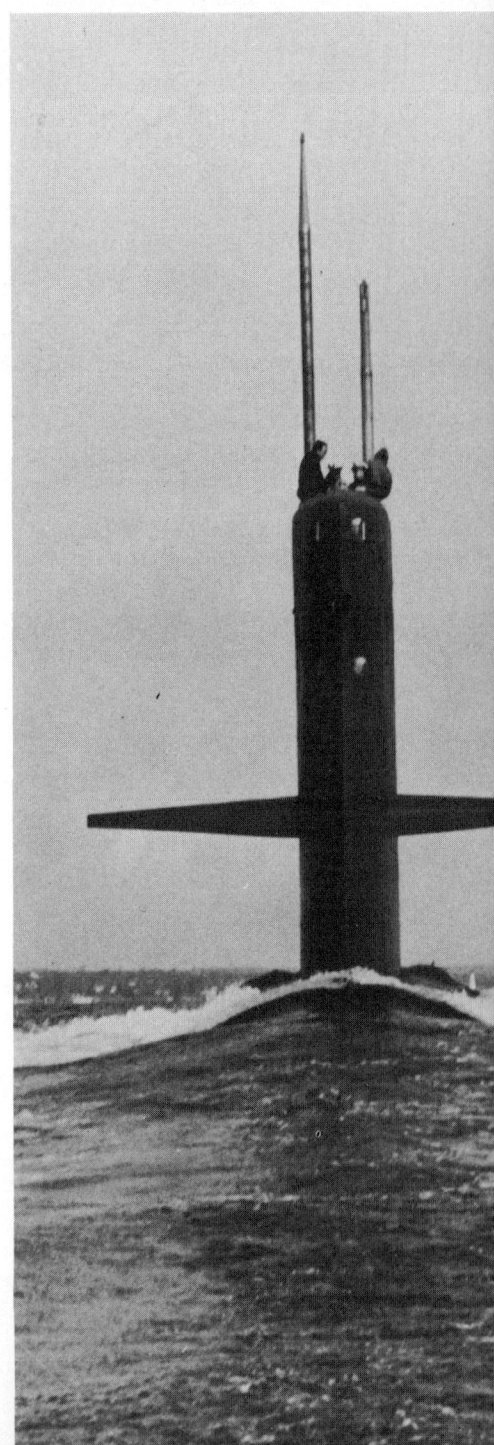

From out of the sea

For the first time in his history, man exists simultaneously in four vital ages that influence his life drastically. These Four Ages—Atomic, Space, Jet (and Rocket), and the one that makes the other three possible, Electronics—have brought to modern warfare an explosive change. The combination of the nuclear-powered submarine; of the compact, solid-propellant rocket of 1,500-mile range; of the compact nuclear warhead of several megatons yield; and of the marvelous, intricate electronic system to allow all these to function with extraordinary precision . . . this means that the sea has suddenly become the province of the ballistic missile. Or, to be more accurate, the *depths* of the sea. In its nuclear-powered submarine fleet carrying Polaris missiles—each of which is a terrible destroyer of a city—the Navy has brought to the nation a desperately needed ballistic weapon that brings new meaning to the term *mobility*. Lost in unimaginable immensity of the deep oceans, free of the rigidity of the fixed base, the submarine-launched Polaris stands to become one of the great classic weapons of all time.

Space buoy

Conceived in an age when astronautics—the science of space flight—was a strange and alien term, the Vanguard satellite-launching program carried out by the Office of Naval Research suffered more from errant public opinion and misguided Congressional wrath than it did from its technical obstacles. When planned, scientists hoped that out of twelve launchings with various Vanguard rockets, they might achieve one satellite in orbit—and this was considered a tremendous achievement. Instead, Vanguard fired three enormously productive scientific packages into orbit about the earth, a credit to the entire program. And from Vanguard comes Transit, the Navy's orbiting navigational satellite.

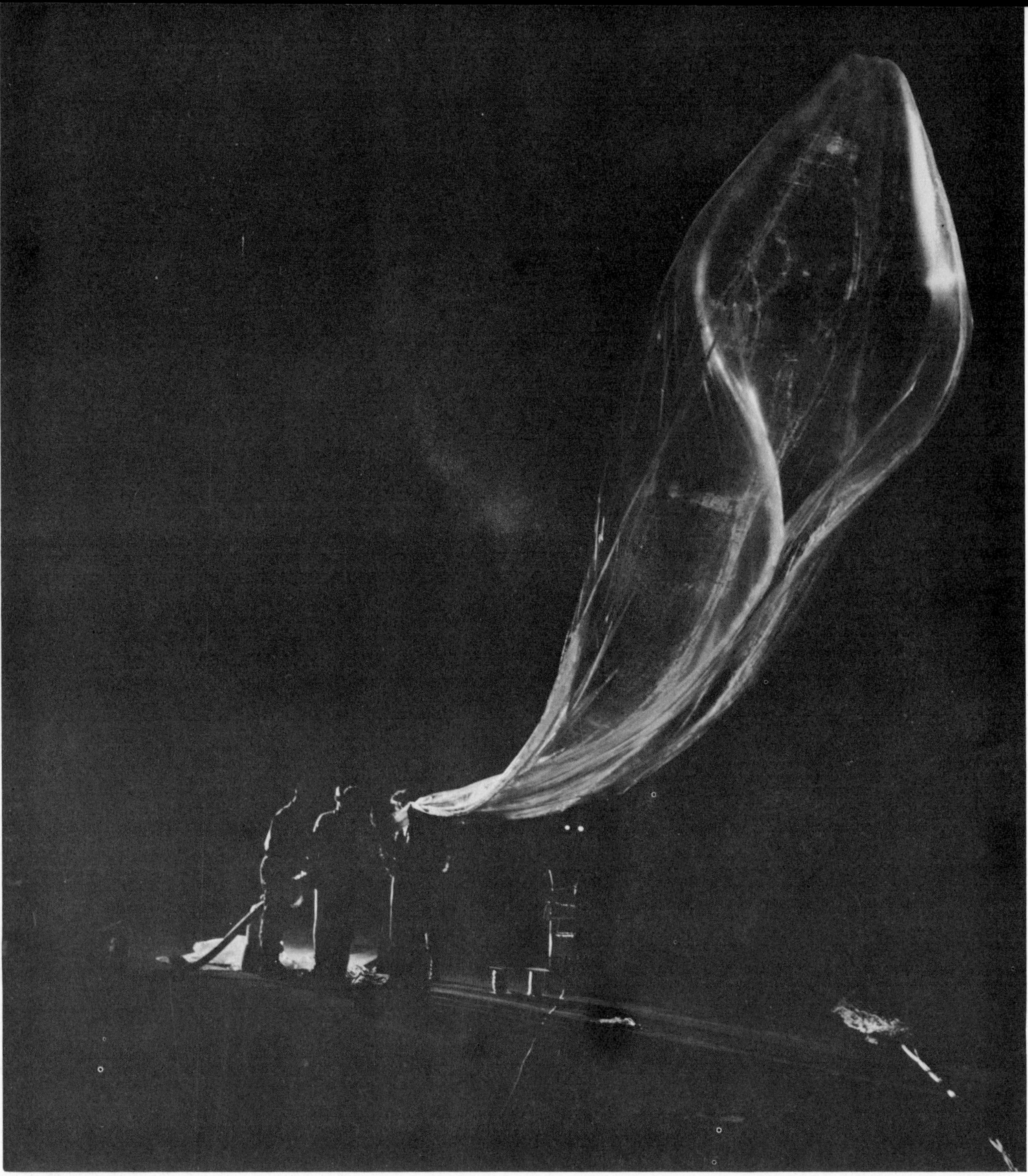

The probing into space is ceaseless—balloons, rockets, aircraft, satellites, robots and man. A strange shape struggles from the ground in Operation Skyhook—great balloons to probe the stratosphere's secrets.

Airpower means manned aircraft; spacepower will call for manned spacecraft. A vital partner in the development of manned machines to reach into space, the Navy has played an important role in the X-15 program, the nation's first hypersonic aircraft, and forerunner of manned satellite vehicles. The result of a combined effort on the part of the Navy, Air Force, and NASA, Project X-15 has depended upon the giant centrifuge at the Johnsville research center in Pennsylvania, where pilots in the X-15 cabin mockup "fly" under great g-forces. (*Right*) Scott Crossfield, North American test pilot, is pictured during experiment in centrifuge.

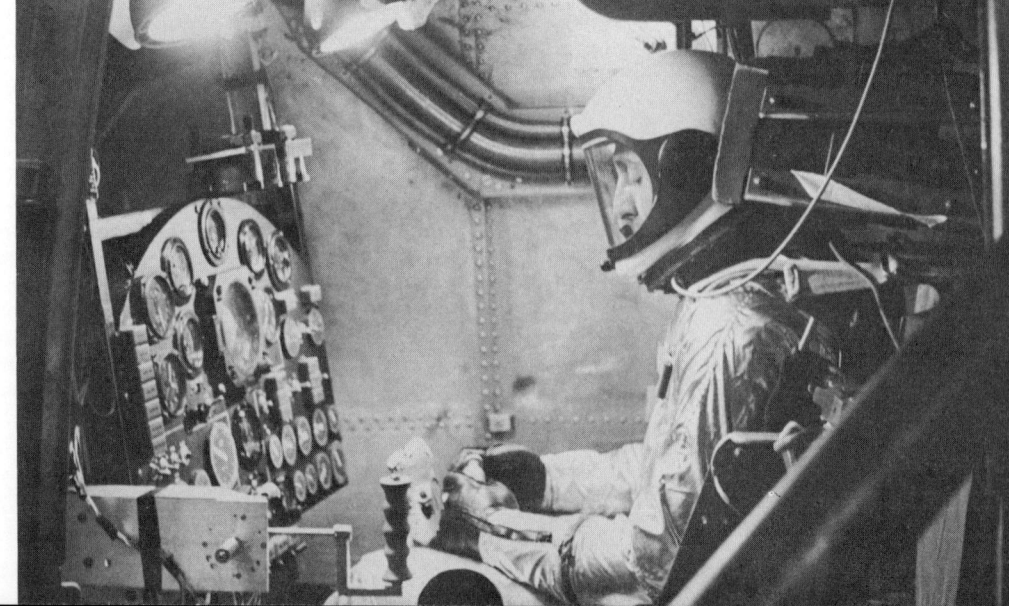

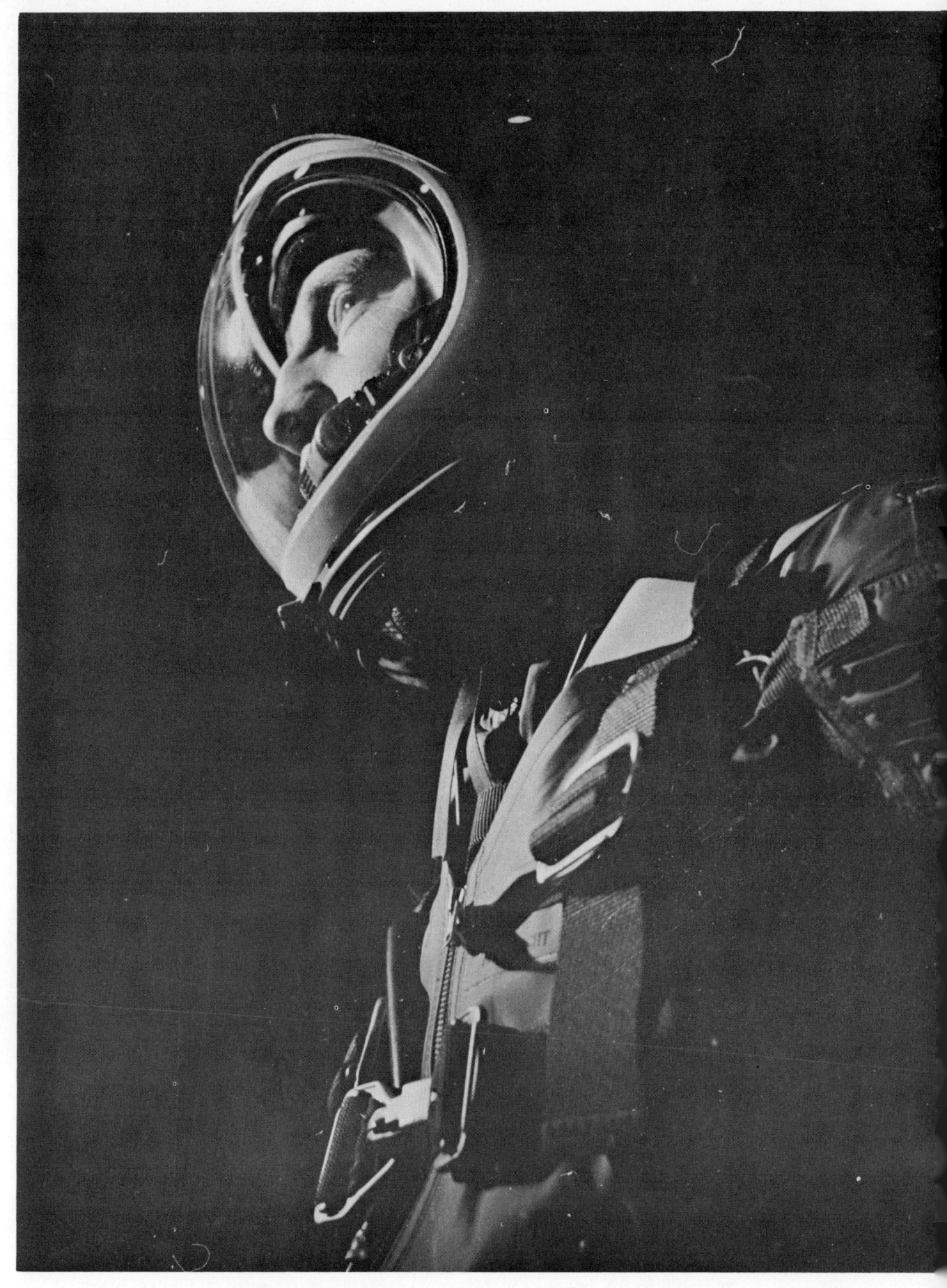

Prelude to space—Navy fighter pilot in full-pressure suit for flight well into stratosphere. Similar suit design will be used for the actual orbital flights by Mercury Astronauts.

PRELUDE TO TOMORROW

For the first time since its warships began to defend this land, the United States Navy no longer carries the specific responsibility to counter another fleet . . . rather, it acts in the capacity of an airpower force, integrated with all the supporting elements of the fleet on the surface of, and beneath, the oceans of this world. As such, our Navy no longer is delineated to specific missions and responsibilities; it has instead become a working instrument of United States policy, unhindered by artificial horizons or boundaries. It is the Naval air arm, the history of which we have just seen, which endows this global force with its speed, versatility, and its tremendous strength. Naval aviators have found in the high, unbounded blue far over our heads a world of sweeping depth and rich beauty; and they have at the same time brought to these endless canyons of flight a purpose with meaning . . . strength to sustain their nation.

. . . ON WINGS OF GOLD